WATKINS SALAD BOOK

BY ELAINE ALLEN

AUTHOR OF WATKINS COOK BOOK, WATKINS HOUSEHOLD
HINTS BOOK AND WATKINS ECONOMY RECIPE BOOK

PRICE $1.50

THE J. R. WATKINS COMPANY

NEWARK • MEMPHIS • WINONA • OAKLAND
MONTREAL • WINNIPEG • VANCOUVER

WATKINS
SALAD BOOK

BY ELAINE ALLEN

AUTHOR OF WATKINS COOK BOOK, WATKINS HOUSEHOLD
HINTS BOOK AND WATKINS ECONOMY HOME BOOK

PRICE $1.50

THE J. R. WATKINS COMPANY

NEWARK · MEMPHIS · WINONA · OAKLAND
MONTREAL · WINNIPEG · VANCOUVER

TABLE OF CONTENTS

Salads

Salads have an important place in the daily diet not only because they furnish the essential mineral salts, phosphorus, iron, calcium, magnesium and lime which are necessary for health, but also because they add variety and color to a meal. Homemakers should serve salads made of crisp, leafy greens, fresh fruits, young, tender vegetables, raw and cooked, and blended with a well-seasoned and appetizing dressing, as an essential part of a balanced meal.

Health experts recommend serving a salad twice a day, to insure a sufficient supply of leafy greens, which are the best source of rich vitamins and minerals, and because they are important body-alkalizers. In addition to their dietetic value, salads aid digestion, and give interest and appetite-appeal to the menu.

It is important that homemakers know the various salad greens and the distinctive flavor of each. The most popular are Boston lettuce, leaf and Iceland lettuce, romaine, French and curly endive, escarole, chicory or American endive, Chinese cabbage, celery, and water cress. There are also the popular garden greens, which include parsley, young dandelion and cabbage leaves, tender spinach, mustard and turnip greens, herbs, celery tops and fennel. The inner crisp yellow leaves of parsnips may be added to a mixed green or combination salad. Highly flavored greens should be used sparingly, as a delicate flavor is more desirable than a pronounced and dominant accent.

The salad should provide a contrast in color, flavor, and consistency to a well-balanced meal; and its flavor should not be repeated elsewhere in the menu. A salad should be thoroughly chilled, and attractively served on a chilled .plate. Do not pack or crush the salad mixture when serving, but arrange ingredients lightly on crisp greens. Have a note of color, such as a sprig of water cress, strips of a green or red ²pepper, or celery or carrot curls, pickled capers, gherkins cut fan shape, fresh herbs, canned pimiento cut into fancy shapes, radish roses, nut meats, with a dash of Watkins Paprika sprinkled over the top of the salad, or dust the edge of crisp salad greens with Paprika. Salads should appeal to the eye as well as to the taste. Appetizing salads made of seasonal fruits and vegetables, with flavorful dressings, make the mealtime hour one of anticipation and surprise.

When To Serve

The salad may be served (1) as the first course, in the form of an appetizer, at an informal luncheon or dinner; (2) as the principal luncheon course; (3) with the meat-course at luncheon or dinner; (4) as a separate course, following the meat-course; or (5) as a dessert, combining the salad and dessert, and served with or without crisp crackers and cheese.

In both France and Italy, a delectable salad is an essential part of the meal; being frequently served first, either as a tossed salad of crisp mixed greens with French dressing, or blended with strips of anchovy, cooked ham, chicken, or julienne strips of red and green peppers. In France, tender salad greens are cut into pieces one inch wide to one and one-half inches long and lightly blended with a dressing made of three parts olive oil to one part vinegar, with salt, Pepper and Paprika added. The dressing is sprinkled over well washed, dry, chilled greens, then tossed with a wooden fork and spoon to coat each leaf.

Salad Should Suit the Meal

Salads may be divided into three classes: (1) Light or Dinner Salads which include all green salads, also those made of non-starchy vegetables, and the citrus fruit combinations, served with French dressing. (2) Luncheon or Supper Salads, such as the protein group, include diced cooked chicken, turkey, ham, veal, tongue, fish, eggs, as well as cheese and nuts. (3) Dessert Salads, which combine the salad and dessert course, are usually of fruit with a tart French dressing; or, if preferred, a mayonnaise or a cooked dressing, plain or blended with cream, or whipped cream.

Dressing Should Suit the Salad

Choose the dressing which best suits the particular salad, the one which will bring out the flavor of the ingredients. French, mayonnaise, and a cooked dressing are the three types most generally used, and there are many variations of each. Both French and mayonnaise have oil foundations, while a cooked dressing is made of eggs, vinegar, water, milk or cream. In all cases, the dressing should be added just before serving the salad. The caloric value of a dressing depends upon the type used; a cooked dressing, made with water or milk, has a lower caloric value than French or mayonnaise. Mineral oil may be partially substituted for olive oil, to reduce the calories of a French or mayonnaise dressing.

Olive Oil In Salad Dressing

Imported Italian olive oil is supreme for salad dressings. One should acquire a discriminating taste, and know the difference between Italian, French, Spanish, and California olive oils. Peanut oil ranks next to olive oil in stability and general quality, and may be blended in equal parts with olive oil to reduce the cost. Corn oil gives off a strong odor, as do some kinds of soybean oil.

Vinegar and Lemon Juice In Salad Dressing

There is a distinct difference in the flavor of various vinegars, and the homemaker should not ask merely for "vinegar", but should specify red wine vinegar, or white wine vinegar, tarragon, malt, cider, wild blackberry, cherry, or an aromatic vinegar, or ask for cucumber vinegar, chili, dill, or spiced tarragon, according to its intended use.

To make tarragon vinegar, blend 3 cups malt vinegar with 1½ cups dried tarragon leaves, cover fruit jar and let stand one week before using. Dilute with water as desired.

Lemon juice is considered by connoisseurs preferable to vinegar in a French dressing, and has the quality of being quickly neutralized in the system, thus preserving the alkalinity of the blood.

Art of Seasoning

Select salad ingredients with care and be creative in making both the salad and the dressing. Just the right seasoning will give the master touch to a salad. Therefore the homemaker should have on hand an assortment of choice seasonings, such as Watkins Red and Black Pepper, Watkins Dry Mustard, Chili Powder, Onion Seasoning, Celery Salt, Garlic Seasoning, Watkins Paprika, Nutmeg, and Watkins Spice Blend with Curry. A delicate sprinkling of Watkins Spice will lift a commonplace salad dressing into a French masterpiece of culinary skill.

Important Points In Salad Making

Wash fresh fruits and vegetables thoroughly under cold running water, drain, dry and chill in a covered enamelled pan in the refrigerator until ready to use. Pick over fresh salad greens carefully to remove all aphids. Use a wire basket and wash greens carefully; shake well, dry on a tea towel. Store greens in a linen cloth, a cellophane bag or in a covered hydrator and chill; salad greens, to be appetizing, must be dry, crisp and cold. Add the dressing just before serving.

Use a chilled wooden bowl for mixing a salad. Break the stiff midribs of lettuce; use a vegetable cutter for slicing vegetables and fruits, and a pair of shears to shred lettuce, or to clip wilted leaves. Use a sharp paring knife of stainless steel or one of glass to cut ingredients. Cut a tough stalk of celery fine and the tender stalks in larger pieces. When both dark and light meat of chicken is used in a salad, dice or cut in uniform, well defined pieces to hold their shape; cut dark meat in small cubes, and the light into larger pieces. If cooked veal or roast pork is blended with the chicken in a salad, dice into finer pieces and let stand one hour in the refrigerator, with a little French dressing, for better flavor.

To Marinate Salads

A marinade is used to give added flavor to a meat, fish, poultry or potato salad. It is prepared by blending salad oil, salt, lemon juice or vinegar and pouring over the mixture and chilling one hour.

Garnishes for Salads

Finely chopped chives, chervil, or parsley may be sprinkled over a green salad. Strips of pimiento or green pepper and a dash of Watkins Paprika, will give a bright garnish to a fruit or vegetable salad. Add red or green maraschino cherries, strawberries, or other berries to a fruit salad; or fresh mint, water cress, parsley, or cheese balls rolled in chopped nuts. Use sprigs of crisp pepper-grass, sorrel, basil or burnet as a garnish with a meat or vegetable salad, or capers, stuffed olives, strips of pimiento, or quartered hard cooked eggs with a dash of Watkins Paprika; or chilled, drained, canned peaches or pears, or slices of canned pineapple, or individual molds of cranberry or fruit gelatin with roast chicken. Tarragon and dill herbs may be served as a garnish for potato salad. Color contrast and color harmony add to the attractive appearance of a salad.

Salad Accompaniments

The accompaniments of a salad depend on the place the salad occupies in the meal. For a formal menu, when the salad is served as a separate course, serve crisp saltines, Melba toast, cheese straws or hot crackers spread with grated cheese and heated under the broiler, or tiny cheese rounds of white bread, toasted.

With a luncheon salad, serve small thin sandwiches of buttered raisin, date, orange or nut bread, or tiny baking powder biscuits buttered and hot, or toast squares spread with butter and heated before serving. Or serve pulled bread, toasted French or Italian bread spread with creamed butter.

With a fruit salad, serve saltine wafers, paprika cheese crackers, or small finger-length sandwiches spread with lemon butter filling, or with cream cheese and chopped nuts. Many unsweetened crackers in packages as rye crisp and Ritz wafers may be served. Ripe and stuffed olives, crisp celery sticks spread with cream cheese and a dash of Watkins Paprika, and crisp raw carrot sticks, may be served with the salad.

Green Salads
Salad Bowls

Salad Greens Rich In Vitamins

Salad greens are rich in Vitamins A, B and C, and the deep green tender leaves are a good source of minerals, iron and calcium. The greener the leaf, the richer the mineral content.

Serve the fresh, tender wild greens so plentiful in the early spring, as dandelion, poke, lambsquarters, plaintain, purslane, wild chicory and dock.

Plant salad greens in the garden. Grow lettuce, romaine, endive, parsley, Swiss chard, kale, Chinese cabbage, celeriac and chicory. Plant herbs such as tarragon, sorrel, mint, thyme, marjoram, chives and mustard to add a piquant flavor.

Lettuce is the most popular of the salad greens. Cabbage is the Vitamin King of vegetables, rich in Vitamin C.

Romaine is a variety of leaf-lettuce with long, coarse leaves, cup shaped; romaine is usually served with a vegetable salad.

Curly endive is a loose head variety of lettuce with wiry, curly leaves. It has a tangy flavor and is best served alone with a well-seasoned French dressing, or as a foundation for a vegetable or a simple fruit salad.

Chicory (American endive) is a popular salad green that grows in short, round white stalks of tightly closed leaves, with a pungent flavor. This salad green is best served with French dressing.

Escarole is a green and yellow leafy vegetable. The inner leaves are small and yellow and are excellent for a salad. The outer green leaves are cooked as greens.

French sorrel is a perennial and the tender leaves can be cut at any time and served with French dressing.

Chives have a mild onion flavor and the leaves may be used in a meat or vegetable salad.

Oriental garlic should be used sparingly. The plant has a long, slender, flat leaf.

Sweet marjoram has a fragrant, mild taste, popular in a mixed green salad. The leaves are small and may be left whole or cut fine and used with tomatoes, peas, beans or a carrot salad.

English thyme may be used whole or chopped in a mixed green or tomato salad.

Fennel leaves may be used in a fish or a mixed green salad.

Dill has feathery, green leaves and gives a delicious flavor to potato, cabbage or a mixed green salad.

Parsley is easily grown and may be used for flavor and for its vitamin content, in almost any salad.

Chervil is similar to parsley but should be used sparingly; the flavor is similar to anise.

Green Salads

A chilled mixed green salad with a well-seasoned French dressing is appetizing to serve for luncheon, dinner or supper. It may be served as an accompaniment, or as the first course, or as a separate course following the meat.

Salad greens should be fresh, young, tender and crisp. Use a variety of greens and serve with a well-seasoned dressing—French, Thousand Island, bacon dressing, horse-radish dressing or Russian dressing.

There are three salient points in making a green salad:

1. Freshness and crispness of the greens. Ingredients should be cold.
2. Quality of the olive oil and vinegar. Oil should be fresh and sweet; wine (not malt) vinegar, or lemon juice, should be used.
3. Blending of the greens and dressing. Blend dressing before adding chilled greens; toss lightly until each leaf is coated with dressing, taking care not to crush the leaves.

Salad Bowl

Salad greens are the foundation of a salad bowl. Combine several—romaine, chicory, endive, lettuce, water cress, escarole, tender spinach and dandelion greens. Have salad greens thoroughly washed, chilled and dry, to avoid diluting dressing.

Any combination of fresh raw vegetables may be blended with salad greens. The salad bowl is an excellent way of using left-over cooked meat. Cube or sliver veal, ham, fish or poultry, marinate in a little French dressing for 30 minutes and add to crisp salad greens.

To Prepare Salad Greens

Pick over greens as soon as delivered. Remove any coarse, dark or bruised outer leaves. Use a wire basket or colander and wash greens under cold, running water, lifting leaves to remove all dirt.

Separate Boston lettuce, chicory, escarole and romaine and wash each leaf. Strip off the outer leaves of iceberg lettuce and store whole; iceberg lettuce turns a rusty pink when cut or bruised and should be prepared by tearing leaves apart by hand, just before serving.

Shake off water after washing salad greens, pat in a clean tea towel, place in a linen or cellophane bag, or keep in a covered hydrator in the refrigerator. Have salad greens crisp before serving.

To separate leaves of head lettuce, remove core and hold the opening under cold running water until the leaves separate easily.

To Prepare Salad Vegetables

Wash carefully and store in a covered container in the refrigerator.

Cut tomatoes in quarters or eighths just before serving. Cut green peppers, remove seeds, and cut in narrow strips. Cabbage should be chilled, and shredded just before serving. Peel cucumbers, slice, and let stand in salted ice water; drain well and marinate with French dressing before serving.

Care of the Salad Bowl

Use an over-size salad bowl to permit room for tossing greens. A chopping bowl may be used as a salad bowl if you do not have one of special wood, such as the hand carved koawood from Hawaii, the myrtlewood of Oregon, the California redwood and oakwood, or a teakwood bowl.

Remove the wax finish from a new bowl with a cloth rinsed in lukewarm water, wash carefully and rub dry. Rub wood inside and out with hot olive oil and let stand 24 hours to dry. The salad bowl should not be washed or exposed to heat. Water will harm the wood. After each use, wipe the bowl with a damp cloth, dry thoroughly with paper towels, and keep in a cloth bag. Season the bowl occasionally by wiping with a cloth dipped in olive oil.

Salad In a Seasoned Wooden Bowl

Rub the salad bowl with a clove of garlic before the greens are added. Add salt, Watkins Black Pepper, and rub into the garlic stained wood. Then add a tablespoon of vinegar or lemon juice and 3 tablespoons of olive oil for each four persons to be served. Blend mixture with a fork, adding fresh or dried herbs, as desired. Add the thoroughly washed, drained, dry chilled greens and toss lightly until coated with dressing.

Unseasoned or China Salad Bowl

To blend a salad served in an unseasoned bowl, place the washed, dry, chilled greens in the bowl and chill. Add dressing just before serving.

Large pottery, china or glass bowls may be used if preferred, especially for fish, fruit and other salads mixed with mayonnaise. These should be chilled before salad is added and should, of course, be washed each time after using.

Fruit salads may be served in a watermelon, cantaloupe or pineapple shell, for variety. Mark off even spaces on the cut edge of melon and cut out triangular sections between each marker, making a notched edge.

California Salad Bowl

3 quarts washed, chilled salad greens
½ cup Parmesan and Bleu cheese grated
Juice of 3 lemons

6 tablespoons olive oil
1 tablespoon Worcestershire sauce
Watkins Paprika
Salt to suit taste

Blend all ingredients in a deep, chilled salad bowl.

Chicory, Endive and Leek Salad

White inner leaves of chicory
2 heads crisp endive
2 medium-sized leeks

6 asparagus tips
¼ teaspoon salt
2 tablespoons red wine vinegar
4 tablespoons olive oil

Cut leeks into small strips, add cut asparagus, seasoning, vinegar and oil. Chill. Blend with chicory and endive and add French dressing.

Hot Chicory or Endive Salad

1⅓ lbs. chicory or endive
½ teaspoon salt
3 tablespoons diced crisp bacon

¼ cup butter
3 tablespoons water
1 tablespoon lemon juice
Watkins Paprika

Pick over greens, remove coarse outer leaves. Wash thoroughly, drain, and place in a saucepan. Add seasoning, dot with butter, add water and lemon juice. Cover and cook slowly over low heat until tender. Remove greens to a hot plate, re-heat sauce until reduced one half, pour over greens, add diced bacon, and serve immediately.

Dutch Salad Bowl

6 slices bacon
1 tablespoon flour
¾ cup water
½ cup vinegar
1 tablespoon sugar
2 eggs, slightly beaten

½ teaspoon salt
Crisp salad greens
1 small onion, chopped
2 hard cooked eggs
Watkins Red Pepper

Cook bacon until crisp. Remove bacon, stir flour into hot bacon fat, add water, vinegar, sugar, salt and pepper. Stir and cook mixture until slightly thickened. Cool. Gradually add mixture to beaten eggs; return to stove, stir constantly over low heat but do not overcook. Pour hot over salad greens and onion. Add bacon broken into small pieces; garnish with quartered hard cooked eggs.

Chiffonade Salad

Romaine	Sliced cucumbers
Lettuce	Quartered
Chicory	tomatoes
Escarole	French dressing

Blend equal parts of crisp salad greens. Add French dressing and toss lightly. Add cucumbers crisped in ice water. Add tomatoes. Serve on chilled salad plates and garnish with chopped beets, chopped eggs and minced parsley.

Combination Salad Bowl

1 bunch water cress	Crisp endive
½ head lettuce	3 strips, diced cooked crisp
½ bunch chicory	bacon
2 stalks crisp celery	Chives
3 tomatoes, quartered	Grated cheese
	Watkins Paprika

Blend all ingredients and add French dressing.

Crab Meat Combination Salad Bowl

1 cup canned crab meat	Crisp romaine
¾ cup diced crisp celery	1 avocado
	1 pimiento
3 tablespoons mayonnaise	2 tomatoes
	1 cucumber
¼ teaspoon salt	Endive
Watkins Red Pepper	French dressing
	Watkins Paprika

Flake crab meat, add celery, mayonnaise and seasoning. Arrange crisp romaine in salad bowl, arrange crab meat on one side of bowl. Arrange sliced avocado and pimiento on crab meat. On opposite side of bowl arrange tomato cut into quarters and sliced cucumber marinated in French dressing. Add endive and French dressing.

Dandelion and Lettuce Salad

½ lb. fresh dandelion greens	1 tablespoon vinegar
1 head lettuce	1 cup thick sour cream
2 hard cooked egg yolks	1 cucumber, sliced thin
1 teaspoon sugar	2 scallions, chopped
½ teaspoon salt	Watkins Paprika
Watkins Red Pepper	

Wash greens, drain, wrap in a cloth and chill. Put egg yolks through a sieve, add seasonings, vinegar, and blend to a paste. Gradually stir in sour cream. Blend greens, add dressing and toss lightly.

Dandelion Salad

Pick over fresh, young dandelion greens, wash thoroughly under cold running water, wrap in a tea towel and chill. Put greens in salad bowl. Fry six thin slices of bacon until crisp and pour hot fat over greens. Add diced cooked bacon and vinegar as desired. Garnish with hard cooked eggs, adding Watkins Paprika.

Egg Salad Bowl

8 hard cooked eggs, halved	1 cup French dressing
4 cups shredded cabbage	¼ cup sweet pickle relish
4 tomatoes, cut into eighths	2 teaspoons Watkins Dry Mustard, dissolved in a little hot water
2 tablespoons chopped scallions	
Crisp chicory	2 teaspoons sugar

Add relish, mustard and sugar to French dressing. Arrange all ingredients in chilled salad bowl and add dressing.

French Endive Salad

Cut endive in half lengthwise, then separate and wash carefully, dry in towel and chill. Serve on crisp lettuce with French dressing. Slices of cooked drained beets may be placed on top of endive. Or serve sections of grapefruit with French dressing.

Hot Endive Salad

1⅓ lbs. endive	¼ cup butter
½ teaspoon salt	2 tablespoons lean bacon, diced
Dash Watkins Red Pepper	
2 tablespoons water	1 tablespoon lemon juice

Pick over greens, remove coarse outer leaves, wash carefully, then pack in a buttered saucepan. Add salt, red pepper, bacon and dot with butter. Add water and lemon juice. Cover and cook over low heat about 35 minutes, or until tender. Place greens in a hot dish and let liquid boil down one half. Pour over greens and serve immediately.

Fruit Salad Bowl

3 oranges
1 banana
1 cup diced fresh
　or canned
　pineapple
½ cup seeded
　grapes
½ cup halved
　walnuts or
　pecans

¼ cup candied
　ginger, cut in
　pieces
1 sliced apple,
　unpeeled
2 tablespoons
　lemon juice
Lime French
　dressing
Crisp water cress

Chill and prepare fruit. Sprinkle lemon juice on sliced apple to prevent discoloration. Arrange fruit on crisp water cress and add French dressing.

Florida Fruit Salad Bowl

2 mangoes
2 avocados
1¼ cups diced
　apple, unpeeled
3 stalks crisp
　celery
1 large banana,
　sliced
Crisp lettuce

2 oranges, cut
　into sections
½ cup whipping
　cream
2 tablespoons
　powdered sugar
½ cup mayon-
　naise
½ cup pecans

Chill and prepare fruit. Blend whipped cream, sugar and mayonnaise and add to cut fruit. Line salad bowl with lettuce, add French dressing, then fruit. Sprinkle top with halved pecans.

Summer Fruit Salad Bowl

1 ripe cantaloupe
2 avocados
3 cups black
　cherries

Crisp lettuce
French dressing
Watkins Paprika

Line a salad bowl with crisp lettuce. Add strips of melon and avocado. Add cherries after removing seed and fill center with cream cheese or nuts. Add French dressing.

Wilted Lettuce

Leaf lettuce
6 slices bacon
⅔ cup vinegar

⅓ cup water
1 teaspoon sugar
Watkins Paprika

Fry bacon until crisp, cut into pieces. Add vinegar and water to hot bacon fat, heat to boiling and pour over lettuce. Add bacon, and diced raw onion if desired. Garnish with quartered hard cooked eggs. Add Watkins Paprika.

Head Lettuce

Wash lettuce under cold running water, drain, wrap in tea towel and chill. Cut head into desired portions, add a generous amount of Thousand Island Dressing with a dash of Watkins Paprika.

Dutch Lettuce

1½ heads lettuce
6 slices bacon
1 medium-sized
  onion
⅓ cup mild
  vinegar

1 tablespoon
  sugar
Dash salt
Watkins Paprika

Wash lettuce, drain, separate leaves, wrap in tea towel and chill. Fry bacon until crisp, remove from pan and cut into pieces. Add onion and cook to a light brown. Pour vinegar slowly into skillet, add seasoning and heat to boiling. Pour mixture over shredded lettuce and toss lightly to blend. Serve hot.

Green Salad with Sour
Cream Dressing

1 large head
  lettuce
2 cups crisp,
  shredded
  cabbage
2 tablespoons
  chopped
  pimiento

½ cup chopped
  celery
2 teaspoons
  lemon juice
1 cup sour cream
Salt
Watkins Paprika

Chill all ingredients. Place shredded lettuce, cabbage and pimiento in a bowl, then add celery. Blend sour cream, lemon juice, seasoning and pour over greens.

Romaine-Endive

½ head romaine
  lettuce
½ head endive
1 cucumber,
  sliced, crisped
  in ice water

½ head lettuce
1 bunch radishes,
  sliced
1 teaspoon
  chopped chives
French dressing

Have all ingredients cold. Add French dressing just before serving.

Supper Salad Bowl

1 cup shredded,
  cooked tongue
  or ham
1¼ cups cooked
  vegetables
6 scallions, cut
  into 1 inch
  pieces
½ bunch
  water cress

½ head escarole
½ head romaine
6 radishes, sliced
¾ cup slivered
  raw carrots
¾ cup slivered
  American or
  Swiss cheese
French dressing

Have all ingredients cold. Blend and serve in a salad bowl.

Salad Bowl As First Course Luncheon or Dinner

¾ cup olive oil
¼ cup lemon juice
¾ teaspoon salt
1 teaspoon sugar
1 ripe avocado
2 grapefruit
2 large oranges

1 head lettuce
½ bunch water cress
1 cup chilled, white grapes, seeded and halved
Watkins Paprika

Blend oil, lemon juice, salt and sugar, and shake briskly. Scoop out avocado, mash with fork and blend with dressing. Remove membrane from sections of grapefruit and orange. Cut chilled lettuce and water cress, place in salad bowl, add fruit, dressing, and blend mixture. Add Watkins Paprika.

Tossed Salad Bowl

1 cup crisp lettuce, shredded
½ cup cabbage, shredded
½ cup diced celery
⅓ cup diced green pepper

⅓ cup raw carrot, shredded
1 small onion, diced
¾ cup bean sprouts
French dressing
Watkins Paprika

Chill all ingredients. Add dressing, toss mixture lightly. Serve on chilled salad plate.

Water Cress and Dandelion Salad

1 cup crisp water cress
1 cup dandelion greens

6 thin slices raw onion
Watkins Paprika
French dressing

Wash greens, drain in a wire basket, wrap in tea towel and chill. Just before serving, add slices of onion, and French dressing. Blend mixture lightly.

Water Cress and Walnut Salad

1 pint crisp water cress
½ cup walnut meats

Juice 1 lemon
French dressing
Watkins Paprika

Add lemon juice to walnut halves. Wash, drain and chill cress. Just before serving, add French dressing to greens and sprinkle top with walnuts.

Foreign Salad Bowl Recipes

Salade Italienne

Blend equal quantities of carrots, diced cooked potatoes, tomatoes and French beans, cut julienne (in long narrow strips). Add peas, stoned olives, capers, diced anchovy fillets. Blend with thinned mayonnaise.

Salade Sicilienne

Blend equal quantities of sliced russet apples, tomatoes, diced celery, and artichoke hearts. Add French dressing made of olive oil and lemon juice with generous sprinkling of Watkins Paprika.

Russian Salad

Blend equal quantities of cooked carrots, potatoes, French beans, peas, truffles, capers, gherkins, sliced cooked mushrooms, lobster meat and baked ham, all cut julienne (in long narrow strips). Add anchovy fillets and blend with mayonnaise.

Salade Monte-Cristo

Blend equal quantities of lobster meat, cooked truffles, diced potatoes and diced hard cooked eggs, adding just enough mayonnaise to blend. Season with a little Watkins Dry Mustard and tarragon vinegar. Arrange on crisp lettuce.

Salade Allemande

Blend equal quantities of raw apple slices, diced boiled potatoes, slivered gherkins and herring fillets. Add French dressing.

Salad Bowl Suggestions with French Dressing

Crisp chicory, escarole, water cress and shredded cabbage.

Escarole, Chinese cabbage, canned hearts of palm.

Chinese cabbage, romaine, shredded carrot and green pepper.

Dandelion greens, sliced onion, sliced cucumber, diced green pepper.

Romaine, radishes, sliced onions, cucumbers and green peppers.

French endive, romaine, curly endive and sliced cucumbers.

Slivered raw turnip, Chinese cabbage, grapefruit and orange sections.

Shredded raw cabbage, chopped onion, diced green pepper, halved grapes (seeds removed).

Shredded cabbage, water cress, celery and raisins.

Cucumber, artichoke hearts, radishes, celery.

Apples, crisp cabbage, grapefruit.

Red cabbage, red apples (sliced not peeled), diced pineapple.

Lettuce with any of the following greens: endive, water cress, spinach leaves, escarole, romaine.

Flowerettes of raw or cooked cauliflower, slivered raw green pepper, bean sprouts, crisp lettuce.

Tomatoes, celery, cucumbers, salad greens.

Tomatoes, pickled pearl onions, julienne strips of green peppers, salad greens.

Salad greens, quartered ripe tomatoes, thin strips pineapple.

Salad greens, quartered tomatoes, onion slices, radishes, sliced cucumbers.

Lettuce, endive, minced onion, diced canned pimiento, crumbled snappy cheese.

Cucumber, onion, tomatoes, lettuce, radishes, celery.

Endive, shredded lettuce, romaine, water cress, chicory, minced onion, diced celery, crumbled cheese, diced stuffed olives.

Cucumber sliced, water cress, romaine, shredded cabbage, minced onion, chopped pimiento.

Chopped cabbage, canned lima beans, chopped celery, crisp lettuce.

Salad greens, tomatoes, onions and strips of green pepper.

Salad greens, ripe tomatoes, crisp hearts of celery, shredded crisp cabbage, raw carrots.

Lettuce, tomatoes, chopped cucumbers, anchovy fillets.

Lettuce, tomatoes, green onions, sliced radishes, sardines, diced cucumbers.

Shredded cabbage, tomatoes, diced crisp celery, diced cucumber, minced onion, radishes.

Tomatoes, avocado, chopped green onions, chopped green peppers, grated Parmesan cheese.

Raw carrots, shredded cabbage, chopped celery, green pepper and cucumber, radishes.

Cooked cauliflower, cooked green beans, cooked asparagus tips, diced pickled beets, crisp lettuce.

Cooked cauliflower, cooked diced carrots, cooked peas, and crisp lettuce with horse-radish cream dressing.

Fruit Salads

Fresh Fruit for Health

Fresh fruit and fresh vegetables are our best alkalizers; most fruits are base forming and have a beneficial effect on the system when they have a prominent place in the daily diet.

Fresh fruit gives an appetite appeal to the most simple meal and contains life-giving vitamins and minerals.

Vitamin Content of Fresh Fruit

Apples	Vitamins A, B and C
Fresh apricots	Vitamins A, B and C
Avocados	Calcium, Vitamins A, B and C
Bananas	Vitamins A, B and C
Cantaloupes	Vitamins A, B and C
Cherries	Vitamins B and C
Dried currants	Calcium, Phosphorus and Iron
Dates	Phosphorus and Iron
Dried figs	Calcium, Phosphorus, Iron and Vitamin B
Grapefruit	Vitamins B and C
Ripe olives	Calcium, Vitamins B and C
Yellow peaches	Vitamin A
Pineapple	Vitamins A, B and C
Raisins	Calcium, Phosphorus, Iron and Vitamin A
Raspberries	Calcium, Phosphorus, Iron, Vitamins A, B and C
Strawberries	Calcium and Iron, Vitamins A and C
Watermelon	Vitamins A and C

Most acid fruits contain either citric acid as lemons, limes, oranges, grapefruit, or malic acid.

Grapes, raisins and figs contain tartaric acid.

Cranberries, prunes and plums contain hippuric acid.

Rhubarb, spinach and beet greens contain oxalic acid.

Fruits rich in available iron include raisins, currants, dates, loganberries, cranberries, dried peaches and prunes.

Fruit Salads

A fruit salad may be served for luncheon, dinner, for a bridge tea or for an evening party with assorted sandwiches, cheese crackers, or with your favorite hot bread.

Use fresh, canned or cooked fruit in any fruit salad recipe. Arrange the drained chilled fruit attractively in a bowl or on individual plates on crisp salad greens, and serve with mayonnaise, cooked or French dressing.

Fruit Salad Buffet

Arrange bowls of chilled mixed salad greens, and have chilled chop plates of assorted fruit such as orange, grapefruit, strips of pineapple, cantaloupe, avocado strips, peach slices, and strawberries. Arrange bowls with French mayonnaise or cooked salad dressing. Platters with assorted cold meat and cheese may be served, with hot rolls, hot buttered baking powder biscuits, or assorted sandwiches.

Hints In Preparing Fruit for A Salad

Wash ripe fruit and chill in the refrigerator. Prepare fruit just before serving, or add lemon or canned pineapple juice to prevent discoloration.

Left-over cut fruit should be wrapped in waxed paper and placed in the refrigerator. Do not remove stone from a cut avocado; wrap in waxed paper and chill.

To Prepare Dried Fruit: Wash thoroughly, soak in warm water and cook only until tender. Add sugar the last five minutes of cooking. To use in a salad, drain and chill.

To Flute Bananas: Before slicing, peel bananas, run tines of a fork lengthwise down the peeled fruit, then slice; prepare just before serving. Do not keep bananas in the refrigerator.

To Flute Lemon or Orange Slices: Cut narrow strips from the bud to the stem-end of the fruit using a sharp knife, then cut crosswise in slices.

To Tint Pears for a Salad: Drain off syrup from canned pears, add a few drops of Watkins Red or Green Color Mixture, bring to boil, add pears and simmer 20 minutes. Remove from syrup and chill.

The Salad Bar

A portable tray or tiered table may serve as a "bar" to mix the dressing and to prepare the salad. Use a large chilled wooden bowl to mix salad greens.

An ingenious way of using left-over fruits and vegetables, is to arrange the assortment on crisp lettuce cups and serve on a platter, for members of the family to make a choice.

Storing Fruit

Berries and all fruits will keep in perfect condition in the refrigerator for days if spread on a platter and covered lightly with waxed paper or cellophane.

Strong-flavored fruit, like cantaloupe, should be wrapped in parchment or waxed paper in refrigeration, as its odor is absorbed by butter and other delicately flavored foods.

Apple-Cheese Salad

1 cup sugar
1 cup water
Few drops Wat-
　kins Red Color
　Mixture
6 apples, pared
　and cored

½ cup cottage
　cheese
2 tablespoons
　tart jelly
Dash salt
¼ cup chopped
　celery
⅓ cup cut nuts

Boil sugar, water and Watkins Red Color Mixture about 7 minutes. Drop apples into syrup, cover and simmer until tender, turning frequently. Drain and chill. Blend cottage cheese, jelly, salt, celery and nuts. Stuff apples and serve on crisp lettuce, adding a little French dressing.

Apple Dessert Salad

1 package pre-
　pared lemon
　gelatin
1 cup hot water
2 cups diced
　apple, unpeeled

1 cup sweet cider
¾ cup diced
　celery
½ cup nuts
Watkins Paprika
Water cress

Dissolve gelatin in hot water, add cider, and chill. When mixture begins to thicken, fold in apple, celery and nuts. Chill until firm. Unmold on crisp water cress. Add cream mayonnaise and Watkins Paprika.

Apple, Pineapple and Cherry Salad

Wash apples, remove core, and slice without peeling. Chill fruit and arrange in alternate sections on crisp romaine. Add French dressing.

Stuffed Apricot Salad

Wash large ripe apricots and chill. Just before serving, peel, remove stone and arrange on crisp salad greens with pitted dates filled with cream cheese and nuts. Serve with French dressing.

Avocado Pear Salad

Cut ripe avocados in half, remove seed, fill center with French dressing, and serve on romaine or crisp lettuce. Or scoop out pear with a large spoon and serve on salad greens with French dressing.

Avocado and Cherry Salad

Peel an avocado, cut in half lengthwise, and remove seed. Fill cavity with chilled Bing cherries pitted and filled with cream cheese or nuts. Serve on crisp salad greens with French dressing.

Avocado and Grapefruit Salad

Peel ripe avocado, remove seed and cut into sections. Marinate in French dressing 30 minutes to flavor. Separate sections of grapefruit and arrange alternately with avocado on crisp endive or lettuce. Or serve sections of ripe cantaloupe, orange, tomato, persimmon or fresh ripe peaches. Cream mayonnaise may be substituted for French dressing.

Avocado, Pineapple and Banana

Blend strips of avocado, pineapple and banana with French dressing. Serve on crisp lettuce.

Avocado Filled with Fresh Fruit Salad

3 avocados
2 cups mixed
   fresh fruit
Crisp lettuce
French dressing

Peel avocados, cut into halves, add lemon or pineapple juice to prevent discoloration. Prepare fruit, add French dressing and fill avocado. Serve on crisp lettuce. Garnish with ripe cherries (remove seed and fill center with cream cheese or nuts).

Avocado Salad Surprise

Stuff a peeled ripe chilled tomato with diced crisp celery, mayonnaise, apple and walnut meats. Scoop out ripe avocados with a teaspoon and place center of the avocados around the stuffed tomato, to cover all but the top. Place on crisp lettuce, garnish with whipped cream and top with a maraschino cherry. Serve cold with lemon dressing.

Stuffed Avocado Salad

1 ripe avocado
2 teaspoons
   lemon juice
1/8 teaspoon salt
1 package (3 oz.)
   cream cheese
1/4 cup mayonnaise
1 tablespoon capers
Watkins Paprika

Cut avocado in half lengthwise, remove seed and peel. Sprinkle with lemon juice. Blend cheese, mayonnaise, capers, salt and fill center of avocado. Press halves together, wrap in waxed paper and chill. Cut lengthwise in slices and serve on crisp lettuce with a dash of Watkins Paprika.

Avocado and Tomato Salad

1 head lettuce
2 tomatoes, quartered
1 avocado, diced
6 green onions, chopped
4 strips crisp bacon

Have all ingredients chilled, toss together with French dressing and Watkins Paprika, and serve on crisp lettuce.

Banana Salad

Serve peeled banana cut lengthwise on crisp salad greens, sprinkle with nut meats and serve with French or cooked salad dressing. Or split banana lengthwise, dip in orange juice and top with orange sections. Add three or four prunes or cherries, pitted and stuffed with cream cheese, and several walnut halves.

Blueberry Salad

3 large grapefruit
1 pint blueberries
Crisp water cress
Mayonnaise

Arrange sections of chilled grapefruit on chilled salad plates and place rows of large berries over fruit. Add salad dressing and a sprig of water cress.

Brazil Nut and Pineapple Salad

½ lb. Brazil nuts
1 small pineapple
1½ pimiento
Juice of 1 lemon
Dash salt
½ cup heavy cream
Watkins Paprika
Crisp lettuce

Shred Brazil nuts. Cut pineapple in julienne strips, two inches in length. Cut pimiento in strips. Blend ingredients in salad bowl, add lemon juice and heavy cream.

Calavo with Orange

Cut calavo in half, remove hard pit, peel and fill center with sections of orange. Add Citrus salad dressing and serve on crisp lettuce. Prepare calavo just before serving to prevent its turning dark, or peel and place in lemon juice.

Cantaloupe Salad

Blend equal parts of cantaloupe balls and whole washed strawberries or raspberries. Add lemon juice and oil dressing, or orange and lemon juice. Serve on crisp lettuce.

California Dessert Salad Bowl

3 ripe cantaloupes
3 fresh peaches
1 cup water-
melon balls
1½ cups grape-
fruit sections

1 cup orange
sections
1 cup ripe pine-
apple, cut in
strips
French fruit
dressing

Prepare chilled fruit. Cut cantaloupe in halves, crosswise, and fill
with fruit; add French dressing.
Serve on curly endive.

Waldorf Cantaloupe Salad

2 cups diced
cantaloupe
1 cup diced
fresh peaches
1 cup diced
pineapple
1 cup diced
orange or
grapefruit

1 cup nut meats,
cut
¼ cup French
dressing
¾ cup whipping
cream
⅓ teaspoon
powdered sugar

Blend fruit and nuts, add French
dressing and chill 15 minutes. Just
before serving, drain off excess
dressing and serve on crisp lettuce.
Add a dash of sweetened whipped
cream with a little Watkins Paprika.

Cherry Dessert Salad

2 cups drained
black cherries
or fresh cherries
1 3-oz. package
cream cheese
2 tablespoons
cream
½ cup walnut
meats

6 slices drained
canned pine-
apple
6 canned peach
or apricot
halves
Cream mayon-
naise
Watkins Paprika

Pit cherries and chill. Blend
cheese, cream, nuts and salt to suit
taste. Fill cherries with mixture.
Arrange pineapple slices on crisp
lettuce, place apricot halves in
center and arrange cherries around
fruit. Serve with cream mayonnaise and a dash of Watkins Paprika.

Escarole and Grapefruit Salad

1 large head
escarole
Grapefruit
sections

Lemon or lime
juice
Radish roses

Wash escarole, separate leaves and
chill. Arrange with grapefruit on
salad plates and add lime juice.
Garnish with radish roses.

Fig Salad

Wash and dry figs, then chill.
Mash cream cheese, add a little
cream, salt and Watkins Paprika.
Make an incision in figs and stuff
with cheese. Serve on crisp lettuce
with fruit mayonnaise.

Dried Fig Salad

1 cup dried figs	1 cup diced apple
½ cup diced crisp celery	Walnut meats
	French dressing

Wash figs, drain, cover with hot water and boil 5 minutes. Drain, cool, use scissors and cut into strips. Blend figs with remaining ingredients and add French or cream dressing. Serve on crisp salad greens.

Fruit Dessert Salad

3 ripe bananas	1 tablespoon lemon juice
1 cup diced canned pineapple	½ cup mayonnaise
1 cup canned diced pears	1 cup heavy cream, whipped
½ cup pitted cherries	Watkins Paprika

Mash ripe bananas, blend with lemon juice, whipped cream and mayonnaise. Add chilled fruit and serve on crisp salad greens. (Prepare just before serving.)

Fruit Dessert Salad

8 peach halves	1 cup sherry wine
2 small avocado pears	Chopped nuts (not fine)
32 dates	2 oranges
1 3-oz. package cream cheese	2 grapefruit
	Watkins Paprika

Soak pitted dates in sherry wine overnight, drain and fill with softened cream cheese blended with chopped nuts. Shred crisp lettuce and arrange on chilled salad plate. Add peach half in center of plate, arrange slices of avocado, orange, grapefruit and dates. Garnish with water cress. Add French dressing.

Fruit Salad Chantilly

Prepare fresh fruit such as strips of ripe pineapple, oranges, grapefruit, peaches, and add a small glass of maraschino and 2 teaspoons sugar. Chill and serve on crisp salad greens with French dressing.

Grilled Fruit Salad

Remove core of half a grapefruit, loosen sections, but do not remove. Fill center with thin strips of apple, ripe strawberries and stoned ripe cherries. Drop honey over mixture and place under broiler with low heat for a few minutes. Serve as a dessert with toasted fruit bread or crisp crackers and cheese.

Fruit Salad In Pineapple Shell

Fresh pineapples
Canned pears, diced
Fresh straw- berries
Bananas, sliced
Honeydew melon balls
Diced ripe peaches

Use half as many small ripe pine-apples as there are salads required. Wash pineapples, cut into halves lengthwise, leave spines on the fruit. Scoop out fruit, dice pine-apple, add a little sugar, sherry and chill. Just before serving, add remaining fruit and serve at once, adding a little orange or grapefruit juice.

Thin bread and butter sandwiches with crisp water cress may be passed with the salad, or rolled chicken sandwiches, or buttered nut or orange bread, cut into nar-row strips.

Frozen Fruit Salad

(May be served without freezing)
1 3-oz. package cream cheese
1 cup mayonnaise
1 cup drained crushed pineapple
1 cup ripe peaches
1 tablespoon lemon juice
½ cup mara- schino cherries
1 cup cream, whipped

Blend cheese and mayonnaise, add fruit, fold in whipped cream. Serve on crisp salad greens.

To Freeze: Pack salad mixture in a mold rinsed out in cold water, then place in the freezing compart-ment of the refrigerator. When firm cut salad in cubes and serve on crisp salad greens.

Grape Salad

Bartlett pear halves
Cream cheese
Cream
Salt
Tokay grapes

Peel ripe pears, cut into halves lengthwise and place core side down, on crisp lettuce. Spread pear surface thickly with cream cheese softened with cream and salted to taste. Press grapes into cream cheese, covering entire pear. Serve with mayonnaise or French dressing. Nuts may be added to cheese.

Grapefruit and Celery Salad

2 grapefruit
2 bunches celery
Crisp lettuce
French dressing
Watkins Paprika

Cut inner stalks of celery into three or four inch pieces. With a sharp knife split each piece into thin strips, stopping within an inch of the end. Drop into ice water and let stand to curl. Arrange crisp lettuce on salad plate. Add sections of grapefruit and curled celery stalks. Add French dressing and Watkins Paprika.

Melon Ring Salad

Medium-sized cantaloupe
White grapes, cut into halves and seeded
Crisp water cress
Lime or lemon juice

Wash melon, cut off ends, then cut into five or six rings, remove seeds and rind. Chill. Prepare grapes, then cover with waxed paper and chill. Just before serving, place melon ring on crisp water cress, fill center with grapes and serve with lime juice or lemon juice, or your favorite French dressing.

Melon Salad

Serve halves of small ripe cantaloupe on crisp salad greens, fill center with blueberries and diced ripe pears. Serve with a fruit salad dressing. Any fruit in season may be used.

Minted Peach Salad

Place peach halves on crisp salad greens, sprinkle with lemon juice and chopped mint. Serve with whipped cream dressing.

Minted Fruit Salad

1½ cups diced fresh pineapple
1 cup diced ripe bananas
1½ cups diced orange sections
1 cup quartered marshmallows
2 tablespoons powdered sugar
2 cups ginger ale
½ cup lemon juice
½ bunch mint, minced

Blend fruit, marshmallows and sugar. Blend ginger ale and lemon juice, pour over fruit and chill. Drain off ginger ale, add mint and serve on crisp lettuce.

Orange Marshmallow Salad

2 large oranges, diced
1 grapefruit, diced
2 cups diced, crisp celery
2 tablespoons chopped walnuts
8 marshmallows, cut into pieces
1 cup seedless grapes
½ cup mayonnaise
2 tablespoons grated orange rind

Blend fruit with mayonnaise and orange rind. Chill one hour. Serve on crisp water cress.

Pear Salad

Peel, halve and core ripe pears. Prepare just before serving to prevent discoloration. Fill center with cream cheese and chopped walnuts, chopped preserved ginger or ripe olives. Place halves together and serve with cooked salad dressing. Add Watkins Paprika.

Pear Dessert Salad

1 tablespoon plain gelatin	1 tablespoon honey
4 tablespoons lime juice	½ cup cut walnuts
1 tablespoon lemon juice	1 tablespoon mayonnaise
1½ tablespoons sugar	1 can pear halves, drained
1½ cups ginger ale	Few drops Watkins Green Color Mixture
1 3-oz. package cream cheese	

Soften gelatin in lime and lemon juice, 5 minutes, then stir over hot water until dissolved. Stir in sugar, then add ginger ale and a few drops of Watkins Green Color Mixture. Chill until slightly thickened. Mash cheese, stir in honey, walnuts and 1 tablespoon mayonnaise. Place 1 tablespoon of cheese mixture in each pear half and arrange pears in a shallow pan, filled side up, then spoon in gelatin mixture. Chill until firm. Cut into squares, serve on crisp lettuce with mayonnaise or cream salad dressing. Add a dash of Watkins Paprika.

Pineapple and Shrimp Salad

1 can shrimp	¾ cup mayonnaise
6 slices pineapple	
1 cup diced celery hearts	¼ cup chili sauce
	Watkins Paprika

Clean shrimp, cut into pieces, and blend with other ingredients. Serve on crisp lettuce and garnish with ripe or stuffed olives.

Pineapple, Apple and Celery Salad

Blend equal parts raw ripe pineapple, apple and celery cut in julienne strips. Add 1 tablespoon sherry, a dash of vinegar and Watkins Paprika to 1 cup mayonnaise, mix well and add to fruit.

Prune Salad

20 cooked prunes	2 cups cubed cantaloupe
Nut meats	
2 cups diced orange or grapefruit	¼ cup honey
	⅓ cup lemon juice

Cut cooked drained prunes, remove pit and fill center with nuts. Blend cantaloupe and grapefruit, add honey mixed with lemon juice. Arrange on crisp salad greens with stuffed prunes.

Royal Salad

Romaine
1 orange
1 grapefruit
1½ pears
1 green pepper

6 strawberries
Strawberry
  cream
  mayonnaise

Arrange romaine on individual salad plates. On this arrange 3 segments of orange, 2 of grapefruit, 2 sections of pear, separating the different fruits with a slice of green pepper. Top with strawberry. Serve with mayonnaise blended with crushed strawberries.

Strawberry Melon Salad

½ honeydew
  melon
1 pint
  strawberries

1 cantaloupe
Lime French
  Dressing

All melons should be served very cold. Melon pulp may be shaped into balls with a French vegetable cutter, diced, or scooped out in large spoonfuls. Arrange berries and melon balls on lettuce. Serve with dressing.

Strawberry Dessert Salad

2 cups large
  strawberries
½ cup cream
  mayonnaise

6 ripe peaches or
  fruit in season
½ head crisp
  lettuce

Arrange peach halves on crisp lettuce. Add strawberries and mayonnaise. Serve cold.

Vienna Fruit Salad

Ripe peach slices
Ripe pear slices
Orange sections
Grapefruit
  sections

Avocado strips
Strawberries
French fruit
  dressing

Chill fruit, prepare just before serving and add a little lemon juice to prevent fruit discoloring. Add French dressing.

Waldorf Salad

2 cups diced,
  peeled apples
1 cup celery,
  diced

½ cup broken
  walnut meats

Blend apple, celery and nuts with mayonnaise. Fill a cup with salad, turn on a crisp lettuce leaf and add a bit of mayonnaise to top. Garnish with half a walnut and a maraschino cherry.

Fruit Salad Combinations

Arrange grapefruit and orange sections alternately on crisp lettuce. Add pitted dates, filled with cheese and nuts. Serve with French dressing.

Separate oranges in sections, cut bananas and apples in julienne strips, marshmallows into quarters. Blend mixture with fruit juice mayonnaise. Add Watkins Paprika.

Mix halved strawberries, cherries, grapefruit and diced pineapple with fruit dressing and serve on shredded lettuce or endive.

Arrange on crisp lettuce, grapefruit and orange sections, pitted cherries, sliced avocado and fresh strawberries. Add a well-seasoned French dressing.

Blend diced canned pineapple, orange and grapefruit sections, grapes or strawberries, and serve with French dressing.

Mix marshmallows, pineapple cubes, orange sections, grapes or cherries and walnuts, add a few grains salt and moisten mixture with cream mayonnaise dressing.

Chill drained canned pears or peaches and pineapple. Fill center of pear with cream cheese and nuts and place pear, hollow side down, on crisp lettuce. Add strips of pineapple and garnish with ripe strawberries or maraschino cherries.

Arrange on crisp romaine, grapefruit sections and avocado or peeled fresh pears cut into strips lengthwise. Sprinkle with lime juice and shredded almonds. Add a dash of Watkins Paprika.

Blend honeydew melon balls, diced pears, preserved ginger and water cress with French dressing made with fruit juices. Chill and serve on salad greens.

Serve strips of ripe melon and quartered ripe peaches on chilled chicory. Add French dressing.

Slice an orange, winter pear, red apple and sweet onion in paper thin slices. Add French dressing and serve on crisp lettuce.

Blend ripe banana cut in finger length strips with orange and grapefruit sections and strips of ripe pineapple. Add French dressing and garnish with ripe strawberries, cherries or ripe olives.

Select large prunes, steam and remove stone. Remove pits from choice dates. Fill centers with cream cheese and nuts and serve on salad greens. Add mayonnaise dressing. Grated pineapple may be added to the cheese and nut filling.

Fill center of chilled canned pear with sliced raisins, cut walnuts or pecans marinated in sherry. Add celery hearts spread with Roquefort cheese and a dash of Watkins Paprika.

On heart of romaine arrange sections of orange, grapefruit, strips of pear and fresh peach. Add French dressing.

Remove seeds from large black cherries and fill centers with cream cheese or nuts. Arrange with sections of orange on crisp salad greens. Add French dressing.

On crisp romaine arrange alternate sections of grapefruit, orange, pear and apple. Add French dressing and garnish with ripe strawberries.

Arrange sections of oranges, pineapple, honeydew melon and strawberries on crisp romaine. Add sour cream dressing blended with a little maraschino.

Arrange chilled sections of orange, avocado, pineapple and grapefruit on chilled greens. Add finely minced preserved ginger and French dressing.

Cut orange and grapefruit sections in half lengthwise and blend with sliced preserved kumquats. Add apple strips sprinkled with lemon juice to prevent discoloration. Fold equal parts whipped cream and mayonnaise together. Add one half of dressing to salad, and use remaining dressing to garnish.

Place a slice of ripe pineapple on crisp salad greens. Cover one quarter of the slice with peeled orange sections, the opposite quarter with sections of ripe grapefruit. In the third quarter place sections of ripe peaches and, in the fourth section, ripe pears, cherries, or avocado strips. Place a rosette of cheese in center of pineapple.

Slice fresh pineapple, sprinkle with sugar and chill. Just before serving, peel avocado, cut into strips and arrange with pineapple strips on salad greens. Ripe peaches may be added.

Cut fresh pineapple into slices, add sugar, and let stand to flavor. Arrange on crisp shredded lettuce with strips of banana or grapefruit sections, and top with sliced ripe strawberries blended with sugar and maraschino. Ripe peaches may be added.

Arrange chilled pineapple slices on lettuce. Remove seeds from whole canned apricots, fill center with blended celery, dates and nuts, and place on pineapple. Add French dressing made with fruit juice instead of vinegar.

Place strips of avocado and sections of chilled orange and melon on romaine. Garnish with thin strips of green pepper. Add French dressing with minced water cress and a dash of chili sauce.

Blend bananas, pineapple, sliced canned or ripe peaches, red cherries, and thinly sliced ripe olives with equal parts of mayonnaise and whipped cream. Add a dash of salt, a dash of tobasco sauce and a teaspoon of lemon juice to the dressing before blending with fruit. Serve on crisp salad greens.

Arrange strips of ripe peaches and peeled apple on crisp endive and add French dressing.

Place a slice of pineapple on romaine, add strips of honeydew melon and sections of orange and grapefruit.

Molded or Gelatin Salads

In making molded salads with flavored gelatin, pour hot liquid over the granules and stir until dissolved. When using plain unflavored gelatin, follow these simple rules:

1. Soak gelatin granules in cold water about 5 minutes to soften.
2. Add softened gelatin to hot liquid and stir until dissolved; if no hot liquid is called for in the recipe, stir the softened gelatin over hot water until dissolved, then add to other ingredients.

Always allow gelatin mixture to cool and begin to thicken before adding salad mixture. If added while the gelatin is warm and in a liquid state, the ingredients will rise to the top.

Pineapple juice or fruit pulp must be cooked before adding it to the gelatin. Unless this is done, the gelatin will not congeal. Drain canned fruit mixture, and chill thoroughly before adding to gelatin.

To Prepare a Gelatin Mold

Rinse the mold in cold water. Drain, but do not wipe mold dry. Add gelatin mixture and chill. Or chill the mold, wipe mold dry, and brush lightly with salad oil.

To Unmold a Gelatin Salad

Immerse the mold nearly to the top for a second in warm, not hot, water; or wrap a hot cloth around the mold; then carefully loosen the gelatin at the top edge with the point of a small knife. Place a chilled serving platter on top of the mold, invert, and lift mold from gelatin, shaking gently if necessary. If gelatin does not at once come out easily, remove from plate and dip mold again in the warm water. Unmold on crisp water cress, feathery endive, or chilled lettuce.

Molded Salad as Garnish for Meat Platter

Serve a garniture salad with a cold meat platter. With fish or dark meat, serve a light colored salad; with white meat, add a molded gelatin salad of fruit, tomato aspic or vegetables.

Individual fancy molds may be used for a salad, or use after-dinner coffee cups or Jello aluminum molds. Gelatin mixtures may be chilled in pans then cut in square or fancy shapes when firm. The cube trays of a mechanical refrigerator may be used to mold gelatin.

The ring mold is a decorative way to serve jellied salad. Have a bowl the exact size of center and fill with decorative fruit, vegetables, or any salad mixture desired, or use for the salad dressing. Have chilled serving platter large enough for garnishing.

Flavor Combinations Important In Molded Salads

Any of the following combinations may be added to either of the foundation gelatin recipes:

Apples, celery and nuts.

Beets, bean sprouts, cooked peas and celery.

Shredded cabbage, celery and crushed canned pineapple.

Cabbage, celery and pimiento.

Cabbage, apple, stuffed olives.

Cabbage, carrot and bean sprouts.

Cabbage, celery and grated raw carrot.

Celery, cucumber, shredded cabbage and horse-radish dressing.

Grapefruit pulp and avocado.

Grapefruit and cucumber.

Grapefruit, celery, nuts.

Marshmallow, pineapple and nuts.

Orange, prunes and nuts.

Orange, apples, seedless raisins and bean sprouts.

Canned pineapple, grapefruit pulp, blanched almonds.

Canned pineapple, cucumber and celery.

Canned pineapple, apple and banana.

Canned pineapple, cherries, dates and nuts.

Canned pineapple, orange and nuts.

Tuna fish, cucumber, celery and horse-radish.

Gelatin Base for Salads

1 envelope plain gelatin
¼ cup cold water
1 cup hot water
¼ cup mild vinegar
¼ cup sugar
1 tablespoon lemon juice
½ teaspoon salt
2 cups diced vegetables or fruit
Watkins Paprika

Soften gelatin in cold water 5 minutes; add sugar, salt, hot water, and stir to dissolve. Add vinegar, lemon juice, and chill.
When mixture begins to thicken, fold in vegetables or fruit. Serve on crisp lettuce with mayonnaise or cream salad dressing, and a dash of Watkins Paprika.

Flavored Gelatin Base for Salads

1 package lemon gelatin
2 cups boiling water
1 tablespoon vinegar or lemon juice
¼ teaspoon salt

Pour water over gelatin and stir to dissolve. Chill. When mixture begins to stiffen, add other ingredients.

Asparagus Salad, New Orleans

1 tablespoon
plain gelatin
¼ cup cold water
1 cup boiling
water
1 cup mayonnaise

¼ cup finely
chopped sweet
gherkins
1 green pepper
Asparagus tips,
canned or fresh
cooked

Soften gelatin in cold water, 5 minutes, add to boiling water, stirring until dissolved. When slightly cooled, beat in mayonnaise with egg beater. Add gherkins and pour into small individual molds. Chill until firm. When ready to serve, unmold on lettuce and top each mold with a thin ring of green pepper. Surround mold with asparagus tips, garnish with stuffed olives.

Avocado or Calavo Salad

1 package lemon
flavored gelatin
1 package lime
flavored gelatin
3 cups boiling
water
1 cup mayonnaise
1 avocado

½ cup diced
celery
½ cup walnut
meats
1 cup apple,
orange and
grapefruit

Stir boiling water into gelatin and chill until slightly thickened, then whip with a rotary beater until light. Add mayonnaise and beat well. Fold in diced avocado and celery. Pour into a ring mold brushed with olive oil and chill. Unmold on salad greens and fill center of mold with fruit and nuts.

Avocado, Grapefruit and Melon Salad

1 package lemon
flavored gelatin
2 cups boiling
water

1 avocado
1 grapefruit
Ripe melon slices

Pour boiling water over gelatin, stir to dissolve. Prepare fruit. Brush bottom of mold with salad oil. In bottom of mold arrange a pattern of the fruit and pour in some of the gelatin and chill. Pour in remaining gelatin, add remaining fruit and chill until firm. Serve on crisp lettuce and add mayonnaise or fruit dressing.

Avocado-Shrimp Aspic

1 tablespoon
gelatin
2 tablespoons
cold water
1 cup boiling
water
1 cup sieved
avocado
1½ tablespoons
lemon juice

¾ teaspoon salt
½ teaspoon
Worcestershire
sauce
Dash of tobasco
1 pimiento,
minced
1½ cups shrimp,
cooked and
shelled

Soften gelatin in cold water, add boiling water and stir to dissolve. Add avocado, seasonings and pimiento. Chill until mixture begins to thicken, then add shrimps. Turn into cold wet mold, chill until firm, and unmold on lettuce.

Avocado Cream Mold

1 package lemon
flavored gelatin
1 cup boiling
water
1 tablespoon
lemon juice
½ teaspoon sugar

1 cup avocado
pulp
½ cup whipped
cream
½ cup
mayonnaise
Watkins Paprika

Stir boiling water into gelatin, add sugar, lemon juice and cool. When mixture begins to thicken, fold in mashed avocado pulp mixed with mayonnaise, then fold in whipped cream. Pour into mold and chill until firm. Unmold on crisp lettuce and garnish with celery curls, radish roses and quartered ripe tomatoes.

Avocado In Tomato Aspic

1½ tablespoons
gelatin
¼ cup cold water
2½ cups tomato
juice
2 bay leaves
4 cloves

1 small onion,
sliced
½ teaspoon salt
2 avocados, diced
1 large apple,
diced
½ cup minced
celery

Soften gelatin in cold water, 5 minutes. Combine tomato juice, bay leaves, cloves, onion, salt, and boil for 5 minutes. Strain. Add gelatin and dissolve. Cool until syrupy. Add avocados, apple and celery. Turn into cold, wet mold and chill until firm.

Cabbage Mold

1 tablespoon
gelatin
¼ cup cold water
½ cup hot water
½ cup grape juice
1 tablespoon
lemon juice
1 teaspoon sugar
⅛ teaspoon salt
½ cup finely
chopped celery

½ cup finely
shredded
cabbage
1 cup diced
cucumber
2 tablespoons
chopped
pimiento
¼ cup heavy
cream

Soften gelatin in cold water; dissolve in hot water. Add grape juice, lemon juice, sugar and salt. Fill 6 small molds half full and chill until firm. Combine vegetables, cream and remaining gelatin, fill molds and chill. Unmold on lettuce.

Cardinal Salad (Beet Salad)

1 package lemon
flavored gelatin
1 cup boiling
water
¾ cup beet juice
½ teaspoon salt
2 teaspoons onion
juice or grated
onion

3 tablespoons
vinegar
1 tablespoon
horse-radish
¾ cup celery,
diced
1 cup cooked or
canned beets,
diced

Dissolve gelatin in boiling water, add beet juice, vinegar, salt, onion juice and horse-radish. Chill and when partly congealed, add celery and beets. Turn into individual molds and chill until firm. Unmold on crisp lettuce and garnish with mayonnaise.

Molded Cheese Salad

1 envelope
  unflavored
  gelatin
¼ cup cold water
1 cup hot water
½ teaspoon salt
¼ cup mild
  vinegar
1½ cups grated
  American
  cheese

⅓ cup cream or
  evaporated
  milk, whipped
½ cup chopped
  stuffed olives
½ cup diced
  crisp celery
¼ cup chopped
  green pepper
Watkins Paprika

Soften gelatin in cold water; add boiling water and stir until dissolved. Add salt and vinegar. Cool. When mixture begins to thicken, beat briskly. Fold in grated cheese, olives, celery, pepper and whipped cream. Turn into a mold and chill. Unmold on crisp salad greens and add mayonnaise dressing.

Cheese and Fruit Salad

1½ tablespoons
  gelatin
1 cup canned
  pineapple juice
3 cups cottage
  cheese
½ cup diced
  apple
¾ cup diced
  pineapple

¼ cup
  mayonanaise
¾ teaspoon salt
¼ teaspoon
  Watkins Dry
  Mustard
2 tablespoons
  lemon juice
Watkins Paprika

Soften gelatin in pineapple juice and dissolve over boiling water. Cool. Blend cheese, apple, pineapple and mayonnaise. Add salt, Watkins Mustard, Paprika and lemon juice. Stir gelatin into cheese mixture. Blend all ingredients and turn into a chilled mold, rinsed out in cold water. Chill until firm.

Cheese, Pineapple and
Cucumber Salad

2 tablespoons
  gelatin
½ cup cold water
¼ cup tarragon
  vinegar
2 cups cottage
  cheese
2 teaspoons salt
1 tablespoon
  granulated
  sugar

1 cup pineapple,
  diced
1 cup cucumber,
  diced
¼ cup green
  pepper, finely
  chopped
Few grains
  Watkins Red
  Pepper

Soften gelatin in cold water, heat over hot water to dissolve, and add tarragon vinegar. Beat cottage cheese until smooth. Blend in seasonings and gelatin. When mixture begins to thicken, add drained pineapple, cucumber and green pepper. Chill.

Special Salad Dressing for
Cherry Salad

White of 1 egg
¼ cup currant
  jelly, melted

1 tablespoon
  cream

Use a rotary whip and beat egg white stiff. Add melted jelly, a little at a time, and whip briskly. Add cream, whip mixture, chill and serve.

Cherry Salad Mold

1 tablespoon gelatin	1½ cups cherry syrup
2 teaspoons cold water	2 tablespoons lemon juice
Few grains salt	⅓ cup heavy cream
2 cups drained cherries	

Soften gelatin in cold water. Heat cherry syrup to boiling point, stir in dissolved gelatin, salt and lemon juice. Chill mixture until gelatin begins to set. Use a rotary whip and beat briskly. Pour half of mixture into a 3-cup ring mold rinsed out of cold water, and chill. Whip cream and fold into remaining gelatin, then whip with rotary beater. Pour into ring mold over first layer and chill in refrigerator several hours. Just before serving, unmold, and fill center of mold with chilled drained cherries. Add dressing and serve. (Fill cherries with cream cheese or nuts.)

Jellied Chicken Ring

1 envelope plain gelatin	2 cups diced cooked chicken
¼ cup cold water	2 tablespoons chopped pimiento
2 eggs	
½ teaspoon salt	
¼ teaspoon Watkins Paprika	2 tablespoons chopped green pepper
1¼ cups hot chicken stock	2 2-oz. cans mushrooms
1 tablespoon lemon juice	Water cress
½ cup cream	

Soften gelatin in cold water, 5 minutes, then stir and dissolve in liquid drained from mushrooms and heated. Beat eggs, add seasoning and stir into chicken stock. Stir and cook in top of double boiler until like custard. Remove from fire, stir in gelatin, then lemon, and cool. Add cream. When mixture begins to thicken, fold in diced chicken, pimiento, green pepper and sliced mushrooms. Turn into salad mold rinsed out in cold water. Chill until firm. Unmold on a chilled platter on crisp salad greens and garnish with stuffed olives and water cress. Serve with mayonnaise.

Molded Chicken Salad

2 teaspoons gelatin	½ green pepper, minced
½ cup cold water	¼ cup chopped olives
2 cups chopped cooked chicken	½ teaspoon salt
½ cup chopped celery	

Soften gelatin in cold water, stir and dissolve over hot water. Add chicken, celery, pepper, olives and salt. Mix well and turn into cold, wet mold until firm. Unmold on lettuce.

Chicken-Pineapple Salad

2 tablespoons gelatin
1/4 cup cold water
1 1/2 cups boiling chicken stock
1/2 teaspoon salt
1/8 teaspoon Watkins Paprika

1 cup canned pineapple juice
3 cups finely cut cooked chicken
1 1/2 cups drained diced pineapple
1 cup shredded toasted almonds

Soften gelatin in cold water 5 minutes, then stir into boiling chicken stock. Add seasoning and pineapple juice. Chill. When slightly thickened, fold in chicken, almonds and diced pineapple. Turn into large mold rinsed in cold water. Chill until firm. Unmold on large platter garnished with chilled chicory. Serve with mayonnaise.

Chicken Vegetable Mold

1 package lemon gelatin
1 pint boiling water
2 chicken bouillon cubes
3 tablespoons vinegar
1 1/2 teaspoons salt
2 teaspoons minced onion

1 cup 1/2-inch raw carrot strips
3/4 cup thinly diced celery
1/4 cup diced dill pickles
2 tablespoons diced pimiento
1 cup diced, cooked chicken or ham
Watkins Paprika

Stir and dissolve gelatin in hot water. Add vinegar, salt, Watkins Paprika and onion. Chill. When mixture thickens slightly, stir in remaining ingredients. Turn into a ring mold rinsed with cold water. Chill until firm. Unmold on crisp lettuce and serve with mayonnaise.

Jellied Crab Salad

1 tablespoon plain gelatin
1/4 cup cold water
3/4 cup mayonnaise
1/4 cup tomato catsup

1 cup crab meat, flaked in small pieces
1/2 cup chopped celery
2 tablespoons lemon juice
1/2 teaspoon salt

Soften gelatin in cold water 5 minutes, then stir and dissolve over hot water. Blend catsup and mayonnaise then add gelatin. Cool. Add remaining ingredients. Pour mixture into salad mold and chill. Unmold on crisp salad greens, garnish with quartered ripe tomatoes and diced cucumbers, crisped in ice water.

Crab Mousse

2 tablespoons gelatin
1/2 cup cold water
1 cup boiling water
1 cup heavy cream
2 cups flaked crab meat

1 cup mayonnaise
2 1/2 tablespoons minced pimiento
6 stuffed olives, sliced
1/2 green pepper, minced
Salt
Watkins Pepper

Soften gelatin in cold water. Dissolve in boiling water, then chill. Fold in mayonnaise, then whipped cream. Add other ingredients and season with salt and Watkins Pepper. Turn into mold.

Corned Beef Salad In Mold

1 envelope un- flavored gelatin	2 cups corned beef, cut into
¼ cup cold water	small pieces
1½ cups tomato juice	¾ cup diced crisp celery
½ teaspoon salt	¼ cup chopped
2 tablespoons lemon juice	pickle
1 teaspoon Worcestershire sauce	Hard cooked eggs Watkins Paprika

Soften gelatin in cold water, stir and dissolve in hot tomato juice. Add salt, lemon juice and Worcestershire sauce. Rinse out loaf pan with cold water and cover bottom with three sliced hard cooked eggs. Pour a little gelatin liquid over eggs and chill until set. When remaining gelatin begins to thicken, fold in the corned beef, celery and pickle. Line sides of pan with sliced cooked eggs and fill with gelatin mixture. Chill. Unmold on crisp lettuce and serve with mayonnaise or cooked salad dressing.

Cranberry Jelly Salad

1 tablespoon gelatin	1 cup finely chopped celery
2 tablespoons cold water	1 cup chopped apple
2 cups cranberry juice	½ cup chopped nuts

Soften gelatin in cold water, stir and dissolve in hot cranberry juice. Chill until mixture begins to thicken. Fold in celery, apple and nuts. Turn into molds. Serve on lettuce with mayonnaise.

Cranberry Salad Mold

1 package lemon gelatin	½ cup chopped celery
1½ cups hot water	½ cup chopped apple
1 cup canned cranberry sauce, chilled	¼ cup chopped nuts

Dissolve gelatin in hot water. Chill until mixture begins to set. Add cranberry sauce, cut into small cubes, celery, apple and nuts. Turn into cold, wet mold. Chill until firm.

Molded Cucumber Salad

1 package lime flavored gelatin	½ teaspoon salt
1 cup water	½ cup cooked dressing
1 cucumber, chopped fine	Dash of Watkins Pepper
1 tablespoon vinegar	Dash of Watkins Paprika
1 teaspoon scraped onion	

Dissolve gelatin in hot water. Add other ingredients when mixture begins to thicken. Chill until firm. Cut in squares and serve on crisp lettuce. Garnish with cooked dressing.

Molded Egg Salad

1 envelope un-
flavored gelatin
¼ cup cold water
4 hard cooked
eggs, sliced
½ cup crisp
celery, diced
2 tablespoons
green pepper,
chopped

1 cup mayonnaise
2 tablespoons
pickle relish
1 tablespoon
pimiento,
chopped
1 tablespoon
lemon juice
½ teaspoon salt
Watkins Paprika

Soften gelatin in cold water, then
stir over hot water to dissolve.
Cool, then beat into mayonnaise.
Add all other ingredients and blend
mixture. Pour into a loaf pan
rinsed out in cold water. Chill.
When ready to serve, unmold and
slice thin. Serve on crisp lettuce
with quartered tomatoes.

Fruit Salad Loaf

1 tablespoon
gelatin
¼ cup water
1 No. 2½ can
fruit cocktail

1 package cream
cheese
1 cup mayonnaise
1 package cherry
gelatin
2 cups hot water

Moisten gelatin in cold water, dissolve in ¾ cup boiling syrup,
drained from fruit cocktail. Cool.
Fold in cream cheese and mayonnaise.
Dissolve cherry gelatin in hot
water; cool.
Place half the drained fruits in a
loaf pan. Cover with 1 cup cherry
gelatin; chill until set. Pour in
cheese mixture. Chill again until
set. Add remaining fruits and
gelatin. Chill and unmold on salad
greens.

Jellied Fruit and Vegetable Salad

1 package lime
flavored gelatin
2 cups hot water
1 cup diced un-
peeled apple

½ cup diced
crisp celery
½ cup shredded
carrots
1 cup shredded
cabbage

Dissolve gelatin in boiling water,
cool. When mixture begins to
thicken add vegetables and blend.
Pour into mold rinsed in cold
water. Add mayonnaise and Watkins Paprika.

Molded Grape Salad

½ cup orange
juice
3 tablespoons
lemon juice
1 tablespoon
plain gelatin

1½ cups hot
grape juice
2 cups seeded
split grapes
¼ cup sugar

Soften gelatin in orange and lemon
juice. Add hot grape juice, sugar
and stir until gelatin is dissolved.
Chill. When mixture begins to
thicken, add grapes. Chill until
firm. Unmold on crisp lettuce and
serve with mayonnaise dressing.

Fruit Salad with Marshmallows

2 eggs
4 tablespoons
  vinegar or
3 tablespoons
  lemon juice
  and 1 table-
  spoon cold
  water
4 tablespoons
  sugar
3 tablespoons
  butter

2 cups diced
  pineapple
2 oranges, diced
2 cups Royal Ann
  cherries, pitted
1 cup seedless
  grapes
2 cups cut
  marshmallows
1 cup whipping
  cream

Beat eggs, stir in vinegar or lemon juice and water, add sugar. Stir constantly and cook over low heat until mixture thickens. Remove from heat, add butter and cool. Fold in fruit, marshmallows and whipped cream. Turn into mold rinsed in cold water. Chill 12 hours or overnight.

Molded Ring with Fruit

2 tablespoons
  plain gelatin
½ cup cold water
1¼ cups boiling
  water
1 cup sugar
1½ cups orange
  juice

2 tablespoons
  lemon juice
Grated rind
  1 lemon
1 cup heavy
  cream, whipped
Watkins Paprika

Soften gelatin in cold water, 5 minutes. Stir in boiling water, add sugar, orange juice, lemon juice and rind. Chill until mixture begins to thicken. Fold in whipped cream and pour into ring mold. Chill until firm. Turn on crisp lettuce and fill center with melon balls, peeled and seeded grapes, diced fresh pineapple, seeded black cherries, orange and grapefruit sections, or any fruit in season. Serve with mayonnaise or French dressing.

Grape and Cabbage Salad

1 tablespoon
  plain gelatin
¼ cup cold water
¼ cup boiling
  water
¼ teaspoon Wat-
  kins Dry
  Mustard
¾ teaspoon sugar
1 tablespoon
  vinegar

¼ teaspoon Wat-
  kins Paprika
1 cup mayonnaise
3 cups finely
  shredded
  cabbage
1 cup white
  grapes, halved
  and seeded

Soften gelatin in cold water, 5 minutes, add boiling water and stir until dissolved. Add Watkins Mustard, sugar, vinegar and Watkins Paprika. Cool, then whip mixture into mayonnaise. Add cabbage and grapes. Pour into salad mold rinsed in cold water. Chill overnight or about 12 hours. Unmold on crisp lettuce or salad greens.

Fruit Salad with Sherry

2 tablespoons
  plain gelatin
¼ cup cold water
1½ cups boiling
  water
¼ cup sugar
1 cup dry sherry
2 grapefruit, peel
  and remove
  sections

3 tablespoons
  lemon juice
4 oranges, peel,
  remove sections
1 lb. white
  grapes, peel,
  remove seeds
1 head romaine
Mayonnaise
Watkins Paprika

Soften gelatin in cold water, stir
and dissolve in boiling water. Add
sugar, lemon juice and mix well.
When cool add sherry. Turn into
mold rinsed in cold water. Chill.
Unmold on crisp romaine and surround with chilled fruit. Add mayonnaise dressing.

Jellied Grapefruit Salad

3 grapefruit
1½ tablespoons
  plain gelatin
4 tablespoons
  cold water
¼ lb. cream
  cheese

2 cups unsweet-
  ened grapefruit
  juice
¼ teaspoon salt
¼ cup chopped
  walnuts

Pare grapefruit, remove white
pulp, separate into sections and
remove membrane; leave sections
whole, and chill after draining off
juice.
Soak gelatin in cold water, stir
over hot water to dissolve. Add
grapefruit juice, salt, and cool.
Place grapefruit segments in mold
and pour over slightly thickened
gelatin mixture. Chill. Form
cream cheese into balls, size of a
walnut, and roll in chopped nuts.
Chill. Unmold gelatin on crisp
lettuce, and arrange cheese balls
around mold. Serve with cream
salad dressing.

Grapefruit-Cherry Dessert Salad

1 package cherry
  flavored gelatin
1½ cups hot
  water
½ cup cherry
  juice
½ cup pecan
  halves

1 tablespoon
  vinegar
¾ cup grapefruit
  sections,
  remove all
  membrane
¾ cup drained
  black cherries
Watkins Paprika

Stir boiling water into gelatin to
dissolve, then add cherry juice and
vinegar. Pour a thin layer into an
oiled ring mold and chill until firm.
Add fruit. Cover fruit with
slightly thickened remaining gelatin and add nuts. Chill until firm.
Unmold on crisp lettuce. Serve
with cream mayonnaise.

Grapefruit-Cheese Salad

1 envelope plain
  gelatin
½ cup cold water
1 cup boiling
  water
2 tablespoons
  sugar
½ teaspoon salt
3 tablespoons
  lemon juice
2 oranges, cut
  into sections

½ cup mara-
  schino cherries,
  halved
1 package lime or
  lemon gelatin
1¾ cup boiling
  water
10 sections
  grapefruit,
  peeled
½ cup cottage
  cheese
Watkins Paprika

First Layer:
Soften gelatin in cold water. Add boiling water, sugar, salt, lemon juice and stir until dissolved. Place orange sections in bottom of an oiled salad mold. Spoon gelatin mixture into mold carefully to prevent disturbing fruit. Chill. When partially set, pour in remaining gelatin.

Second Layer:
Dissolve lemon gelatin in boiling water and stir. Divide into two parts reserving one part to blend with cheese.
Arrange grapefruit sections on top of first layer. When lemon gelatin is partially set, spoon mixture carefully over grapefruit. Chill.

Third Layer:
Blend cottage cheese with reserved lemon gelatin and mix well. Pour cheese mixture over second layer when partly congealed. Chill until firm.

Ham and Cheese Salad Mold

Tomato Aspic
  (Page 98 Wat-
  kins Cook Book)
2 packages cream
  cheese
1 cup cottage
  cheese
Salt
Watkins Pepper
1 tablespoon
  gelatin
3 cups ground,
  cooked ham
½ cup mayon-
  naise

¼ cup cold water
2 tablespoons
  chopped celery
2 tablespoons
  chopped green
  pepper
1 teaspoon Wat-
  kins Dry
  Mustard,
  dissolved in
1 tablespoon
  hot water
Watkins Paprika
Salt to suit taste

Prepare tomato aspic. Cool and pour one-third of the mixture into a salad mold brushed with salad oil; chill until firm. Add seasoning to cheese, mash, and spread over jellied aspic. Carefully pour second-third of tomato aspic over cheese and chill until firm.
Mix ham, celery, green pepper, mayonnaise and seasonings, add gelatin softened in cold water and dissolved over hot water. Spread ham mixture over aspic and chill. For the final layer, cover ham with remaining tomato aspic and chill until firm.

Ham Salad Mold

1 tablespoon
  plain gelatin
1/4 cup cold water
2 cups boiling
  stock or
  bouillon
1/2 cup
  mayonnaise
3/4 cup diced
  crisp celery

1/4 cup diced
  dill pickle
1/2 cup chopped
  stuffed olives
2 cups diced
  cooked ham
Watkins Celery
  Salt
Watkins Paprika

Soften gelatin in cold water, 5 minutes, then stir into hot stock. Chill until slightly thickened, then whip in mayonnaise. Add remaining ingredients and pour into ring mold rinsed out with cold water. Chill until firm. Unmold on crisp salad greens.

Ham Mousse Salad

1 tablespoon
  gelatin
1/4 cup cold water
2 cups minced
  cooked ham
1/4 cup minced
  celery
1/2 cup heavy
  cream

2 tablespoons
  minced
  pimiento
1/2 teaspoon
  Watkins Dry
  Mustard
1/4 cup mayon-
  naise

Soften gelatin in cold water. Dissolve over hot water. Chill. Mix ham, celery, pimiento and mustard. Fold into chilled gelatin. Add whipped cream, mayonnaise and turn into cold mold. Chill until firm.

Deviled Ham and Cheese Loaf

2 packages lemon
  flavored gelatin
2 cups water
2 packages (3-oz.)
  cream cheese

1 7-oz. jar
  deviled ham
1 cup mayonnaise
Watkins Paprika

Dissolve gelatin in hot water. While hot, beat in cheese and ham. Cool. Fold in mayonnaise. Pour into loaf pan rinsed with cold water, and chill.

Perfection Salad

1 envelope plain
  gelatin
1/2 cup cold water
1 cup hot water
1/4 cup sugar
1/2 teaspoon salt
1/4 teaspoon
  mild vinegar
1 tablespoon
  lemon juice

1/2 cup cabbage,
  finely shredded
1 cup celery,
  chopped
1 pimiento,
  chopped, or
2 tablespoons
  sweet red or
  green peppers,
  chopped

Soften gelatin in cold water. Stir in hot water, sugar, salt, and stir until dissolved. Add vinegar and lemon juice. Cool. When mixture begins to thicken, fold in remaining ingredients. Turn into mold rinsed in cold water. When firm, unmold on lettuce and serve with desired dressing.

Molded Macaroni Salad

4 ounces
(½ package)
elbow macaroni
2 tablespoons
gelatin
½ cup cold water
½ cup cottage
cheese
¾ cup minced
celery
¼ cup minced
green pepper

1 cup mayonnaise
2 tablespoons
lemon juice
2 teaspoons
minced onion
1 tablespoon
sugar
1 teaspoon salt
½ cup heavy
cream, whipped

Cook macaroni in boiling, salted water until tender. Drain.
Soften gelatin in cold water and dissolve over hot water. Add cheese and mix well. Cool. Add macaroni, vegetables, mayonnaise and seasonings. Chill until slightly thickened, then fold in cream. Turn into cold wet ring-mold and chill until firm. Unmold and serve on lettuce.

Pineapple Up-Side-Down Salad

2 tablespoons
plain gelatin
½ cup cold water
1¼ cups boiling
water
½ cup sugar
1 teaspoon salt
½ cup pineapple
syrup
½ cup mild
vinegar

¼ cup lemon
juice
3 slices pineapple
3 cups finely
shredded crisp
cabbage
1 cup diced crisp
celery
¼ cup diced
pimiento
¼ cup diced
green pepper

Soften gelatin in cold water, 5 minutes, add to boiling water, sugar and salt and stir until dissolved. Add pineapple syrup, vinegar, lemon juice and cool. Pour into a loaf pan to depth of ¼ inch and chill until almost firm. Arrange two slices of pineapple over gelatin. Blend the other ingredients and fold into remaining gelatin. Pour over pineapple slices and chill. Serve with mayonnaise and a dash of Watkins Paprika.

Pineapple Pickle Salad

1 package lemon
gelatin
1 small can
pineapple
½ pound salted
almonds

1 dozen small
sweet pickles
1 pint boiling
water

Mix gelatin with boiling water and stir until dissolved. Cool. When mixture begins to thicken add pickles, almonds and pineapple cut into small pieces. Chill until firm. When solid cut in cubes and serve on lettuce with mayonnaise dressing. The salt from the almonds dissolves in the gelatin and flavors the salad agreeably. If blanched almonds are substituted for salted almonds be sure and add salt, about ¼ teaspoon.

Rhubarb Salad

2 cups rhubarb,
cut in pieces
⅔ cup sugar
1 tablespoon
gelatin
Few drops
Watkins Red
Coloring

½ cup cold water
¾ cup chopped
nut meats
1 cup chopped
celery
1 tablespoon
lemon juice

Simmer sugar and rhubarb a few minutes. Soften gelatin in cold water, then stir into rhubarb and cook one minute longer. Remove from heat, add a drop or two of Watkins Red Coloring, and cool. When mixture begins to thicken, add nut meats, celery and lemon juice. Pour into individual molds and chill. Unmold on shredded lettuce and serve with mayonnaise.

Salad Supreme
(Illustrated)

1 envelope plain
gelatin
½ cup cold water
1 cup hot water
⅓ cup sugar
½ teaspoon salt
Black cherries

¼ cup lemon
juice
Queene Anne
cherries
Sliced banana
Pineapple slices
Strawberries

Soften gelatin in cold water, add sugar, salt and hot water and stir until dissolved. Add lemon juice and mix thoroughly. Substitute fruit juice for part of hot water if canned fruit is used, using less sugar. Rinse mold in cold water and pour in jelly to the depth of about one-half inch, and allow to congeal. Arrange banana slices and cherries in rows in mold, add slightly thickened gelatin mixture carefully, and chill. Mix remaining cherries and gelatin and pour into mold. Serve with pineapple slices and garnish with ripe strawberries and sprigs of fresh mint.

Molded Salmon Salad

2 cups cold flaked
cooked salmon
1 teaspoon salt
1 tablespoon
sugar
1 teaspoon Wat-
kins Mustard
1 tablespoon flour
2 egg yolks
2 tablespoons
vinegar

1 cup milk
2 tablespoons
lemon juice
1 tablespoon
granulated
gelatin
3 tablespoons
cold water
2 tablespoons
butter
Watkins Paprika

Blend salt, sugar, mustard and flour in top of double boiler. Stir, add beaten egg yolks and blend to a smooth paste. Stir in milk, then vinegar and lemon juice. Stir constantly and cook over hot water until mixture thickens. Add gelatin which has been softened in cold water, then butter. When melted, carefully add salmon flakes to prevent breaking. Pour into mold and chill. Unmold on crisp lettuce and serve with sour cream salad dressing. Add Watkins Paprika.

Stuffed Tomatoes in Aspic

1 package lemon
  gelatin
1 tablespoon
  vinegar or
  lemon juice

2 cups water
6 small tomatoes
1 package (3-oz.)
  cream cheese
Cole slaw

Dissolve gelatin in water according to directions on package. Chill until mixture begins to thicken. Peel tomatoes, scoop out center and fill with cream cheese. Arrange in ring mold, filled side down, pour gelatin around tomatoes, and chill until firm. Unmold on lettuce and fill center with cole slaw.

Tomato Aspic Ring

3½ cups stewed
  tomatoes
1 tablespoon
  chopped onion
1 stalk celery
  with leaves
1 bay leaf
1 teaspoon sugar

½ teaspoon salt
2 tablespoons
  gelatin
½ cup cold water
3 tablespoons
  lemon juice
  or vinegar

Combine tomatoes and seasoning and cook mixture. Bring to boiling point, then simmer 15 minutes. Strain, add gelatin softened in cold water. Measure, and add enough water to make 3½ cups. Add lemon juice; pour into a ring-mold and chill in refrigerator.
Unmold on platter, using crisp salad greens. Fill center with chicken salad.

Tomato Aspic Variations

1.

Pepper Salad: Remove core and seeds from large green peppers. When aspic begins to thicken, fill prepared peppers. When firm, serve two or three slices to a serving, garnishing with lettuce, hard cooked egg or a cheese ball.

2.

Favorite Salad: When aspic begins to thicken add 1 cup finely chopped celery and 1 cup blanched, chopped almonds. Turn into individual molds and chill until firm.

3.

Shrimp Aspic: When aspic begins to thicken add 1 cup flaked shrimp and ½ cup finely chopped celery. Turn into individual molds and chill until firm.

4.

Artichoke: Add 1 teaspoon grated horse-radish to aspic before chilling. Pour into ring-mold; when firm unmold on lettuce and fill center with 2 cups artichoke hearts marinated in French dressing.

Molded Tuna Salad

1 tablespoon plain gelatin	2 tablespoons sliced pimiento
¼ cup cold water	3 tablespoons minced parsley
¼ cup lemon juice	½ cup finely chopped celery
1¾ cups ginger ale	Watkins Celery Salt
1 6-oz. can tuna	Watkins Paprika

Soften gelatin in cold water, 5 minutes, place over hot water and stir until dissolved. Cool. Stir in lemon juice, ginger ale, and chill until mixture begins to thicken. Break tuna in small pieces, fold into gelatin mixture, blend with pimiento, parsley and celery. Turn into salad mold brushed lightly with salad oil and chill until firm. Unmold on shredded crisp lettuce and garnish with sections of grapefruit. Serve with French or mayonnaise dressing.

Vegetable Salad Mold

1 tablespoon gelatin	⅛ teaspoon salt
¼ cup cold water	½ cup finely shredded cabbage
½ cup hot water	½ cup finely chopped celery
½ cup grape juice	¼ cup heavy cream
1 tablespoon lemon juice	
1 teaspoon sugar	

Soften gelatin in cold water; dissolve in hot water. Add grape juice, lemon juice, sugar and salt. Fill small molds half full and chill until firm. Combine vegetables and cream. Fill molds and chill one hour; unmold.

Jellied Vegetable Salad

1 envelope plain unflavored gelatin	½ teaspoon salt
½ cup cold water	½ cup cooked peas
1 cup hot chicken broth	1 tablespoon celery, chopped
½ cup diced carrots	2 tablespoons green pepper, chopped

Soften gelatin in cold water and dissolve in hot chicken broth. Add salt and cool. When mixture begins to thicken, fold in remaining ingredients. Pour into mold and chill. When firm, unmold and serve with mayonnaise or cooked dressing.

Gelatin Waldorf Salad

1½ tablespoons gelatin	1 cup diced crisp celery
½ cup cold water	⅓ cup nut meats
1½ cups hot water	½ teaspoon salt
2 cups diced apples	¼ teaspoon Watkins Paprika
	2 tablespoons lemon juice

Soften gelatin in cold water, dissolve in hot water.
Place diced apple, celery, nuts and salt in a bowl and add lemon juice. Blend lightly with a fork. When gelatin is almost ready to set, add to fruit and turn into a mold. Chill. Unmold on crisp lettuce and serve with mayonnaise or cooked dressing. Add a dash of Watkins Paprika.

Frozen Salads

Frozen fruit salads may be used as the last course of a simple meal. Marshmallows are excellent to use in a frozen salad because they help to absorb liquids and prevent their freezing into ice particles. Combined with whipped cream and mayonnaise, the salad should only be frozen until firm, not enough to harden the fruit or vegetable. The freezing can be done in the tray of an automatic refrigerator or packed in a mold and chilled in ice and salt.

Lime, lemon, pineapple or orange ice may be purchased and frozen in molds until firm, then filled with fruit mixture and garnished with crisp mint.

Frozen salads are practical for entertaining because they can be prepared in advance. When ready to serve, cut a slice or square, and serve on crisp lettuce or other salad greens. Add a dash of mayonnaise or cooked salad dressing and Watkins Paprika.

To Freeze a Salad

Automatic Refrigerator: Place salad mixture in refrigerator tray and set control at coldest point. When frozen, turn cold control back to No. 4 to hold until serving time. Do not freeze salad until mixture is frozen and icy, only until firm.

To Pack Salad in Ice: Pack mixture into an oiled salad mold, seal tightly with paraffin or adhesive tape (a baking powder tin may be used). Pack tin in five parts ice to one part salt and let stand about four hours, or until firm.

Apricot Cheese Salad

1 tablespoon granulated gelatin
1 cup cottage cheese
½ cup fruit jelly, melted over hot water
¼ cup cold water
1 tablespoon lemon juice
1 cup whipping cream
1¾ cups canned drained apricot halves

Soften gelatin in cold water 5 minutes, then stir and dissolve over hot water. Put cheese through a sieve, stir in melted jelly and lemon juice. Fold in dissolved gelatin and whipped cream. Pour blended mixture into refrigerator tray and freeze until firm. Serve on crisp lettuce and add apricot halves.

Frozen Dried Apricot Salad

1 lb. dried apricots	4 tablespoons sugar
1 pint water	1 tablespoon grated lemon rind
2 tablespoons lemon juice	
Few grains salt	

Wash apricots thoroughly, drain, add pint of water, salt, lemon rind, and simmer until soft. Add sugar last 5 minutes of cooking. Put apricots through a sieve. Add lemon juice, pour into refrigerator tray and freeze. Serve on crisp greens and add mayonnaise.

Frozen Banana Salad

4 ripe bananas	½ lb. marshmallows, cut
2 tablespoons lemon juice	3 pimientoes, put through sieve
1 cup heavy cream, whipped	½ teaspoon salt
½ cup mayonnaise	

Slice bananas and add lemon juice. Fold in whipped cream, mayonnaise and marshmallows cut into small pieces. Add pimiento and salt. Pour mixture into refrigerator tray and freeze until firm.

Frozen Banana-Cheese Salad

2 3-oz. cakes cream cheese	Juice of 1 lemon
1 teaspoon salt	2 bananas
½ cup mayonnaise	½ cup walnut meats
½ cup crushed pineapple, drained	½ cup maraschino cherries
	1 cup whipping cream

Blend cheese, salt, mayonnaise and lemon juice. Stir in drained pineapple, sliced bananas, nuts, and cherries cut in half. Fold in whipped cream and pour into freezing tray. When frozen, serve in slices on crisp lettuce and garnish with ripe strawberries.

American Cheese Salad with Pears

1 cup heavy cream, whipped	1 cup mayonnaise Watkins Paprika
1 cup grated American cheese	2 cups canned pear halves, drained

Blend all ingredients and pour into freezing tray. Sprinkle grated cheese over top in addition to cheese in salad. Freeze quickly until firm. Serve on crisp lettuce.

Frozen Cheese and Olive Salad

2 3-oz. packages cream cheese	¾ cup stuffed olives, sliced
1 cup mayonnaise	⅔ cup whipping cream
¾ cup ripe olives, chopped	Watkins Paprika

Cream the cheese, blend in mayonnaise, add remaining ingredients and pour mixture into refrigerator tray. When firm, (do not overfreeze), slice crosswise and place each section on crisp lettuce. Garnish with mayonnaise, Watkins Paprika and stuffed olives.

Frozen Cheese Salad

1½ cups fresh
  cream cheese
¾ teaspoon salt
¼ teaspoon Wat-
  kins Paprika
½ cup green
  pepper,
  chopped

½ cup pecans
½ cup chopped
  pimiento
½ cup
  mayonnaise
½ cup heavy
  cream, whipped

Blend all ingredients and turn into refrigerator tray. Freeze until firm. Serve on crisp salad greens and garnish with crisp water cress.

Cottage Cheese and Fruit Salad

¾ lb. cottage
  cheese
1 tablespoon
  mayonnaise
1 tablespoon
  lemon juice
¼ teaspoon salt
2 oranges, cut
  into small
  pieces

2 ripe bananas,
  diced
1 cup grated
  pineapple,
  drained
Maraschino
  cherries, diced
1 cup whipping
  cream
Watkins Paprika

Mash cheese until smooth, then blend in all ingredients, adding whipped cream last. Pour mixture into refrigerator tray and freeze until firm. Slice and serve on crisp salad greens. Add Watkins Paprika.

Frozen Cream Cheese and Fruit Salad

1 3-oz. package
  cream cheese
3 tablespoons
  mayonnaise
1 cup heavy
  cream
Watkins Paprika

1 cup fruit (diced
  drained pine-
  apple, cherries
  and candied
  ginger)
½ cup salted
  almonds

Cream the cheese, stir in mayonnaise and blend well. Add whipped cream, fruit and salted almonds. Pour into freezing tray and chill until firm. Serve on crisp lettuce.

Frozen Cheese and Pistachio Salad

3 3-oz. packages
  cream cheese
2 ounces
  Roquefort
  cheese
¼ cup whipping
  cream
¼ teaspoon salt

1 tablespoon
  lemon juice
Few drops Wat-
  kins Green
  Color
¾ cup shelled
  pistachio nuts

Cream cheese thoroughly, add lemon juice, salt, and a little Watkins Green Color to tint slightly. Add nuts, fold in whipped cream. Pour mixture in refrigerator tray and freeze until firm. Cut into squares and serve on chilled salad greens. Add stuffed olives to garnish.

Frozen Cheese and Water Cress Salad

2 packages cream cheese
½ cup coffee cream
½ cup mayonnaise
4 cups water cress, loosely packed
½ cup sliced stuffed olives
1 pint whipping cream
¾ teaspoon salt
1 cup nuts, cut
Watkins Paprika

Cream the cheese until smooth, add coffee cream, mayonnaise, and blend thoroughly. Break water cress into inch lengths, discarding coarse stalks. Blend all ingredients, folding in whipped cream last. Pour into refrigerator tray and freeze only until firm. Serve on crisp salad greens and add a dash of mayonnaise.

Frozen Chicken Salad

1 teaspoon plain gelatin
2 tablespoons cold water
⅔ cup mayonnaise
⅔ cup whipping cream
⅛ teaspoon salt
1½ cups diced cooked chicken
⅓ cup chopped blanched almonds
½ cup peeled and seeded Malaga grapes
Watkins Paprika

Soften gelatin in cold water 5 minutes, then stir and dissolve over boiling water. Cool, then combine with mayonnaise. Add other ingredients and fold in whipped cream. Turn into refrigerator tray and freeze until firm. Slice and serve on crisp salad greens. Add mayonnaise and a dash of Watkins Paprika.

Frozen Chicken and Pineapple Salad

1½ cups diced cooked chicken
¾ cup drained crushed pineapple (canned)
¾ cup cut pecan meats
1 cup whipping cream
1 cup cooked dressing or mayonnaise
Watkins Paprika

Toss together chicken, pineapple and nuts. Fold in whipped cream and salad dressing blended together. Freeze mixture until firm and serve on crisp salad greens.

Coconut Fruit Salad

¾ cup Watkins shredded coconut
1 cup maraschino cherries, halved
2 oranges, remove sections, peel and dice
Watkins Paprika
1 cup crushed drained pineapple (canned)
2 ripe bananas, diced
1 cup whipping cream
½ cup mayonnaise

Blend coconut and fruit, chill. Fold in whipped cream and mayonnaise. Pour into refrigerator tray and chill until firm. Unmold on salad greens.

Frozen Date-Pineapple Salad

1 3-oz. package
cream cheese
¼ cup cooked
salad dressing
½ cup whipping
cream

½ cup chopped
dates
½ cup crushed
drained pine-
apple (canned)
2 tablespoons
lemon juice

Mash cheese until smooth, blend in salad dressing. Fold in whipped cream, add fruit mixture. Pour into freezing tray and chill until firm.

Frozen Fig Salad

2 3-oz. packages
cream cheese
¼ cup
mayonnaise
1 tablespoon
lemon juice

¼ teaspoon salt
1 dozen preserved
figs or dates
½ cup whipping
cream

Blend cheese and mayonnaise. Add lemon juice, salt, figs and fold in whipped cream. Pour into refrigerator tray and chill until firm.

Frozen Fruit Salad

1 orange
¾ cup diced
pineapple
¾ cup Royal
Anne cherries
1 ripe banana
⅓ cup blanched
chopped
almonds

3 canned pear
halves
⅓ cup cut mar-
aschino cherries
½ cup cooked
salad dressing
½ cup whipping
cream
Watkins Paprika

Dice orange segments, add fruit, nuts, dressing, then fold in whipped cream. Pour into refrigerator tray and chill until firm. Serve on crisp lettuce and garnish with strawberries.

Frozen Fruit Salad

¾ cup diced
ripe melon
¾ cup ripe pears,
chopped
¾ cup ripe plums,
chopped
½ tablespoon
lemon juice
¼ cup cottage
cheese
Dash salt

½ cup orange
juice
⅓ cup cream
1 egg
1 tablespoon
corn starch
½ cup
mayonnaise
½ cup heavy
cream, whipped

Add lemon juice to prepared fruit, and chill. Blend cottage cheese with ⅓ cup cream and whip mixture. Heat orange juice and stir into corn starch, blended with a little cold water; stir and cook over hot water until mixture thickens. Stir in beaten egg yolk and cook 2 minutes. Remove from heat and add salt; chill. Fold in stiffly beaten egg white, then whipped cream. Blend cheese and fruit, fold in mayonnaise, add whipped cream mixture and pour into refrigerator tray. Freeze until firm. Serve in slices on crisp lettuce. Garnish with toasted almonds.

Frozen Fruit Salad

1 cup peeled
  seeded grapes
1 ripe banana,
  diced
1 orange, diced

¾ cup drained
  pineapple
½ cup mara-
  schino cherries
1 cup heavy
  cream, whipped

Blend all ingredients, pour into refrigerator tray and chill.

Frozen Party Fruit Salad

1 tablespoon
  plain gelatin
2 tablespoons
  cold water
¼ cup boiling
  water
2 tablespoons
  sugar
½ cup lemon
  juice
1 cup whipping
  cream
1 cup mayonnaise
1 cup drained
  crushed
  pineapple

1 cup finely cut
  orange sections
½ cup finely cut
  grapefruit
1 cup peeled cut
  grapes, seeded
1 cup marsh-
  mallows, cut
  into pieces
½ cup fresh
  coconut,
  shredded
⅓ cup sliced
  maraschino
  cherries

Soften gelatin in cold water 5 minutes. Add boiling water and sugar and stir until dissolved. Cool and add lemon juice. Chill until mixture slightly thickens. Fold whipped cream into mayonnaise and add to gelatin mixture. Add fruit, pour mixture into refrigerator tray and chill until firm. Unmold on crisp lettuce.

Quick Frozen Fruit Salad

Add ½ cup fruit salad dressing (or honey dressing) to contents of a No. 1 can of mixed fruit, then fold in ½ cup of heavy cream, whipped. Pour into refrigerator tray and freeze until firm. Serve on crisp salad greens. Drain canned fruit mixture and chill thoroughly before using.

Frozen Peach and Pecan Dessert Salad

6 canned peach
  halves
1 cup heavy
  cream, whipped
½ cup
  mayonnaise

1 cup cream
  cheese
1 cup chopped
  pecans

Drain peaches, place hollow side up in freezing tray of refrigerator. Combine cream, mayonnaise and cheese, mixing until smooth. Add nuts and pour over peaches. Freeze until firm, cut in squares and serve on lettuce, peach side up.

Marshmallows, Pineapple, Cherries

1 3-oz. package
  cream cheese
¼ cup
  mayonnaise
1 cup cream,
  whipped

1 small can
  crushed pine-
  apple, drained
⅓ cup mara-
  schino cherries
½ pound
  marshmallows

Blend cheese and mayonnaise. Add fruit, and marshmallows cut into small pieces. Fold in whipped cream and pour mixture into refrigerator tray. Chill until firm.

Frozen Peanut Butter Salad

1 3-oz. package
  cream cheese
½ cup chopped
  green pepper
¼ cup chopped
  pimiento
⅓ cup peanut
  butter

½ cup chopped
  celery
Salt
Juice of 1 lime
¼ cup
  mayonnaise
¼ cup heavy
  cream, whipped

Blend all ingredients and fold in whipped cream. Pour mixture into refrigerator tray and chill until firm. Unmold on crisp lettuce.

Frozen Pears

Fill center of small halved canned drained pears with cut maraschino cherries, nuts and raisins moistened with sherry wine. Place two halves together and insert a whole clove for stem. Place in refrigerator tray and freeze rapidly until firm, but not hard. Serve on crisp salad greens with mayonnaise.

Frozen Pineapple Salad

1 cup pineapple
  juice (canned)
2 tablespoons
  flour
½ cup butter
⅛ cup sugar
1-16 teaspoon
  salt
1 egg
2 tablespoons
  lemon juice

4 slices pineapple,
  cut fine
2 oranges
⅛ cup nuts
10 marshmallows,
  cut fine
10 maraschino
  cherries, cut
2 cups whipping
  cream

Make a paste of flour and a little pineapple juice, then stir in rest of juice. Add butter, sugar and salt. Stir and cook mixture in top of double boiler about 10 minutes. Take from fire, add beaten egg gradually. Cool, then stir in lemon juice. When cold, add fruit, nuts and marshmallows, and fold in whipped cream. Pour into refrigerator tray and chill until firm.

Frozen Pear-Cherry Salad

2 cups diced
  fresh pear
Juice 1 lemon
⅓ cup cut
  walnut meats
⅓ cup sliced
  fresh dates
Watkins Paprika

⅓ cup sliced
  maraschino
  cherries
½ cup
  mayonnaise
½ cup cream
  cheese
¼ teaspoon salt

Peel pear, dice and sprinkle with lemon juice. Mix mayonnaise and cream cheese until smooth, and blend with other ingredients. Press mixture into refrigerator tray and freeze until firm. Cut into squares and serve on crisp water cress or curly endive.

Frozen Pear Salad

1 cup heavy
  cream, whipped
1 cup grated
  American
  cheese

1 cup mayonnaise
2 cups drained
  canned pears
Watkins Paprika

Whip cream, blend in mayonnaise and grated cheese. Spread part of mixture in refrigerator tray, add pear halves and pack in remaining mixture. Sprinkle top with additional grated cheese and freeze until firm. Serve on crisp salad greens.

Prune, Pineapple, Coconut Salad

1 cup cooked
  drained prunes,
  seeded
1 cup crushed
  pineapple
1 cup moist
  coconut

¼ cup diced
  green pepper
1 cup whipping
  cream, whipped
½ cup
  mayonnaise
Watkins Paprika

Cut prunes into quarters. Blend all ingredients and pour into a refrigerator tray; chill until firm. Unmold on crisp lettuce.

Frozen Stuffed Tomatoes

6 firm ripe
  tomatoes
½ cup chopped
  cucumber
2 tablespoons
  finely chopped
  chives
3 tablespoons
  chopped green
  peppers
½ teaspoon salt

1 cup cottage
  cheese
2 tablespoons
  chopped
  pimiento
1 cup cooked or
  mayonnaise
  dressing
1 cup heavy
  cream, whipped

Wash and peel tomatoes, remove stem end, scoop out center, turn upside down to drain, and chill. Mix cheese, cucumber, chives, green pepper, pimiento, salt and 3 tablespoons salad dressing. Stuff tomatoes, place in refrigerator tray, cut-side down, taking care not to disturb filling.
Mix dressing and whipped cream and pour around tomatoes. Freeze until firm. When ready to serve, cut into squares with each portion a stuffed tomato. Add a little salad dressing and serve on crisp lettuce.

Frozen Roquefort Cheese Salad

¼ lb. Roquefort cheese	1 cup celery chopped fine
1 teaspoon lemon juice	1 tablespoon minced chives, if desired
2 tablespoons cream cheese	1 cup cream, whipped
Watkins Paprika	

Blend cheese and lemon juice. Add remaining ingredients and fold in whipped cream. Turn into refrigerator tray and freeze until firm. Serve on crisp salad greens.

Frozen Rhubarb-Cheese Salad

2 cups cottage cheese	1 teaspoon granulated gelatin
2 cups cooked rhubarb sauce, sweetened	2 tablespoons cold water
Watkins Paprika	1 cup heavy cream

Sieve cheese. Soften gelatin in cold water 5 minutes, then stir into hot rhubarb sauce until dissolved. Add cottage cheese, fold in whipped cream and chill mixture in refrigerator tray until firm. Cut into squares and serve on crisp salad greens. Add a dash of mayonnaise and Watkins Paprika.

Frozen Shrimp Salad

1 tablespoon gelatin	1 cup minced shrimp
½ cup chicken stock	Watkins Red Pepper
½ cup cooked white sauce, cold	½ cup mayonnaise
⅓ teaspoon salt	¾ cup whipping cream, whipped

Soften gelatin in stock, then stir and heat over hot water. Add shrimp, white sauce and seasoning. Cool. When partly set, fold in mayonnaise mixed with whipped cream. Pour into refrigerator tray and chill until firm. Cut into squares and serve on crisp lettuce. Add mayonnaise and garnish with stuffed olives.

Frozen Tomato Salad

1 tablespoon plain gelatin	½ cup mayonnaise
¼ cup cold water	½ cup whipping cream
1½ cups canned tomato soup	⅛ teaspoon salt
1 3-oz. package cream cheese	⅓ cup sliced stuffed olives
1 tablespoon onion juice	⅓ cup diced celery

Soften gelatin in cold water 5 minutes. Heat soup in top of double boiler, add gelatin and stir until dissolved. Cool. Add cheese, and mayonnaise blended with whipped cream. Add other ingredients and turn into refrigerator tray. Chill until firm. Unmold on salad greens.

Frozen Salmon Salad

2 cups cold
    cooked rice
1½ cups canned
    drained salmon
1 cup cooked peas
½ teaspoon salt

⅛ teaspoon Wat-
    kins Paprika
1 tablespoon
    lemon juice
¼ cup
    mayonnaise

Blend all ingredients, pour into refrigerator tray and freeze until firm. Unmold on crisp salad greens and garnish with stuffed olives.

Frozen Vegetable Salad

¼ cup sugar
2 tablespoons
    flour
½ teaspoon salt
¼ teaspoon
    Watkins Dry
    Mustard
Dash Watkins
    Paprika
½ cup cider
    vinegar
3 tablespoons
    butter

2 eggs, beaten
¾ cup diced
    cucumber
¾ cup diced
    celery
¾ cup diced
    fresh tomatoes
2 tablespoons
    minced green
    pepper
2 tablespoons
    minced
    pimiento

Sift together sugar, flour, salt, mustard and paprika. Add beaten eggs and vinegar. Stir and cook in top of double boiler until mixture thickens. Add butter and cool. Turn into refrigerator tray and chill slightly. Remove tray and stir in vegetables; return to refrigerator and chill until firm. Serve on crisp lettuce and add a dash of mayonnaise.

Frozen Vegetable Salad

2 teaspoons
    gelatin
¼ cup cold water
¾ cup
    mayonnaise
¼ cup whipping
    cream
¾ cup diced
    tomatoes
¾ cup diced
    cucumbers

¾ cup diced
    celery
3 tablespoons
    chopped green
    peppers
2 tablespoons
    chopped chives
¾ teaspoon salt
¼ teaspoon Wat-
    kins Paprika
2 tablespoons
    lemon juice

Soften gelatin in cold water 5 minutes, then stir until dissolved, over hot water. Cool slightly, add mayonnaise and whipped cream. Add remaining ingredients and pour into refrigerator tray. Chill until firm.

Frozen Water Cress Salad

½ lb. cream
    cheese
½ cup
    mayonnaise

1 cup top milk
1 bunch water
    cress
Watkins Paprika

Mash cream cheese and add mayonnaise. Gradually whip in top milk and blend. Add crisp water cress, turn mixture into freezing tray and freeze until firm. Serve on a slice of chilled tomato and crisp lettuce.

Vegetable Salads

Vegetables of all kinds are important in the diet because of their various vitamins and minerals. They contain protein and carbohydrates in the form of sugar, starch and cellulose; they furnish iron for red blood, give resistance to disease, and stimulate the appetite. Vegetables are base-forming and help to neutralize acid-forming foods. By eating fresh raw vegetables in a salad, we get the essential mineral salts which are often lost in cooking. Fresh raw vegetables provide an abundance of health food, furnish Vitamins A and C; in lesser amounts, Vitamins B and G, and give variety and flavor to a meal.

The most popular of the salad vegetables are tomatoes, shredded green cabbage in form of cole slaw, carrots, turnips, celery hearts, onions, radishes, green pepper, cucumbers, and salad greens. Other vegetables used raw in a salad are chopped broccoli, spinach, cauliflower, and parsley.

In the present fad of "counting calories", those who wish to avoid gaining in weight, will find that raw vegetable salads satisfy hunger but do not add extra pounds. Raw vegetables and fruit are high in water content and thus insure against dehydrated body tissue. The natural palatable uncooked vegetables contain minerals which aid in reducing, as well as counter-acting any tendency to acidosis. They safeguard a proper acid-base balance in the system, and supply Vitamin C, a vitamin that must be taken into the system daily for health.

Crisp green leaves of tender cabbage and salad greens are rich sources of Vitamin C; two ounces of raw green cabbage, the king of vegetables, contain nearly as much of this health giving vitamin, as forty ounces of cooked cabbage.

Purchase perishable vegetables in small quantities and use promptly. Clean vegetables, remove unedible parts, wash thoroughly under cold running water to remove sand and soil, drain and store in a cellophane or oil silk bag, or in a covered container in the refrigerator. Prepare a vegetable salad just before serving.

Artichoke Salad

6 cooked French artichoke bottoms

French salad dressing
Watkins Paprika

Pour French dressing over hot artichoke bottoms and let stand in the refrigerator 1 hour to flavor. Serve on crisp lettuce and garnish with strips of pimiento. Minced chives may be added if desired. Add French dressing.

Artichoke Salad

1 cup thinly sliced raw artichoke hearts

1 cup diced cucumber
1 cup chicory
1 or 2 tablespoons chopped chives

Blend with French salad dressing.

Artichoke Hearts and Foie Gras

Artichokes
Truffled goose liver
Crisp lettuce

Olive oil
Lemon juice
Mayonnaise
Watkins Paprika

Wash, tie each artichoke with white string to hold leaves together and cook in boiling salted water (allowing one artichoke for each person). Remove outside leaves, trim hearts and place in a dressing of 1 part olive oil and 4 of lemon juice). Let stand to flavor. Top each artichoke heart with truffled goose liver and serve on crisp salad greens. Add mayonnaise dressing and a dash of Watkins Paprika. Or omit goose liver and serve with mayonnaise.

Artichoke Salad

¾ cup grated raw artichoke hearts
¾ cup crisp shredded cabbage

¾ cup sliced raw carrots
Diced green pepper
4 tablespoons slivered Swiss cheese

Soak artichokes, cabbage and carrots in salted ice water until crisp. Drain and dry on a tea towel. Add pepper and cheese. Add sufficient French dressing to blend.

Asparagus Gelatin Salad

1 tablespoon gelatin
¼ cup cold water
1 cup boiling water
1 cup mayonnaise
Crisp lettuce

¼ cup chopped sweet gherkins
1 green pepper
30 asparagus tips, cooked or canned
Watkins Paprika

Soften gelatin in cold water 5 minutes, stir in boiling water. Cool. Beat in mayonnaise with a rotary beater, add gherkins and pour into individual molds. Chill until firm. Unmold on crisp lettuce and garnish with strips of green pepper. Top with asparagus tips marinated in French dressing.

Asparagus Salad

Wash asparagus stalks thoroughly, using a sharp knife to remove scales along the stalk, as the scales are pockets for sand and soil. Use cold running water to wash tips. Cut stalk in 4 to 5 inch lengths and tie in bunches. Cook in boiling salted water in an uncovered pan, only until tender.

Or serve drained chilled canned asparagus tips. Let asparagus tips stand in French dressing 1 hour before serving, for better flavor. Serve on crisp lettuce or other salad greens and serve with French, mayonnaise or chiffonade dressing. Add a dash of Watkins Paprika. Or arrange marinated (adding French dressing) asparagus tips on a slice of ripe tomato and serve on crisp lettuce. Garnish with strips of pimiento.

Green Bean Salad

Cooked string
  beans
Beet root

Corn salad
Chopped chives
French dressing

Cook green beans and beet root separately in boiling salted water and cook only until tender; drain. While warm, add French dressing. Chill. Add fresh corn salad and French dressing. Garnish with radish roses.

Kidney Bean Salad

3 cups cooked or
  canned red
  kidney beans
1 cup diced celery
4 hard cooked
  eggs, diced
½ green pepper,
  diced
4 green onions,
  sliced
Salt
¾ cup sliced
  radishes

¾ cup diced crisp
  cucumbers
⅓ cup chopped
  sweet pickle
1 cup diced boiled
  potatoes
  blended with
  French dressing
Watkins Paprika
Cooked or
  mayonnaise
  dressing

Blend ingredients and chill several hours before using. Use a sharp dressing made with vinegar, a little Watkins Mustard for added flavor.

Baked Bean Salad

2 cups canned
baked beans
1 cup drained
canned bean
sprouts
¼ cup minced
canned
pimiento

¼ cup chopped
green peppers
2 tablespoons
lemon juice
¼ cup diced
celery
Salt and
Watkins Pepper
French dressing

Chill all ingredients and serve on crisp salad greens.

Bean Sprout Salad

1 cup bean
sprouts
½ cup crisp
celery, chopped
½ cup green
pepper, sliced

1 sliced cucumber
⅓ cup sliced
radishes, do
not peel
French dressing
Watkins Paprika

Have all ingredients cold, blend mixture and serve on crisp lettuce. Add a little soy sauce to bean sprouts for better flavor.

Kidney Bean Salad

2½ cups canned
kidney beans
¾ cup diced
tart apple
½ cup chopped
sweet pickle

½ cup chopped
cabbage
Crisp lettuce
Mayonnaise
Watkins Paprika
½ teaspoon salt

Drain beans, add other ingredients and enough mayonnaise to blend. Chill. Serve on crisp lettuce.

Lima Bean Salad

2 cups cooked
lima beans
2 sweet pickles,
minced
Pimiento strips

2 ripe tomatoes,
peeled and
sliced
Lettuce
French dressing

Drain lima beans, blend with pickles and add dressing. Arrange on lettuce, add quartered tomatoes, and garnish with pimiento strips.

Lima Bean and Celery Salad

1 can drained
lima beans,
chill
1 bunch onions,
chopped

1 bunch radishes,
slice, do not
peel
¾ cup diced
celery

Have all ingredients cold. Blend mixture and serve with mayonnaise or French dressing and a dash of Watkins Paprika.

Lima Bean Salad

1½ cups cooked lima beans
½ cup diced pickled beets
2 tablespoons minced onion
2 tablespoons chopped parsley

Toss with cut crisp lettuce and French salad dressing, adding a little Worcestershire sauce.

String Bean Salad

Serve cooked or canned green or wax string beans. Add French dressing one hour before serving, for added flavor. Chill and serve on crisp salad greens. Add pimiento strips for a garnish. Minced chives may be added.

String Bean and Onion Salad

1½ lbs. green beans
1 large sweet onion
2 tablespoons olive oil
1 teaspoon sugar
½ cup vinegar (dilute with water if too strong)
Watkins Pepper

Wash beans thoroughly, remove strings and ends, and cut lengthwise. Cook in boiling salted water (1 teaspoon salt to a quart of water) only until tender. Drain. Cut onion fine, add hot beans, olive oil, sugar, pepper and vinegar. Chill and let stand an hour to flavor. Serve on crisp lettuce.

Beet Salad

Cut off tops of beets, about two inches above root. Do not peel. Wash thoroughly and cook in boiling salted water until tender. Plunge into cold water, then rub off skin. Chill.
Slice thin or dice, serve with French dressing on crisp lettuce. Sliced hard cooked eggs may be added, with a garnish of pickled mushrooms or green onions.

Beet and Cabbage Salad

Blend equal parts of sliced cooked beets, diced crisp celery, pimiento, shredded cabbage, sliced onion and green pepper. Add French or mayonnaise dressing.

Beet-Celery Salad

Blend equal parts of crisp salad greens, sliced boiled celery root and pickled beets; add French dressing.

Deviled Beets

3 tablespoons
  melted butter
2 tablespoons
  vinegar
½ teaspoon salt
¼ teaspoon Wat-
  kins Paprika

¼ teaspoon Wat-
  kins Mustard
1 tablespoon
  powdered sugar
1 teaspoon
  Worcestershire
  sauce

Blend mixture and serve over diced cooked beets.

Vinegar Beets

2 lbs. beets
⅓ cup water
⅓ cup vinegar
½ teaspoon salt

⅛ teaspoon
  Watkins
  Paprika
1 teaspoon sugar

Blend dressing and pour over 3 cups hot sliced beets and chill. Serve on crisp salad greens.

Beet Gelatin Salad

1 No. 2 can beets
2 tablespoons
  cider vinegar
2 packages lemon
  flavored gelatin
1 teaspoon salt

1 tablespoon
  horse-radish
½ teaspoon Wat-
  kins Celery Salt
Watkins Paprika

Drain liquid from beets, dice beets and add vinegar to flavor. Chill. Dissolve gelatin in boiling water, add beet liquid to make 4 cups. Add seasoning and chill. When mixture begins to stiffen, drain beets and fold into gelatin. Turn into salad mold and chill until firm. Serve on crisp greens with mayonnaise.

Beet Salad

Blend 6 medium-sized cooked beets and 1 small onion, sliced, in ⅓ cup French dressing and chill 1 hour. Serve on crisp lettuce with a dash of mayonnaise. Diced oranges may be added if desired.

Broccoli Salad

Wash broccoli thoroughly. Remove large leaves, then peel woody outer skin from main stem. Split large stem into pieces for serving. Cook, uncovered, in large amount of boiling salted water until tender. Drain and chill. Serve with a well-seasoned French, mayonnaise, or hot Hollandaise dressing.
Or arrange cooked flowerets of broccoli on crisp salad greens and garnish with radish roses. Add French dressing.

Cabbage Salad

3 cups crisp shredded cabbage	1 tablespoon ground caraway seeds, if desired
2 cups diced oranges	Salt
2 tablespoons chopped chives	Watkins Paprika
	Romaine or lettuce
Watkins Celery Salt	Salad dressing

Soak shredded cabbage in ice water 1 hour to crisp; drain, dry in a tea towel, add a little French dressing and chill. Add remaining ingredients just before serving with enough cooked dressing to hold mixture together. Chopped green peppers and diced crisp celery may be added.

Cabbage Bowl Salad
(Illustrated)

Carefully remove outer leaves of a large head of cabbage and soak them in ice water. Wash head under cold running water, cut off top. Remove center, leaving a shell about ⅓ inch thick. Chill. Shred cabbage, red cabbage and raw carrots. Add salt and French dressing, and chill. Diced raw apples, diced pineapple and cut walnut meats may be added. Just before serving moisten with cooked salad dressing, fill cabbage shell and place in bowl or on platter lined with the outer leaves of the cabbage.

Cabbage Salad with Whipped
Cream Dressing

3 cups shredded green cabbage	12 drops tabasco sauce
1 cup cream, whipped	Watkins Onion Seasoning
4 tablespoons lemon juice	2 tablespoons ground horse-radish
1 teaspoon salt	Watkins Paprika
1 teaspoon sugar	

Chill cabbage. Blend all ingredients just before serving. Garnish with strips of pimiento.

Cabbage Nut Salad

2 cups shredded cabbage	Dash Watkins Paprika
½ cup diced celery	Dash salt
1 cup walnuts or peanuts	⅓ cup cooked salad dressing

Shred cabbage, chill. Blend crisp diced celery and nuts. lightly with salad dressing. Watkins Paprika and garnish strips of pineapple.

Creamed Slaw

1 small head
  crisp cabbage
1 green pepper,
  remove seeds,
  chop
1 cup sweet cream
½ cup vinegar

3 tablespoons
  granulated
  sugar
Watkins Celery
  Salt
Watkins Paprika

Chop crisp cabbage fine. Blend mixture, chill and serve.

Combination Salad with Avocado Pear

2 avocado pears
Lemon juice
Salt
¾ cup diced
  celery
½ cup cubed
  tomatoes

⅛ cup sliced
  radishes, do
  not peel
¼ cup shredded
  green pepper
Mayonnaise

Cut pear lengthwise, peel, remove seed and brush pear with lemon juice. Blend remaining ingredients, fill avocado and serve on crisp salad greens. Garnish with stuffed olives. Or fill avocado with tuna fish salad mixture.

French Combination Salad

½ crisp head
  lettuce
2 ripe tomatoes
4 green onions
½ cucumber
5 radishes

2 outside stalks
  celery
1 individual
  Roquefort
  cheese

Wash lettuce, dry in clean towel, and chill. Peel cucumber, cut in half lengthwise, scrape out seeds, and slice thin. Place all ingredients in a mixing bowl, add cheese broken into pieces, and French dressing. Toss lightly to blend, and serve cold.

Combination Salad

1 cucumber
6 scallions
6 radishes
2 ripe tomatoes,
  cut into eighths

1 green pepper
Crisp lettuce
Crisp shredded
  cabbage

Chill all ingredients, add French dressing and serve.

Cosmopolitan Salad

String beans
Cauliflower

Brussels sprouts
Asparagus

Arrange freshly cooked vegetables in a salad bowl with crisp salad greens. In center of bowl place cooked shrimp, canned lobster or crab meat. Serve with a well-seasoned French dressing and Watkins Paprika.

Peel cucumbers, slice and crisp in ice water and salt. Drain, chill, and marinate in French dressing about an hour. Serve with any chilled salad greens.

Variations:

(1)
Blend with diced celery, pecan nuts, shredded red and green peppers. Add a little mayonnaise thinned with whipped cream. Arrange on thick slices of ripe tomato and serve on crisp lettuce.

(2)
Hollow out thick slices of cucumber and fill center with a curled anchovy or with anchovy paste. Add French dressing and Watkins Paprika.

(3)
Cover cucumber slices with thick cream, add salt and Watkins Paprika. Just before serving, add juice of a lemon.

Cucumber Salad

Cucumber Salad with Sour Cream Dressing

1 cucumber, peeled and sliced	2 hard cooked eggs
1 head lettuce	1 tablespoon vinegar
½ teaspoon salt	½ cup sour cream
¼ teaspoon Watkins Red Pepper	Watkins Celery Salt

Wash lettuce, drain, dry and chill; crisp cucumber slices in ice water and salt. Just before serving, blend with dressing.

To prepare dressing, mash egg yolks, add seasoning, vinegar and sour cream.

Cucumber and String Bean Salad

Peel cucumber, cut in half lengthwise, scrape out seeds, cut into thin slices, chill in salted ice water 15 minutes, then squeeze dry in a clean towel. Add drained canned string beans cut into 1 inch pieces, 1 tablespoon minced onion, and French dressing. Chill. Serve on crisp lettuce.

Stuffed Cucumber Salad

2 medium-sized cucumbers	Watkins Pepper
Salt	¼ cup chopped onion
Worcestershire sauce	¼ cup chopped green pepper
2 3-oz. packages cream cheese	Watkins Paprika
	Pimiento strips

Cut cucumbers in half crosswise; peel thinly, remove seeds, leaving centers hollow; sprinkle with salt, pepper, Worcestershire sauce, and chill 30 minutes. Combine cream cheese, onion and green pepper, season with salt and paprika, and stuff firmly into cucumber shells. Put shells together, fasten with toothpick and roll in French dressing; chill. To serve, cut in ¼ inch slices, place on shredded crisp lettuce and garnish with strips of pimiento; pour French dressing over salad.

French Dandelion Salad

Crisp young dandelions	Vinegar
Diced crisp bacon	Salt
Potatoes	Watkins Paprika

Pick over and wash dandelions, dry in a cloth and chill. Scrub potatoes, cook in jackets in boiling salted water. Peel and slice potatoes while hot and add French dressing for added flavor. Place potatoes in a Pyrex salad bowl, over a pan of hot water.
Just before serving, fry bacon crisp. Add dandelions to potatoes, and pour hot bacon fat blended with vinegar over the mixture. Add chopped bacon, and blend.

Garden Salad

2 heads romaine	6 hard cooked eggs, chopped
Water cress, minced	6 pickled beets, chopped
6 young carrots, shredded	

Wash romaine, pat in a cloth and chill. Cut lengthwise in halves and place on chilled salad plate. Add carrots, water cress, beets and eggs. Add French dressing made with lemon juice.

Spring Garden Salad

½ cup cooked asparagus tips	3 green onions, minced
½ cup sliced radishes	1 tablespoon minced parsley
½ cup sliced cucumbers	⅓ cup grated cheese
2 tablespoons minced green pepper	Watkins Celery Salt
	Watkins Paprika

Chill vegetables, add seasoning, cheese, and toss mixture with French dressing.

Health Salad

Place ½ inch slice of ripe tomato on crisp lettuce. On top of tomato place 1 tablespoon cottage cheese. Sprinkle chopped chives over cheese and add a dash of Watkins Paprika. Garnish with crisp water cress.

Hot Salads

A hot salad may be served for luncheon or dinner.

Asparagus or cauliflower may be served hot with hot Hollandaise dressing as a salad with the meat course.

Hot potato salad is appetizing with smoked tongue or baked ham.

Hot string bean salad with French dressing may be served with a roast.

Hot Slaw

4 cups shredded cabbage
⅛ teaspoon Watkins Paprika

1 teaspoon salt
2 tablespoons vinegar
1 cup cream

Heat vinegar, cream and seasoning, stirring lightly with a fork. When mixture comes to boiling point, pour over the chilled crisp cabbage. Add Watkins Paprika and serve. Garnish with quartered hard cooked eggs.

Hot Red Cabbage Slaw

2 medium heads of red cabbage
3 tablespoons fat
1 cup mild vinegar
2 teaspoons salt

½ cup sugar
3 unpeeled chopped apples
½ glass currant jelly

Remove outer leaves and core from cabbage. Shred fine. Melt fat in a large kettle, add cabbage, vinegar, salt, sugar and apples. Cook over low heat until tender, adding jelly or fruit juice. Serve on crisp lettuce or garnish with water cress.

Italian Salad

Blend equal parts of cooked carrot strips, peas, turnips, potatoes and string beans; add tomatoes cut into eighths, diced celery, chopped anchovies and mayonnaise. Chill thoroughly and serve on crisp salad greens.

Lentil Salad

Wash lentils thoroughly and cook in boiling salted water only until tender. Drain and add French dressing to flavor. Chill and serve with additional French dressing, if needed.

Lettuce and Tomato Salad

Cut ½ head of lettuce into 3 sections. Place on crisp lettuce leaves with 3 sections of quartered tomato between lettuce sections. Add French dressing.

Onions for Salad

Buy the large Italian red onion called Torpedo or Bottleneck, a mild, sweet onion excellent in a salad. Peel onions under cold running water.

For a delicate onion flavor, rub the inside of the salad bowl with a sliced spring onion before the other ingredients are added.

To extract onion juice, wash onion under cold running water, peel, mince fine and press out juice by twisting onion in the corner of a cloth.

Onion Salad

3 Bermuda onions
⅓ cup cold water
⅓ cup vinegar
½ teaspoon salt
1 tablespoon sugar, if desired

⅓ cup French dressing to which has been added ½ teaspoon Worcestershire sauce and ½ teaspoon Watkins Dry Mustard

Peel onions under cold running water; cut in thin slices. Blend water, vinegar, salt and sugar, pour over onions and let stand one hour to flavor. Chill. Drain and arrange onion slices on crisp salad greens or lettuce. Add French dressing and a dash of Watkins Paprika.

Onion Salad

Small white onions
Seedless raisins
Bay leaf
Tomato paste

Olive oil
Salt
Watkins Red Pepper
Sugar to suit taste

Place onions, raisins and bay leaf in a heavy saucepan, cover with a mixture of ⅔ white wine and ⅓ vinegar. Cook until onions are tender. Drain and chill. Serve on crisp lettuce with dressing made of tomato paste, olive oil, salt, Watkins Red Pepper and sugar.

Parsnip Salad

Blend boiled, chilled, sliced parsnips, crisp celery and walnut meats with a well-seasoned mayonnaise and serve on crisp salad greens or lettuce.

Green Pepper Salad

2 3-oz. packages cream cheese	⅓ cup mayonnaise
2 large green peppers	Salt
	Watkins Paprika

Wash peppers, cut off tops and remove seeds. Chop tops for filling. Use a fork and mash cheese to a paste, add mayonnaise and blend well. Add salt to taste, Watkins Paprika and tops from peppers. Press mixture into peppers and chill. Slice thin and arrange on crisp salad greens. Serve with French or Russian dressing. Chopped walnuts may be added.

Green Pepper with Tomato Aspic

1¼ tablespoons gelatin	1 teaspoon sugar
1 cup cold tomato juice	½ teaspoon salt
1 cup boiling tomato juice	1 teaspoon Worcestershire sauce
2 teaspoons lemon juice	3 large green peppers

Soften gelatin in ¼ cup cold tomato juice, 5 minutes. Add hot liquid and stir until dissolved. Add seasoning and remaining tomato juice. Wash green peppers, cut off tops and remove seeds, being careful not to puncture shell. Drain well. Place peppers upright in a shallow bowl. Fill cavity with tomato mixture almost to the top. Chill until firm. To serve, place a ring shaped slice on a bed of crisp salad greens. Serve with celery sticks spread with cheese.

Hints for Potato Salad

Select potatoes the same size and scrub well. Cover with boiling, salted water and cook until tender. Drain. Peel and slice, while hot, into ¼ inch slices, place in a shallow dish and sprinkle with French dressing to coat each piece. Cover with wax paper and chill in refrigerator. The vinegar in the French dressing will prevent potatoes from turning dark; the olive oil and seasonings will flavor the potatoes. When using left-over potatoes for a salad, pare off the dry surface, heat in top of double boiler and follow directions given above.

Potato Salad

3 cups hot cooked
  potatoes
2 hard cooked
  eggs
6 sweet pickles,
  chopped
6 pickled onions,
  minced
¾ cup sliced
  radishes

2 pimientoes
  chopped
(Diced celery,
  sliced olives,
  diced cu-
  cumbers may
  be added)
Lettuce
Dressing

Add French dressing to sliced, hot potatoes and chill. Have all ingredients cold. Before serving add French, cooked or mayonnaise dressing. Arrange on crisp lettuce and garnish with radish roses.

VARIATIONS:

To 3 to 4 cups hot, sliced, boiled potatoes, marinated in French dressing, add:

(1)
1 cup diced cucumbers
1 cup chopped green pepper
1 tablespoon grated onion
2 medium-sized tomatoes, peeled
  and diced
⅓ cup mayonnaise or cooked
  dressing
Watkins Paprika
1½ teaspoons salt

(3)
½ cup diced crisp celery
2 teaspoons minced onion
2 teaspoons minced parsley
2 hard cooked eggs
½ cup mayonnaise blended with
½ cup sour cream
2 tablespoons prepared mustard
2 tablespoons pickle juice or mild
  vinegar
Watkins Celery Salt
Watkins Paprika

(2)
½ cup diced crisp celery
½ cup sliced crisp radishes
1 cup cooked string beans,
  cut lengthwise
1 cup cooked peas
2 teaspoons chopped onion
Watkins Paprika

(4)
½ cup diced crisp celery
2 tablespoons chopped chives
½ cup diced cucumber
1 hard cooked egg
¼ cup chopped stuffed olives
5 slices diced crisp bacon
Watkins Paprika

(5)
½ cup diced crisp celery
¼ cup pimiento olives sliced
½ cup shredded cooked ham
½ cup shredded cheddar cheese
Diced canned meat may be
  substituted for ham

Chef's Potato Salad

1 can chicken
bouillon
3 cups hot cubed
potatoes
2 tablespoons dry
white wine
½ cup French
dressing
1 cup thinly
sliced celery

¼ teaspoon
Watkins Dry
Mustard
2 tablespoons
scraped white
onion
Mayonnaise
Watkins Paprika
½ cup sliced
pimiento olives

Pour hot bouillon over hot potatoes and chill. Drain. Add wine and French dressing blended with onion and seasoning, add celery and blend. Chill. Place on a serving platter and top with mayonnaise. Garnish platter with hard cooked eggs, minced parsley and strips of green or red sweet pepper. Slivered cooked ham may be added.

French Potato Salad

Slice hot cooked potatoes in a salad bowl and add white wine to flavor (⅔ pint for 2 pounds potatoes). Drain after one hour, and chill. Add French salad dressing and chervil, chopped fine. Diced celery may be added.

Hot Potato Salad

4 cups sliced hot
potatoes
¼ lb. thinly
sliced bacon
½ cup chopped
green onions
⅛ cup vinegar
⅓ cup water
1 teaspoon salt

⅛ teaspoon Watkins Pepper
1 teaspoon Watkins Dry
Mustard
1 tablespoon flour
1 tablespoon
sugar
Watkins Paprika

Fry bacon in a heavy skillet until crisp; remove bacon and chop. Cook onions in hot bacon fat, then add flour and seasonings, stirring well. Add vinegar and water, and cook. Add sliced potatoes, heat thoroughly, add bacon and serve warm on salad greens.

Hot Potato Salad

6 medium-sized
potatoes, boiled
in jackets
⅛ cup diced
celery
¼ cup vinegar
¼ cup salad oil
Salt
Slice lemon

6 slices crisp
bacon,
crumbled
Watkins Paprika
2 tablespoons
chopped onions
or chives, if
desired

Peel and slice potatoes while hot. Place in shallow baking dish, adding salt, Watkins Paprika and celery. Heat vinegar, oil and lemon to boiling and pour over potatoes. Add bacon and heat in moderate oven until dressing is absorbed. Serve hot. Garnish with lettuce.

Potato Salad with Ham

4 large baking
   potatoes
3 hard cooked
   eggs
⅔ cup diced
   crisp celery
½ cup dry white
   wine
Salt

Watkins Celery
   Salt
Watkins Paprika
½ cup sliced
   ripe olives
⅓ cup slivered
   cold ham,
   chicken or veal
Mayonnaise

Scrub potatoes and cook in boiling water in jackets until tender. Peel potatoes, slice while hot, add wine and chill one hour. Marinate slivered ham in French dressing. Blend all ingredients, adding enough mayonnaise to moisten. One-half cup blanched almonds may be added.

Potato and Water Cress Salad

3 cups potatoes
   marinated in
   French dressing
½ cup minced
   water cress
6 slices crisp
   bacon,
   crumbled

2 tablespoons
   chopped chives
2 chopped hard
   cooked eggs
Watkins Celery
   Salt
Watkins Paprika

Blend all ingredients and serve with hot bacon dressing.

Sweet Potato Salad

2 cups cooked
   sweet potatoes
1 cup chopped
   celery
1 small chili
   pepper, diced

¼ cup French
   dressing
1 cup slivered
   cooked ham
Mayonnaise

Boil potatoes in jackets; peel and slice while hot, add chili pepper and marinate in French dressing. Just before serving, blend all ingredients with enough mayonnaise to moisten. Serve on crisp lettuce and garnish with quartered stuffed eggs. Add Watkins Paprika.

Wild Rice Salad

Blend cooked (dry) wild rice with an equal amount of crisp diced celery, diced pineapple and seedless raisins (moistened in grape juice). Turn into a salad mold brushed with olive oil and chill. Unmold on crisp salad greens and serve with cooked or mayonnaise dressing. Garnish with stuffed olives. (For recipe to cook wild rice, see page 85, Watkins Cook Book).

Sauerkraut Salad

1 diced cooked
  carrot
1 diced cooked
  beet
1 small onion,
  minced
1 diced cooked
  potato
Salt

1 dill pickle,
  diced
1 cup sauerkraut,
  drained
2 hard cooked
  eggs, quartered
  for a garnish
¼ cup
  mayonnaise

Chill vegetables. Blend all ingredients and serve on crisp salad greens.

Soybean Sprouts in Salad

Blend equal portions of bean sprouts, diced celery, and seedless raisins soaked in a little grape juice. Chill. Add mayonnaise dressing thinned with a little cream or evaporated milk. Arrange on crisp lettuce and add Watkins Paprika.

Spanish Salad

1½ cups shredded
  white cabbage
1 cup diced
  cucumbers
½ cup thinly
  sliced onions
½ cup diced
  celery

2 large tomatoes
½ cup diced
  green pepper
2 hard cooked
  eggs
French dressing
Mayonnaise
Lettuce

Crisp cabbage and cucumber in salted ice water, drain and chill. Add French dressing to cabbage and cucumber, then add mayonnaise to cabbage and onion. Arrange a mound of cabbage mixture in center of salad plate, add quartered tomato, cucumber, and garnish with quartered hard cooked egg and a dash of Watkins Paprika.

Spanish Salad

2 large tomatoes
2 green peppers
2 oranges

1 tablespoon
  minced onion

Wash, peel and chill tomato; cut into 3 slices and top each slice with pepper ring and orange sections. Add minced onion to French dressing. Add dressing just before serving salad.

Spanish Broccoli Salad

1 bunch tender
  broccoli
½ chili pepper
1 hard cooked
  egg
½ teaspoon salt

Juice 1 lime
Dash Watkins
  Red Pepper
4 tablespoons
  olive oil
¾ cup peanuts

Cook broccoli in boiling salted water with the chili pepper; drain and chill. Mash egg, beat in lime juice; add seasoning and olive oil and mix well. Blend with broccoli and serve on crisp lettuce. Add chopped peanuts fried until brown in a little butter.

Spring Salad

½ cup diced
  celery
12 spring onions

12 radishes
½ lb. crisp lettuce
French dressing

Chill ingredients, toss lightly with French dressing and serve on a chilled plate.

Spring Vegetable Salad

1 large cucumber
2 heads endive
10 radishes
½ cup diced
  celery
1 green pepper,
  cut in strips

¼ head chicory
4 tomatoes, peel,
  cut into
  quarters
1 head romaine
1 cup French
  dressing

Peel, slice cucumber and crisp in salted ice water. Slice crisp endive, slice radishes (do not peel). Have all ingredients washed, drained and chilled. Arrange romaine around a salad bowl, add salad mixture and blend with French dressing.

Supper Salad

4 large boiled
  potatoes
1 onion, chopped
1 small can
  pimiento,
  chopped
6 hard cooked
  eggs
Salt
Watkins Paprika
1 cup mayonnaise

1 cup sour cream
  dressing
1 head crisp
  lettuce
1 can asparagus
  tips
1 red pepper, cut
  into strips
3 ripe tomatoes
½ lb. boiled
  shrimp

Cook potatoes in jackets, peel, slice hot and add a little French dressing. Chill. Add salt, Watkins Paprika, 3 chopped hard cooked eggs, and the sour cream and mayonnaise dressing blended together. Just before serving arrange potato salad on a large chilled platter with crisp lettuce. Place stalks of asparagus in clusters around platter, adding strip of pimiento; alternate half of hard cooked egg cut lengthwise and sprinkled with Watkins Paprika (or use stuffed eggs), and a slice of peeled ripe tomato. Around the rim of the platter arrange shrimp. Pass additional mayonnaise when serving salad.

Stuffed Tomato Salad
(Illustrated)

Select small ripe tomatoes of uniform size. Use a fork, dip tomato in hot water one minute, then remove skin. Carefully scoop center so as not to break shell, and turn tomato upside down to drain. Chill. Use any filling desired and serve on chilled salad greens.
Shallow cuts may be made into outside of tomato shell and half slices of fluted cucumber inserted.

Filling Variations for Stuffed Tomato Salad

1. Well seasoned salad of lobster, chicken, shrimp, crab meat, tuna fish or sweetbreads.

2. Cottage cheese blended with finely diced cucumber, Watkins Celery Salt, Watkins Onion Seasoning and French dressing.

3. Shredded pineapple, minced cucumber and cottage cheese with Watkins Onion Seasoning and Watkins Paprika.

4. Chopped hard cooked egg moistened with cooked dressing and seasoned with salt, Watkins Mustard and chopped pickles with diced celery.

5. Asparagus tips with Russian dressing.

6. Deviled ham blended with chopped hard cooked egg and chopped celery.

7. Mashed avocado moistened with a little lemon juice, cottage cheese, chopped canned shrimp and chopped pickle.

Tomato Aspic Salad

2 tablespoons gelatin	1½ teaspoons sugar
½ cup cold water	1 bay leaf
3 cups cooked tomatoes	4 pieces celery with leaves
3 tablespoons chopped onion	1 teaspoon salt
	2 tablespoons lemon juice

Soften gelatin in cold water, 5 minutes. Blend remaining ingredients, except lemon juice, boil 15 minutes and strain. Add softened gelatin and lemon juice; measure, and add water to make 4 cups. Chill. When mixture begins to thicken, add sliced pimiento olives, green pepper rings, strips of pimiento and pour into a salad mold brushed with olive oil. When firm turn on crisp salad greens. Garnish with mayonnaise. Add Watkins Paprika.

VARIATIONS:
When aspic begins to thicken, add
(1)
2 cups shredded cabbage
1 cup diced celery
1 pepper, chopped
(2)
1 cup blanched chopped almonds
1 cup diced celery

(3)
1 cup flaked shrimps
½ cup diced celery
(4)
Mold tomato aspic in a thin sheet, in a baking pan; when firm cut into squares and spread with cream cheese, as for a sandwich. Serve on crisp lettuce.

Tomato Salad-Princesse

For individual service: Place half inch slice of chilled ripe tomato on crisp lettuce. Add cooked asparagus tips, marinated in French dressing. Decorate with a strip of green pepper and pimiento.

Stuffed Tomatoes in Aspic

1½ tablespoons gelatin
½ cup cold water
1¼ cups boiling water
1½ tablespoons sugar
2 tablespoons vinegar
1 teaspoon salt
2 tablespoons lemon juice
½ teaspoon minced onion
6 tomatoes
1 3-oz. package cream cheese
Watkins Paprika

Soften gelatin in cold water, 5 minutes, then stir into boiling water. Add sugar, salt, vinegar, lemon juice and onion. Peel tomatoes, scoop out center, fill with cream cheese and arrange in a ring mold, filled side down. Pour a little gelatin mixture around tomatoes and chill. When firm, fill mold with remaining gelatin and chill. Unmold on crisp lettuce and add mayonnaise.

Tossed Tomato Salad

Combine chilled diced tomato, diced crisp celery, young radishes, diced crisp cucumber, green onion and crisp lettuce broken into pieces. Add French dressing and Watkins Paprika.

Vegetable Salad

1 cup shredded cabbage, crisp
1 cup diced, cooked string beans
½ cup sliced radishes, do not peel
¾ cup diced cooked asparagus tips
½ cup diced carrot sticks
Diced pickled beets
2 tablespoons minced onion
½ cup French dressing
Salad greens
Mayonnaise or cooked dressing

Blend cabbage, beans, radishes, carrot, onion and asparagus tips with French dressing and chill. Just before serving add enough mayonnaise to hold mixture together. Serve on salad greens with asparagus tips, sliced pickled beets and radish roses for a garnish.

Vegetable Salad

1 clove garlic
1 bunch crisp water cress
1 small head lettuce
2 stalks endive
1 bunch radishes
1 raw carrot
3 stalks crisp celery
3 tomatoes
1 bunch scallions
3 tablespoons Roquefort cheese
3 slices crisp bacon, diced

Rub salad bowl with clove of garlic, then discard. Wash vegetables, drain and crisp in refrigerator. Break chilled greens into pieces, prepare vegetables. Toss mixture lightly in salad bowl, add French dressing, cheese and diced cooked bacon.

Vegetable Salad

½ bunch crisp
water cress
3 tomatoes,
peeled and
chopped
6 radishes, sliced
1 small onion,
minced

1 green pepper,
chopped
½ cup diced
crisp celery
2 carrots, thinly
sliced
½ cup Roquefort
cheese dressing
Watkins Paprika

Chill all ingredients.   Add dressing just before serving.

Raw Vegetable Salad

1 cup shredded
cabbage
1 cup grated
carrots
1 cup diced celery
1 cucumber,
chopped

⅓ cup green
pepper,
chopped
¾ cup radishes,
sliced thin
do not peel
1 cup Russian
dressing

Blend all ingredients just before serving on crisp lettuce.

Cooked Vegetable Salad

String beans, cut
in long strips
Peas, fresh or
frozen

Carrots, diced
Cauliflower,
diced
Asparagus tips

Cook vegetables separately in boiling salted water, only until tender. Drain and add French dressing while vegetables are hot, for better flavor.   Just before serving, blend and serve on crisp lettuce.

VARIATIONS:
(1)
Cauliflower, cooked
Peas, cooked
Baby lima beans, cooked
Sliced raw tomatoes
Crisp water cress
Raw carrot sticks

(2)
String beans, cooked
Peas, cooked
Artichoke hearts, cooked
Sliced raw cucumbers

Walnut and Green Pea Salad

Season cooked peas with salt and Watkins Paprika and blend with half the amount of cut walnut meats or blanched almonds. Add French dressing and serve on salad greens or in a crisp lettuce cup. Diced crisp celery may be added.

Suggestions for Additional Vegetable Salad Combinations, French Dressing

Lettuce, salad greens, quartered tomatoes, crumbled bleu cheese and green pepper.

Cauliflower flowerets, green pepper, turnip strips, carrot sticks, and water cress.

Shredded cabbage, diced celery, diced cucumber, sliced onion, quartered tomato, slivered green pepper.

Carrot sticks, green pepper, red sweet pepper, diced celery, sliced cucumber, bean sprouts and salad greens.

Lettuce, sliced radishes (do not peel), celery, tomato, onion, green pepper, hard cooked eggs and water cress.

Shredded lettuce, shredded raw carrots, turnips, shredded apple, and diced celery, with endive.

Chopped onion, raw carrot strips, diced celery, radishes and salad greens.

Shredded cabbage, diced apple, diced pineapple, banana and water cress.

Salad greens, diced celery, peeled white grapes, grapefruit, orange and water cress.

Sliced onions, cooked string beans, sliced radishes, celery, lettuce and water cress.

Raw Vegetable Platter

Arrange a combination of raw vegetables on a large plate with French or Thousand Island dressing in the center in a lettuce cup.

Carrot Sticks: Wash and scrape tender young carrots, cut into quarters lengthwise, then into narrow strips. Wrap in waxed paper or in a damp cloth to chill. Or spread carrot sticks in a tray on ice, cover and chill.

Carrot Curls: Shave thin lengthwise pieces from peeled long carrots. Curl around finger then crisp in ice water until curled, dry and serve.

Raw Cauliflower Buds: Remove outside stalks from cauliflower (save stalks and cook as a vegetable). Wash and break the cauliflower head into flowerets. Chill and serve.

Green Pepper Sticks: Prepare the same as carrot sticks.

Radish Roses: Select firm radishes with unwilted leaves. Leave only the last small leaf as garnish. With a sharp knife cut uniform thin strips of red, peel almost through to the stem on each radish. Place on ice; as radishes chill, the peel will curl back like petals.

Cucumber Fingers: Peel a narrow cucumber, cut in half lengthwise. Remove seeds, then cut solid portion into narrow strips about 3 inches long. Wrap in a damp cloth and chill at least one hour before serving.

Meat Salads

Use well seasoned cooked ham, tongue, veal, lamb, cooked or canned chicken or turkey, or cooked or canned fish in a meat salad. Remove bone, skin, gristle and fat from meat and poultry, cut into ¼ to ½ inch cubes; cut or flake fish. Add French dressing to moisten and chill one hour in the refrigerator before preparing salad. Diced cooked ham, veal, tongue, chicken or turkey may be cut into julienne (long thin strips) pieces, blended with French dressing and added to any mixed green salad.

Serve a chilled meat salad on crisp greens, add a dash of mayonnaise and Watkins Paprika to top salad. Garnish with green, ripe or pimiento olives, radish roses, deviled eggs, celery hearts spread with cheese, or strips of green pepper or pimiento.

Bacon, Tongue and Chicken Salad

Arrange artichoke hearts, marinated in French dressing, in a bowl with crisp salad greens. Add slivered cooked tongue and white meat of chicken with diced crisp bacon.

Bacon and Rice Salad

1 small onion, chopped	3 cups cooked brown (unpolished) rice
1 tablespoon minced parsley	
2 teaspoons salt	4 slices crisp bacon, diced
¼ teaspoon Watkins Pepper	Hot bacon drippings
½ cup vinegar	3 hard cooked eggs
4 stalks celery, cut fine	Watkins Paprika

Place chopped onion, parsley, salt, pepper and vinegar in a large bowl, let stand 10 minutes to flavor, then blend in hot rice. Add celery, crisp bacon, hot bacon drippings, and blend. Arrange on crisp lettuce and garnish with sliced eggs.

Molded Chicken Salad

See Page 97

Cheese and Frankfurter Salad

1 bunch scallions
½ lb. Swiss
cheese, cut
into strips
4 cooked frank-
furters, peeled
and sliced

6 hard cooked
eggs, sliced
Crisp lettuce
Mayonnaise or
French dressing
Watkins Paprika

Trim tops and roots from scallions, wash well and drain. Arrange all ingredients in a chilled salad bowl.

Chef Salad Bowl

1 cup crisp
shredded
cabbage
1 cup cooked
chicken, diced
1 cup cooked
ham, diced
1 cup cooked
tongue, diced
1 cup diced celery

1 cup diced
cucumbers
2 cups finely cut
tomatoes
1 cup cooked
green lima
beans
Crisp lettuce
Russian dressing
Watkins Paprika

Crisp cabbage and celery in ice water, drain and chill. Dice meat, add a little French dressing to moisten and chill 1 hour. Dice cucumbers and crisp in ice water. Blend ingredients just before serving on crisp lettuce.

Cold Meat Salad

2 cups cold cooked
lamb, veal, ham
or chicken, cut
in cubes
½ cup asparagus
tips, cooked
½ cup diced
celery
1 tablespoon
olive oil

½ tablespoon
vinegar
¼ teaspoon salt
Mayonnaise or
cooked dressing
Crisp lettuce
6 hard cooked
eggs
Watkins Paprika

Blend diced meat, asparagus and celery, add olive oil, vinegar and seasonings. Chill to flavor. Add mayonnaise and blend lightly. Serve on crisp lettuce, garnish with eggs cut into eighths, and cooked asparagus tips.

Cold Meat Salad

2 cups diced
cooked meat
1 small green
pepper, sliced
1 cup raw carrots,
sliced
¼ cup diced
celery
¼ cup scallions,
sliced

¾ teaspoon salt
Crisp lettuce,
cut into pieces
1 cup diced
cooked beets
¼ cup
mayonnaise
Watkins Paprika

Blend all ingredients and chill thoroughly.

Corned Beef and Macaroni Salad

1 12-oz. can corned beef, chilled
2 cups cooked elbow macaroni
1 cup chopped celery
4 sweet pickles, chopped
Watkins Paprika
Mayonnaise to moisten

Cut beef into small even cubes. Cook macaroni in boiling salted water 20 minutes, drain and rinse with cold water. Blend all ingredients and serve on crisp salad greens.

Frankfurter and Baked Bean Salad

4 frankfurters
1 1-lb. can baked beans in tomato sauce
⅓ cup minced sour pickle
Watkins Paprika

Use skinless frankfurters and follow directions on can, or wash and boil 5 minutes, chill and cut in ¼ inch slices. Arrange in a salad bowl lined with crisp lettuce, or break lettuce into small pieces, add French dressing, toss mixture and serve.

Frankfurter and Macaroni Salad

¾ cup raw macaroni
4 cups boiling water
¾ lb. frankfurters
¼ cup French dressing
1 small onion, minced
2 teaspoons lemon juice
4 teaspoons salt
¼ cup diced celery
½ cup diced cucumber
1 tablespoon slivered green pepper
1 cup diced ripe tomatoes
¼ cup French or mayonnaise dressing
½ head crisp romaine
Watkins Paprika

Cook macaroni in boiling salted water until tender. Five minutes before macaroni is done, add well-washed frankfurters and boil 5 minutes, drain. Remove frankfurters and rinse macaroni in boiling water, drain. Cut frankfurters in quarters, lengthwise, then in 1-inch pieces. Add French dressing, onion, lemon juice, and seasonings. Chill. Combine with other ingredients, add additional dressing, and serve on crisp romaine or other salad greens.

Ham Salad

Blend equal quantities of slivered baked or boiled ham (remove all fat), with diced crisp celery, diced apples and Thousand Island dressing. Serve on crisp salad greens and garnish with ripe olives and strips of green pepper.

Ham and Cheese Salad

2 cups diced
   baked ham
2 cups diced
   American
   cheese
¾ cup cooked
   peas
¾ cup diced
   crisp celery
French dressing

Blend mixture, add French dressing and chill for better flavor. Serve on crisp lettuce and add a garnish of mayonnaise and stuffed olives.

Ham and Egg Salad

Blend equal quantities of slivered baked ham (remove all fat), hard cooked eggs, diced celery and add French dressing. Serve on crisp water cress or lettuce.

Ham and Macaroni Salad

½ lb. elbow
   macaroni
1 cup diced celery
1 cup slivered
   cooked ham
1 tablespoon
   chopped
   pimiento
2 tablespoons
   chopped green
   pepper
1 tablespoon
   minced onion
3 hard cooked
   eggs, diced
Watkins Paprika

Cook macaroni in boiling salted water until tender. Pour hot water over drained macaroni. Drain and chill.
Marinate ham in French dressing and chill. Blend all ingredients and serve on crisp lettuce.
Crumbled bleu or Parmesan cheese may be used instead of ham.

Ham and Pineapple Salad

Blend 2 cups cubed cooked ham, 1 cup diced pineapple, 1 cup diced celery, ½ cup French dressing. Top with mayonnaise.

Ham Salad Sandwich Rolls

2 cups cooked
   ground ham
⅓ cup minced
   crisp celery
Mayonnaise
2 hard cooked
   eggs, chopped
¼ cup minced
   sweet pickle
Long rolls

Split rolls lengthwise, remove part of inside of roll. Spread with softened butter. Blend salad ingredients with enough mayonnaise to hold mixture together, and fill rolls. Garnish with large stuffed olives.

Ham, Tongue and Chicken Salad

Cut cooked meat in long narrow strips, add French dressing and chill. Blend equal parts of meat, diced crisp celery, and add ½ cup blanched almonds. Serve on chilled salad greens and top with a little mayonnaise. Garnish with pimiento olives.

Ham and Vegetable Salad

1 cup cooked peas
1 cup cooked carrots, diced
1 cup cooked potatoes, diced
1 tablespoon minced onion
4 slices boiled ham, (remove fat)
12 stuffed olives
Salt
Watkins Paprika
Mayonnaise

Cut ham into cubes and blend all ingredients. Serve on crisp lettuce and garnish with chicory.

Molded Ham Salad

See Molded Salad Section, page 45.

Virginia Ham and Endive Salad

Soak cooked ham in hot maple syrup and then broil. Cut in julienne strips and serve on crisp endive with French dressing.

Virginia Ham and Tomato Salad

Fill peeled, hollowed-out ripe, chilled tomatoes with finely slivered boiled ham, strips of crisp celery, diced apple and enough mayonnaise to blend. Or blend diced cooked ham, celery, caviar, chopped chervil, chives and mayonnaise.

Or blend 2 cups cubed cooked ham, 2 cups cubed boiled potatoes, blended with French dressing, 2 tablespoons chopped chives, diced green pepper, ½ cup diced celery and French dressing.

Left-Over Cooked Meat Salad

Blend diced white meat of turkey or chicken, tongue and ham, with finely diced sweet pickle, celery and equal parts of mayonnaise and whipped cream. Chill mixture and serve on crisp lettuce.

Or sliver the left-over meat, add French dressing and chill. Toss with shredded cabbage, water cress, or with a mixed green salad and French dressing. Cooked or raw vegetables may be added.

Pork and Veal Salad

Cook meat until tender. When cold, dice and marinate in French dressing. Use in any recipe for chicken salad.

Sunday Night Meat Salad

2 cups cooked cold meat, cut into thin strips (Use chicken, veal, ham or tongue)
1 cup diced crisp celery
1 cup minced pineapple
¾ cup pecans
1 teaspoon salt
1 cup mayonnaise
Watkins Paprika
Crisp salad greens

Chill all ingredients and blend just before serving. Garnish with quartered hard cooked eggs.

Swedish Salad

1 cup diced cooked ham
1 cup diced cooked veal or chicken
1½ cups diced boiled potato
½ cup diced raw apple
⅓ cup chopped sweet pickle
½ cup diced crisp celery
¼ cup chopped onion, if desired
¾ teaspoon salt
⅛ teaspoon Watkins Paprika
½ cup French dressing
½ cup mayonnaise
3 hard cooked eggs, quartered

Add French dressing to cubed cooked meat, chill 1 hour to flavor. Add a little French dressing to hot sliced potatoes. Just before serving, blend all ingredients. Serve on crisp lettuce and garnish with quartered hard cooked eggs and a dash of Watkins Paprika.

Sweetbread Salad

1 pair sweetbreads
French dressing
Crisp lettuce
½ cup diced celery
½ cup blanched almonds
Watkins Paprika
Mayonnaise

Wash sweetbreads under cold running water, soak one hour in cold salted water. Drain, cover with boiling water and boil 20 minutes. Drain, when cool remove all membranes and cut into cubes. Add French dressing with considerable Watkins Paprika and chill. Just before serving, blend with diced celery marinated in French dressing; add almonds and serve on crisp lettuce. Or blend mixture and use as a filling for stuffed tomatoes.

Sweetbread Salad

Blanch mushrooms in boiling water 10 minutes, drain; slice and marinate in French dressing. Blend parboiled (see above recipe) sweetbreads, mushrooms, walnuts and black olives. Add French dressing and serve on crisp lettuce.

Thrift Salad

1½ cups diced cooked meat, preferably veal, ham or chicken
½ cup diced hot boiled potatoes
1 slice onion
Cooked peas or green beans

French dressing
1 teaspoon Watkins Dry Mustard
1 tablespoon Worcestershire sauce
Watkins Paprika

Add mustard and sauce to dressing, pour over meat and potatoes and let stand in refrigerator one hour to flavor. Blend with other ingredients and serve on crisp lettuce.

Tongue Salad

½ lb. cold cooked tongue
½ cup chopped olives

¾ cup cooked string beans
1 tomato

Dice tongue, olives and add French dressing; chill. Add French dressing to hot cooked beans, and chill. Blend mixture, serve on crisp lettuce and add quartered tomato.

Tongue and Asparagus Salad

2 cups slivered cooked tongue
Watkins Paprika
Crisp salad greens

1 cup asparagus tips, marinated with French dressing

Blend all ingredients and add French or mayonnaise dressing.

Tongue and Cabbage Salad

2 cups chopped crisp cabbage
4 hard cooked eggs
½ green pepper, chopped
Watkins Onion Seasoning

Watkins Celery Salt
Watkins Paprika
2 cups slivered tongue or boiled ham
Mustard dressing

Add French dressing to cabbage and chill. Just before serving blend all ingredients and serve in a salad bowl or on crisp lettuce.

Tongue and Pepper Salad

Serve julienne strips of smoked tongue, sweet red pepper and crisp celery on crisp salad greens. Add mayonnaise and garnish with stuffed olives.

Veal, Ham, Roast Pork or Chicken and Apple Salad

Arrange a salad bowl of crisp, greens and add equal quantities of julienne strips of cooked veal, ham, chicken or pork (remove all fat). Add seasoning, diced crisp celery and diced apples. Blend mixture and add mayonnaise dressing.

Veal Salad

1 lb. veal
1 chili pepper
1 cup red wine vinegar
½ lb. water chestnuts, peeled and diced
Heart leaves of 1 head of curly chicory
½ bunch water cress
Chives
⅛ teaspoon ginger
2 egg yolks
1½ teaspoons salt
½ teaspoon black pepper
½ teaspoon Watkins Dry Mustard
½ cup olive oil
3 tablespoons lemon juice

Simmer veal until tender with 1 teaspoon of salt and the chili pepper. Remove from water and cover with red wine vinegar; let stand several hours to flavor.

Make thin mayonnaise, combining egg yolks and seasonings, adding olive oil, gradually, and adding enough lemon juice to make quite tart.

Drain veal, dice, and combine with chestnuts, chicory and water cress. Blend with dressing. Add a sprinkling of chopped chives. Chill and serve.

Jellied Veal Salad

Mold jellied, cooked veal with slices of hard cooked egg. Unmold on a chilled platter and surround with potato salad molded in a cup, on crisp lettuce. Garnish with radish roses and sliced dill pickles. Add mayonnaise or cooked salad dressing.

Chicken Salads

Dress chicken and cook (whole) in a small amount of boiling water until tender, then let stand several hours in the chicken stock to flavor. Remove bone, skin, gristle and fat; use all white meat or part dark and part white meat of chicken. Cut meat into ½ inch cubes but cut the dark meat into smaller cubes, and the white meat will predominate in appearance.

Chicken Salad
(BASIC RECIPE)

3 cups cooked chicken	1½ cups diced celery
½ teaspoon salt	Mayonnaise
4 tablespoons tarragon vinegar	Watkins Paprika
	Crisp lettuce
½ cup olive oil	Stuffed olives

Place salt and vinegar in a chilled bowl, add olive oil and mix thoroughly. Add cubed chicken and chill 2 hours in the refrigerator. When ready to serve, drain off the dressing, add chilled crisp celery and just enough mayonnaise to blend mixture. Arrange crisp lettuce in a chilled bowl or on chilled salad plates, add salad and top with a little mayonnaise, a few of the white chicken cubes and pimiento cut into fancy shapes for a garnish. Or add a dash of Watkins Paprika, pimiento or ripe olives, chopped truffle, chopped pistachio nuts, capers, strips of canned chili pepper or hard cooked eggs cut in attractive forms.

VARIATIONS OF CHICKEN SALAD

1. Add 1 cup of toasted sliced almonds to the diced cooked chicken and follow recipe given above. If walnuts are used, sprinkle nuts lightly with salt, add 1 tablespoon butter, stir occasionally and heat in oven. Cut into pieces, do not chop, and add to chicken and celery.

2. Add 1½ cups chilled peeled seedless grapes or diced oranges.

3. Add 1 tablespoon chopped pimiento and 2 tablespoons diced green pepper, or ½ cup chopped stuffed olives.

4. Substitute 1 cup of julienne strips of cold boiled Virginia ham for 1 cup of chicken, in above recipe.

5. Add 1½ cups diced pineapple, ½ cup diced ripe olives, and ¾ cup sliced toasted almonds, to the basic recipe.

6. Diced cooked veal may be substituted for part of the chicken, or 1 cup diced cooked sweetbreads marinated in French dressing.

7. Add 1 cup sliced boiled chestnuts and follow above recipe.

8. Add 1 cup diced cooked artichokes marinated 1 hour in French dressing.

9. A tablespoon of chow chow added to the mayonnaise will give a different flavor to chicken salad, or minced ripe olives may be used.

For a more creamy mayonnaise dressing, add ½ cup whipped cream to the dressing, before blending with the chicken.

10. In making a jellied chicken salad, use boiling-hot chicken broth in place of boiling water, to dissolve the hydrated gelatin.

Chicken and Almond Salad

2 cups diced
cooked chicken
¼ cup tarragon
vinegar
¼ cup olive oil
3 tablespoons
lemon juice
½ teaspoon salt
8 olives, cut fine

½ cup finely
diced celery
2 hard cooked
eggs, cut in
eighths
4 sweet pickles,
cut fine
½ cup toasted
almonds, sliced

Blend vinegar, olive oil, lemon juice and salt, add diced chicken and chill several hours. Just before serving, add remaining ingredients and toss lightly, with just enough mayonnaise to moisten. Garnish with stuffed olives and eggs. Add Watkins Paprika.

Canned Chicken Salad

1 No. ½ can
boneless
chicken
2 cups diced
crisp celery
½ cup toasted
almonds, sliced

4 hard cooked
eggs
¾ cup
mayonnaise
Crisp parsley
French dressing
Watkins Paprika

Cut chicken in ½ inch cubes, add celery and enough French dressing to moisten. Chill. Just before serving, add almonds and mayonnaise. Serve on crisp lettuce and garnish with hard cooked eggs cut into eighths, parsley, and strips of pimiento. Add a dash of Watkins Paprika.

Chicken Salad with Capers

2 cups cooked
diced chicken
1½ cups diced
celery
1 tablespoon
capers

4 hard cooked
eggs
Mayonnaise
Watkins Paprika

Mix diced chicken and celery with a little French dressing and chill. Just before serving add mayonnaise, toss lightly to blend, and serve on crisp lettuce. Garnish with capers and hard cooked eggs cut into quarters. Add Watkins Paprika.

Chef's Chicken Salad

1½ cups diced
cooked chicken
⅓ cup diced
celery
2 tomatoes, diced
2 hard cooked
eggs, chopped
½ avocado, diced

½ cup spiced
beets, chopped
½ cup cucumber,
diced
French dressing
Russian dressing
Watkins Paprika

Add French dressing to diced chicken and celery and chill. Just before serving have all ingredients cold and blend with a little Russian dressing. Garnish with ripe olives, stuffed celery, radish roses or pimiento olives.

Chicken Chow Mein Salad

2½ cups diced
cooked chicken
1 cup drained
canned bean
sprouts
1 small can water
chestnuts,
sliced

½ cup diced
pineapple
½ cup diced
crisp celery
1 teaspoon
minced
pimiento
Salt
Watkins Paprika

Add French dressing to cooked chicken and chill 2 hours. Add other ingredients and mayonnaise, toss together lightly, and serve on crisp lettuce. Garnish with ripe olives and deviled eggs, cut into quarters. Add a dash of Watkins Paprika.

Chicken-Cranberry Salad

2 cups diced
cooked chicken
2 cups diced
crisp celery
⅓ cup minced
olives

1 can cranberry
sauce, chilled
Crisp salad greens
Watkins Paprika
Mayonnaise

Blend chicken and celery with French dressing and chill 2 hours. Cut cranberry mold into 6 slices and each slice into quarters. Arrange cranberry on crisp greens and add chicken blended with a little mayonnaise. One-half cup toasted almonds (sliced) may be added. Garnish with strips of pimiento.

Chicken Salad with Fruit

½ cup diced
canned
pineapple
(chilled)
3 diced ripe
bananas
2 cups diced
cooked chicken
¼ teaspoon salt

⅓ cup diced
celery
¼ cup French
dressing
¾ cup toasted
almonds, cut
Mayonnaise
Lettuce

Blend chicken, salt, celery, add French dressing and chill. Just before serving, prepare fruit, blend all ingredients and serve on crisp lettuce. Garnish with capers.

Chicken and Ham Salad

2 cups diced
  cooked chicken
1 cup diced
  cooked ham
⅓ cup pickle
  relish
1 cup diced celery
⅓ cup French
  dressing
Lettuce
Mayonnaise
Watkins Paprika

Combine chicken, ham, celery, relish, add French dressing and chill 2 hours. Add mayonnaise to blend. Serve on crisp lettuce and garnish with sliced stuffed olives.

Chicken and Pineapple Salad

3 cups diced
  cooked chicken
1 cup diced celery
1½ cups diced
  canned
  pineapple
¼ teaspoon Wat-
  kins Paprika
¼ cup French
  dressing
Salt to suit taste
Mayonnaise

Blend chicken and celery, add French dressing, and chill. Just before serving add pineapple cubes and mayonnaise. Toss together lightly. Serve on crisp lettuce and garnish with stuffed olives.

Chicken Relish Salad

1 package lemon
  Jello
1 pint boiling
  water
2 chicken bouillon
  cubes
3 tablespoons
  tarragon
  vinegar
Watkins Paprika
Watkins Onion
  Seasoning
½ teaspoon salt
Watkins Celery
  Salt
¾ cup diced
  crisp celery
2 tablespoons
  diced pimiento
¼ cup diced
  sweet pickle
1½ cups chopped
  cooked chicken

Dissolve Jello and bouillon cubes in hot water. Stir in vinegar, seasonings, and chill. When slightly thickened, stir in remaining ingredients. Turn into mold rinsed in cold water. Chill until firm. Unmold on a chilled platter, garnish with crisp salad greens, and radish roses.

Chicken Salad with String Beans

2 cups cooked
  chicken
1 cup string
  beans, cooked
1 cup cooked
  wild rice
1 sliced truffle
Salt
Watkins Paprika
Few chives, to
  suit taste
French dressing

Cut breast of a boiled chicken in ½ inch squares, add a little French dressing and chill. Cut string beans julienne (long narrow strips). Add a little French dressing to the beans while hot, then chill. Just before serving blend all ingredients and serve on crisp lettuce.

Chicken and Sweetbread Salad

1½ cups cooked chicken
1 cup boiled sweetbreads
¼ cup French dressing
½ cup diced crisp celery
½ cup diced cucumbers
1 tablespoon chopped capers

Dice chicken and sweetbreads, add French dressing and chill 2 hours. Marinate celery and cucumbers in a little French dressing and chill. Before serving blend all ingredients. Add a little mayonnaise, and a dash of Watkins Paprika.

Chicken Salad in Chilled Tomato

6 large firm ripe tomatoes
Mayonnaise
Crisp lettuce
2 cups chicken salad (See Basic Recipe)
Watkins Paprika

Wash tomatoes, cut a slice from the top, scoop the inside out carefully, turn upside down to drain and chill. Just before serving, fill tomato shells with salad and place on crisp lettuce. Add a dash of oil mayonnaise to top salad and Watkins Paprika.

Variation:
The salad may be served in Cream Puff shells if desired. Decorate with olives or radish roses.

Chicken and Vegetable Salad

2 cups cooked chicken
½ cup diced cucumbers
½ cup cooked lima beans
½ teaspoon salt
½ cup cooked string beans, cut in thin strips
½ cup diced crisp celery
Watkins Paprika

Dice cooked chicken, add French dressing and chill 2 hours. Cook vegetables in a little of the hot chicken stock for better flavor, drain and chill. Add a little French dressing. When ready to serve, drain off dressing from chicken and cooked vegetables, add diced crisp celery and just enough mayonnaise to blend mixture. Serve on crisp lettuce and garnish with pimiento olives.

Hawaiian Chicken Salad

Follow basic recipe for chicken salad, fill an after-dinner coffee cup or individual Jello mold with chilled salad and turn on crisp lettuce. Garnish with strips of pineapple, or serve salad on a drained slice of chilled, canned pineapple and top with a maraschino cherry.

Jellied Chicken Ring Mold

1 envelope plain gelatin
¼ cup cold water
2 eggs
½ teaspoon salt
¼ teaspoon Watkins Paprika
1¼ cups hot chicken stock
½ cup cream

1 tablespoon lemon juice
2 cups diced cooked chicken (½ inch cubes)
2 tablespoons chopped pimiento
2 2-oz. cans mushrooms

Soften gelatin in ¼ cup cold water 5 minutes. Beat eggs, add salt, Watkins Paprika, chicken stock; stir constantly and cook in top of a double boiler until mixture begins to thicken. Stir in softened gelatin. Cool. Fold in diced chicken, pimiento and drained cut mushrooms. Turn into a chilled mold rinsed in cold water and chill until firm. Unmold on crisp lettuce or water cress and serve with mayonnaise. Garnish with stuffed olives.

Julienne Chicken and Fruit Salad

2 cups cooked chicken
1 cup orange sections
1 cup grapefruit sections

1 cup peeled white grapes, remove seeds
French dressing
Watkins Paprika

Cut chicken into long thin strips, add a little French dressing and chill two hours. Blend with remaining ingredients, and add additional French dressing. Serve on crisp salad greens.

Molded Chicken Salad

4 cups cooked chicken, cut into ½ inch cubes
½ cup diced celery
2¼ cups rich chicken broth (remove all fat)

1½ tablespoons granulated gelatin
3 tablespoons cold water
Mayonnaise
Crisp lettuce
Watkins Paprika

Heat broth and season to suit taste. Soften gelatin in the 3 tablespoons cold water, 5 minutes, then stir into hot chicken broth. Cool stock. Place diced chicken and celery in individual or a large mold, arrange carefully. Pour cooled chicken stock over chicken and celery and chill until firm. Unmold on crisp lettuce and serve with mayonnaise.

Fish Salads

Popular fish salads include canned or cooked lobster, salmon, tuna, shrimp, crab meat, flaked white fish, herring and anchovy fillets.

Flaked cooked fish should be marinated in French dressing one-half to one hour in the refrigerator, then drained before using.

Fish may be combined with diced cucumbers, diced celery, with any chilled mixed salad greens, with diced raw tomatoes, or with cooked French lima beans, adding mayonnaise or a cooked dressing, with Watkins Paprika.

Fish are a body-building food, and being high in complete protein, are a good substitute for meat. Shellfish, such as crabs and lobster are rich in phosphorus and calcium, while shrimp is an excellent source of iron. The intestinal tract of both canned and cooked shrimp must be removed before they are served. This tract, located under the outer curved surface, should be cut out with a sharp knife.

Cod, halibut and salmon are rich in Vitamins A, D, and G; while all salt-water fish and shellfish supply iodine in the diet.

Fish roe, codfish and sardines contain thiamin, and haddock contains niacin, both B-complex vitamins.

Salmon furnishes some Vitamin A, and is a good source of Vitamin G. The flesh of all fish is highly perishable, and must be stored at a low temperature; freezing does not affect the food value of fish. Shellfish should be strictly fresh and used promptly, as they deteriorate rapidly; keep on ice until ready to use.

Garnishes for Fish Salad

Use lemon cut into slices, in quarters, halves or wedges. One half of the lemon may be sprinkled with minced parsley, the other with Watkins Paprika. Scallop the edge of the lemon. Cut a pimiento, green pepper or cucumber into fancy shapes, as stars and crescents, or into slices and scallop the edge. Crisp celery sticks spread with cream, pimiento or American cheese and Watkins Paprika may be used, or cut the peel of crisp radishes in downward slices from tip to stem, and crisp in ice water. Or use chilled tomatoes cut into eighths, or hard cooked eggs, or stuffed eggs, garnished with a small crescent of pimiento and a dash of Watkins Paprika.

Sprigs of crisp water cress or parsley give an attractive color note to a fish salad, or stuffed olives, a dill pickle cut fan-shape, chilled capers, or sweet pickles may be used.

To Boil Shrimp

Cover shrimp with boiling salted water and boil 15 minutes or until shells turn pink. Drain, add cold water. When cold remove shell, cut shrimp along the outside and remove the intestinal tract, a slender black line in the meat. All other part of a shrimp is edible. Chill thoroughly. One pound fresh shrimp will yield two cups when cooked. Quick-frozen shrimp may be purchased all the year. Follow directions on the container.

To Boil Lobster

Buy lobster that weighs from 1¼ to 2 pounds; over three pounds the meat is tough and coarse. Use vegetable tongs and plunge a live lobster into a large kettle of rapidly boiling water, to which 1 tablespoon of salt is added for each quart of water. When water boils vigorously, cover kettle and boil 20 to 25 minutes, depending upon the size of the lobster; the lobster will turn red and the tail draw up. Over-cooking will toughen the meat. Use tongs or two tablespoons and drop lobster into cold water. When cold, twist or chop off claws close to the body and use the meat from the small claws to garnish the salad. Crack the large claws with a hammer and remove the meat with a silver fork.

Place lobster on its back, drain, pull back tail; cut lengthwise from head to end of tail, remove stomach near the head, also the spongy tissue or lungs, and the intestinal vein. Remove meat from lobster in large pieces and cut meat for a salad, using a silver or stainless steel knife; other metal will discolor the meat. Chill meat thoroughly. Marinate cut lobster meat in French dressing and chill before using in a salad.

To Boil Salmon or White Fish

Select a thick piece of choice fish, rub a little salt over it, then wrap in cooking parchment paper, or in clean cheesecloth, or place in a wire frying basket or steamer, then in a kettle, cover with hot, not boiling water, and add ½ teaspoon salt and ½ tablespoon lemon juice, to each quart of water. Onion, celery stalks, bay leaf, peppercorns and parsley may be added. Bring to boiling, cover kettle, then **simmer** until fish separates from bone. Allow from 10 to 15 minutes per pound for large pieces of salmon, and 5 to 10 minutes per pound for small pieces. Cook only until tender, then drain and cool. Remove skin, bones and chill. Flake fish, add a little French dressing and chill, before using in a salad.

A fish salad is better when made from cooked fish that will flake well, such as salmon, cod, haddock or halibut. Remove the bones, separate meat into flakes, add French dressing and chill.

If canned salmon is used, turn from the can, drain off oil, remove skin, add French dressing and chill. Then follow recipe.

Crab Meat and Avocado Salad

3 avocados
¼ lb. crab meat
½ cup diced celery
Juice of ¼ lemon

6 tablespoons Russian dressing
Watkins Paprika

Cut avocado lengthwise, remove pit, carefully remove pulp with a large spoon without breaking shell. Cut pear into cubes, add other ingredients, fill shell and serve on crisp lettuce. The flavor will be improved if a little French dressing is added to the avocado and crab meat and the two ingredients chilled for one hour before adding Russian dressing.

Crab Meat and Avocado Salad

Peel and pare as many halves of avocado as persons to be served. Flake crab meat and blend with a dressing made of equal parts of mayonnaise and chili sauce. Fill centers of avocado with mixture. Serve well chilled on crisp salad greens.

Crab Meat Salad

2 cups crab meat
1 cup chopped celery
1 tablespoon minced pepper
⅛ teaspoon Watkins Paprika

⅓ teaspoon salt
3 tablespoons French dressing
⅔ cup mayonnaise
Crisp lettuce

Pick over crab meat carefully to remove any shell. Add celery, French dressing and chill. Add mayonnaise and serve on crisp lettuce. Garnish with stuffed olives.

Variation:
Blend crab meat with cleaned shrimp and follow above recipe. Garnish with ripe tomato cut into eighths.

Crab Meat Salad

3 cups crab meat (in large pieces) chill
¼ cup tart mayonnaise
2 cups shredded lettuce

⅓ cup French dressing
3 small tomatoes
3 hard cooked eggs, quartered
Watkins Paprika

Blend crab meat with mayonnaise. Toss lettuce with French dressing. Arrange lettuce on salad plate, add crab meat, and garnish with quartered tomatoes and hard cooked eggs.

Crab Meat and Macaroni Salad

1½ cups flaked crab meat
1½ cups cooked elbow macaroni, seasoned with salt
1 cup crisp diced celery
2 tablespoons chopped green pepper
1 tablespoon minced pimiento
1 tablespoon minced sweet pickle
½ teaspoon salt
¼ cup mayonnaise
Crisp lettuce

Blend all ingredients and chill mixture. Serve on crisp lettuce and garnish with stuffed olives.

Crab Meat and Shrimp Salad

2 3-oz. packages cream cheese
1 can tomato soup
1⅓ tablespoons gelatin
⅓ cup cold water
½ cup diced celery
⅓ cup finely diced green pepper
Watkins Paprika
⅛ cup minced parsley
1⅓ cups well-flaked crab meat
1⅓ cups lobster or shrimp, broken into pieces
½ cup mayonnaise

Soften gelatin in cold water 5 minutes. Heat tomato soup over hot water until steaming, stir in softened gelatin until dissolved. Add cream cheese and chill until mixture begins to thicken. Add remaining ingredients, turn into a square loaf pan and chill until firm. Unmold and cut into squares. Serve on crisp lettuce, top with mayonnaise and garnish with stuffed olives.

Crab Meat, Shrimp and Tuna Salad

1 cup crab meat
1 cup shrimp
1 cup tuna
3 hard cooked eggs, diced
½ cup diced celery
½ cup mayonnaise
1 tablespoon chopped, sweet pickle
2 tablespoons French dressing
1 tablespoon lemon juice
⅛ teaspoon salt
Watkins Paprika

Add French dressing to crab meat, shrimp and tuna and chill. Blend all ingredients and serve on crisp lettuce.

Crab Meat Rolls

1 cup crab meat　　Salt
1 cup diced celery　Watkins Paprika
1 hard cooked　　　Finger Rolls,
　egg, chopped　　　buttered
Mayonnaise

Blend crab meat, celery, egg and salad dressing, adding seasoning to suit taste. Cut roll lengthwise, remove part of bread, and fill with salad. Serve on crisp lettuce with sliced dill pickle. Diced cooked chicken or shrimp may be substituted.

Crab Meat with Tomato

6 ripe tomatoes　　　1 tablespoon
1½ cups crab　　　　　pickle relish
　meat　　　　　　　　1 tablespoon
2 hard cooked　　　　　Worcestershire
　eggs, chopped　　　　sauce
2 tablespoons　　　　Watkins Celery
　lemon juice　　　　　Salt
2 tablespoons　　　　Watkins Onion
　tarragon　　　　　　Seasoning
　vinegar　　　　　　Watkins Paprika
¼ cup olive oil

Blend olive oil, vinegar and pickle relish, pour over crab meat and chill. Peel tomatoes, scoop out center, place cut-side down to drain, and chill. Blend all ingredients, add enough mayonnaise to moisten mixture, fill tomato and serve on crisp salad greens.

Crab Mousse Salad

2 tablespoons　　　　2 cups flaked
　gelatin　　　　　　　crab meat
½ cup cold water　　2½ tablespoons
1 cup boiling　　　　　pimiento
　water　　　　　　　⅓ cup stuffed
1 cup mayonnaise　　　olives, sliced
1 cup whipping　　　½ green pepper,
　cream　　　　　　　minced
Salt　　　　　　　　Watkins Paprika

Soften gelatin 5 minutes in cold water, add boiling water and stir until dissolved. Chill. When mixture begins to thicken, fold in mayonnaise, whipped cream, and add other ingredients. Turn into salad mold rinsed in cold water, and chill until firm. Unmold on crisp lettuce.

Fish Salad

1 cup cooked or　　　¼ teaspoon Wat-
　canned flaked　　　　kins Paprika
　fish　　　　　　　　1 teaspoon
2 hard cooked　　　　　lemon juice
　eggs　　　　　　　　½ cup
½ cup crisp celery　　mayonnaise or
　diced　　　　　　　　cooked dressing
2 tablespoons　　　　½ cup diced
　celery hearts,　　　　cucumbers,
　diced　　　　　　　　crisped in ice
¼ teaspoon salt　　　　water

Chill all ingredients, blend mixture and serve on chilled lettuce.

Fish and Apple Salad

Blend 1½ cups flaked fish with 1½ cups diced tart apple, add ⅓ cup diced celery and enough mayonnaise to moisten. Serve on crisp lettuce.

Fish, Celery and Olives

Blend 2 cups diced canned salmon, 1 cup sliced stuffed olives, ⅓ cup diced cucumbers, ¼ cup diced sweet pickle. Add French dressing and serve cold on crisp lettuce.

Jellied Fish Salad

¾ tablespoon gelatin
2 tablespoons cold water
1 cup chopped halibut blended with a little French dressing
1½ teaspoon salt
1 teaspoon sugar
1 teaspoon Watkins Dry Mustard
¼ teaspoon Watkins Paprika
2 egg yolks
1½ tablespoons melted butter
¼ cup vinegar

Soften gelatin in cold water 5 minutes. Chop halibut, then blend with a little French dressing and chill. Beat egg yolks, stir in vinegar, then dry ingredients. Stir and cook egg mixture over boiling water until thickened. Add softened gelatin to hot egg mixture. Cool. Add fish. Pour into mold rinsed in cold water and chill until firm. Unmold on crisp lettuce, slice and serve on crisp salad greens with a dash of mayonnaise and Watkins Paprika.

Herring Salad

2 salt herring
3 medium-sized cooked potatoes
1 medium-sized cucumber
1 small onion, grated
1 tablespoon capers, chopped
4 hard cooked eggs, chopped
3 tablespoons olive oil
3 tablespoons vinegar
Salt
Watkins Paprika
Crisp lettuce

Soak herring overnight, drain, remove skin, bone and cut into small pieces. Blend all ingredients and serve on crisp lettuce.

Herring Salad

4 potatoes boiled in jackets
3 raw apples
6 medium-sized cooked beets
3 dill pickles
4 pickled herring
French dressing
¼ teaspoon salt
Watkins Paprika
3 hard cooked eggs
Mayonnaise

Slice hot potatoes, add French dressing and chill. Add diced ingredients and enough mayonnaise to moisten.
Serve on crisp lettuce, garnish with quartered hard cooked eggs and Watkins Paprika.

Herring Salad

2 cups diced,
cooked potatoes
(cook in jackets,
peel, slice hot
and add French
dressing)
2 cups diced raw
apples
1 cup diced beets
½ cup chopped
salt herring
(soak overnight)

1 dill pickle,
chopped
1 small onion,
chopped
½ teaspoon Watkins Dry
Mustard
¼ teaspoon Watkins Paprika
1 teaspoon sugar
¼ cup vinegar
1 cup sour cream

Blend all ingredients, except sour cream, and chill. Add cream and serve on crisp lettuce with Watkins Paprika.

Herring and Veal Salad

5 medium boiled
potatoes
3 large green
apples
4 hard cooked
eggs
1 onion
1 cup diced celery
3 dill pickles
2 cups cooked
diced veal or
chicken

4 smoked or
pickled herring
1 tablespoon
vinegar
1 teaspoon sugar
1 teaspoon salt
¼ cup capers
1 cup sliced
stuffed olives
Watkins Paprika
Watkins Celery
Salt

Blend French dressing with sliced, hot, boiled potatoes and chill. Mix together potatoes, diced apples, sliced eggs, onion, pickles, meat and add a little mayonnaise. Chill 2 hours. Just before serving on crisp salad greens, add additional dressing if needed and blend a little sour cream with the mayonnaise. Garnish with radish roses and strips of pimiento.

Lobster in Cucumber Jelly

1 can lobster
2 sliced
cucumbers
2 cups salted
water
¾ teaspoon salt
½ teaspoon onion
juice
Watkins Green
Vegetable
Coloring

2 tablespoons
vinegar
1½ teaspoons
gelatin
3 tablespoons
cold water
Worcestershire
sauce
½ pimiento cut
into strips
Crisp water cress

Boil cucumber in salted water until soft. Soften gelatin in cold water; add salt, onion juice, vinegar and softened gelatin to cooked cucumbers and water. Strain and add a drop of green vegetable coloring to strained liquid. Cool.
When mixture begins to thicken, stir in flaked lobster and add Worcestershire sauce. Add chilled diced cucumber. Turn mixture into a chilled mold brushed with olive oil, adding a few strips of pimiento. Chill until firm and serve on crisp water cress.

Lobster Salad

2 cups diced
  canned lobster
3 stuffed olives,
  cut fine
⅛ teaspoon salt

½ cup chopped
  celery
Watkins Paprika
3 hard cooked
  eggs

Add French dressing to lobster, cover container with waxed paper, and chill 30 minutes. Blend ingredients and add enough mayonnaise to moisten. Serve on crisp lettuce, add quartered cooked eggs with a dash of Watkins Paprika.

Or follow your favorite recipe for chicken salad and substitute diced canned lobster. Garnish with strips of red or green pepper.

Mock Lobster Salad

2 lbs. fillet of
  haddock
1 medium-sized
  onion, sliced
1 stalk celery
½ tablespoon
  Watkins
  Paprika
1 teaspoon salt

1½ cups boiling
  water
¼ cup French
  dressing
Lettuce
Mayonnaise
3 hard cooked
  eggs

Place fish in a kettle, add onion, celery, parsley, salt, boiling water and simmer until fish is tender, but not broken; cook about 7 minutes. Drain, remove vegetables and flake fish. Add French dressing and Watkins Paprika to fish and chill thoroughly. Serve on crisp lettuce with mayonnaise and add a garnish of quartered hard cooked eggs.

Lobster Salad Supreme

4 eggs, beaten
1½ teaspoons salt
1 tablespoon
  Watkins Dry
  Mustard mixed
  with 1 table-
  spoon boiling
  water
¾ cup vinegar

½ teaspoon Wat-
  kins Paprika
2 tablespoons
  butter, melted
6 cups chopped
  canned lobster
1 scallion,
  chopped

Beat eggs, add seasonings, butter, gradually add vinegar, stir and cook over hot water until mixture begins to thicken. Remove from fire and chill. Pour over chilled lobster and garnish with water cress.

Salmon Salad

1 small can (6 oz.)
  salmon
½ cup
  mayonnaise
Dash Worcester-
  shire sauce
Crisp lettuce

2 tablespoons
  shredded
  blanched
  almonds
½ cup minced
  crisp celery
Watkins Paprika

Remove bone and skin from salmon and flake fish. Add all ingredients and serve on crisp lettuce with a dash of Watkins Paprika.

Salmon or Shrimp Salad

2 cups flaked
   salmon, or cut
   shrimp
2 cups crisp,
   shredded
   cabbage
½ cup crisp
   celery, diced
½ cup chopped
   green pepper

6 green olives,
   sliced
1 cup diced
   American or
   Parmesan
   cheese
1¼ cups
   mayonnaise
Watkins Paprika

Blend all ingredients, chill and serve on crisp lettuce. Or blend equal parts of mayonnaise or cooked dressing with sour cream.

Molded Salmon

2 cups flaked
   cooked or
   canned salmon
¾ teaspoon salt
1 teaspoon sugar
1 teaspoon
   Watkins Dry
   Mustard
1 tablespoon flour
2 egg yolks
2 tablespoons
   vinegar

1 cup milk
2 tablespoons
   lemon juice
2 tablespoons
   butter
1 tablespoon
   plain gelatin
3 tablespoons
   cold water
Crisp lettuce
Crisp water cress
Watkins Paprika

Soften gelatin in cold water while preparing other ingredients. Mix salt, sugar, Watkins Mustard, flour in top of double boiler, stir in beaten egg yolks to a smooth paste. Stir in milk, then vinegar gradually, then lemon juice. Use a wooden spoon, stir mixture constantly over boiling water. When mixture thickens, stir in gelatin, then add butter. Remove from fire, add salmon flakes, pour into salad mold rinsed with cold water. Chill. Unmold on crisp lettuce, add mayonnaise and garnish with capers.

Sardine Salad

Remove skin and bones from can of sardines. Chill. Add French dressing and serve on crisp lettuce. Garnish with pimiento olives.

Sardine Salad

3¾ oz. can
   sardines
3 hard cooked
   eggs
½ teaspoon
   Watkins Dry
   Mustard
¾ teaspoon salt
2 teaspoons
   Worcestershire
   sauce

5 tablespoons
   tarragon
   vinegar
1 cup finely
   chopped celery
3 tablespoons
   minced onion,
   if desired
Watkins Paprika

Drain sardines, remove skin and bones carefully and reserve oil. Make a dressing of one mashed egg yolk blended with a little sardine oil, add Watkins Mustard, salt, Worcestershire sauce, vinegar, onion and one finely chopped egg white. Blend lightly with sardines and celery, and serve on crisp lettuce. Garnish with sliced or quartered eggs and Watkins Paprika.

Shad Roe Salad

½ cup salad oil
1 teaspoon Watkins Dry Mustard
4 hard cooked eggs
1½ teaspoon salt
Dash Watkins Red Pepper
¾ cup vinegar
2 lbs. shad roe, cooked
16 asparagus tips, cooked
½ bunch crisp water cress
½ green pepper, cut into strips

Blend olive oil, Watkins Mustard and mashed yolks of hard cooked eggs. Add salt, Watkins Pepper, gradually stir in vinegar, and beat until smooth. Cut roe in small pieces and add to dressing. Add pepper strips, chopped egg whites, asparagus cut into 1 inch pieces, and chopped water cress. Serve on crisp lettuce.

Shrimp Salad

Blend equal parts of cooked, cleaned chilled shrimp and crisp diced celery. Add a little French dressing and chill. Serve on crisp lettuce and add a dash of mayonnaise and a few capers.

Shrimp Salad

1 lb. canned shrimp
2 cups cooked diced boiled potatoes
⅔ cup diced crisp celery
3 tablespoons chopped green onion
1 cup cooked peas
Salt
Watkins Paprika
French dressing

Blend shrimp, vegetables, French dressing and chill 30 minutes. Serve on crisp lettuce and add a dash of mayonnaise with Watkins Paprika.

Shrimp Main Dish Salad

¾ cup mayonnaise
¾ cup grated carrot
1 cup diced celery
3 dozen shrimp
1 head lettuce, shredded
1 large grapefruit, cut in sections
3 tablespoons French dressing

Remove black vein from canned shrimp, add a little French dressing and chill. Blend mayonnaise, carrot, celery and chill. Combine shrimp, celery mixture and add shredded lettuce with French dressing. Serve with grapefruit sections.

Shrimp and Pineapple Salad

1 can shrimp
6 slices pineapple, diced
1 cup diced celery
¾ cup mayonnaise
¼ cup chili sauce
Watkins Paprika

Remove black vein from shrimp, chill fish, cut into ½ inch pieces and add pineapple and celery. Blend mayonnaise and chili sauce, and mix with salad. Serve on crisp salad greens and garnish with stuffed olives.

Shrimp Salad Bowl

1 cup cooked or
canned shrimp
2 tablespoons
anchovy fillets
½ cup French
dressing

2 hard cooked
eggs, put
through ricer
Crisp lettuce
Crisp romaine
Watkins Paprika

Wash, chill greens; break into pieces and arrange in a salad bowl. Chill. Blend all ingredients, toss lightly with French dressing and serve.

Shrimp Luncheon Salad

2 tablespoons
gelatin
½ cup cold water
2 cups hot tomato
juice
1 cup cooked or
canned shrimp,
cleaned
½ cup stuffed
olives, chopped

1 cup minced
celery
¼ teaspoon salt
½ teaspoon Wat-
kins Paprika
1 tablespoon
lemon juice
2 hard cooked
eggs, sliced

Soften gelatin in cold water 5 minutes, then stir into hot tomato juice. Chill until slightly thickened. Blend remaining ingredients in order given and pour into mold rinsed in cold water. Pour tomato juice over mixture and chill until firm. Unmold on crisp lettuce and add mayonnaise with a dash of Watkins Paprika.

Molded Shrimp and Potato Salad

2 tablespoons
gelatin
½ cup cold water
2½ cups hot
tomato juice
1 teaspoon salt
Watkins Paprika
1 cup cleaned,
cooked or
canned shrimp
1½ cups cooked
diced potatoes

⅓ cup finely
chopped celery
2 tablespoons
minced green
pepper
¼ cup
mayonnaise
1 tablespoon
vinegar
1 teaspoon
grated onion

Soften gelatin in cold water 5 minutes, then stir and dissolve in hot tomato juice. Add salt, Watkins Paprika and chill until mixture begins to thicken. Blend diced shrimp, potatoes, celery, vinegar, green pepper, onion, mayonnaise, and fold into tomato mixture. Pour into salad mold rinsed with cold water. Chill. Serve with mayonnaise, adding chopped chives.

Tuna Fish Salad

For each cup of flaked canned tuna fish, add ½ cup diced crisp celery. Toss mixture lightly to blend and add enough mayonnaise to moisten. Garnish with quartered hard cooked eggs and serve on crisp lettuce. Or serve tuna salad on chilled drained canned pineapple slices, placed on salad greens.

Tuna Fish and Fruit

1½ cups white
    tuna fish, drain
    off oil
1 cup seedless
    grapes, chilled
Mayonnaise

½ cup diced
    crisp celery
¾ cup diced
    avocado
Watkins Paprika

Add French dressing to tuna fish after flaking with a silver fork and remove any bones. Chill. Just before serving, blend all ingredients and serve on a chilled salad plate.

Swedish Tuna Fish Salad

1 small can white
    tuna fish
4 sweet gherkins
Stuffed olives
⅓ cup juice
    from gherkins

1 bunch crisp
    water cress
1 head crisp
    lettuce
French or Mayon-
    naise dressing
Watkins Paprika

Drain oil from tuna fish, flake fish, add gherkins cut into narrow strips, sliced olives, and gherkin juice. Chill 1 hour. Line a salad bowl with crisp lettuce, add fish mixture, dressing, and serve.

Jellied Tuna Fish Salad

1 envelope plain
    gelatin
¼ cup cold water
¾ cup hot water
1 tablespoon
    lemon juice
½ teaspoon Wat-
    kins Paprika

¾ teaspoon salt
¾ cup flaked tuna
    or halibut
⅓ cup crisp
    diced celery
¼ cup chopped
    cucumber

Soften gelatin in cold water 5 minutes. Add hot water and stir until dissolved. Add salt, lemon juice and Watkins Paprika. Chill until partly congealed, then add fish, celery and cucumber. Blend and pour into a mold brushed with salad oil. Chill until firm and serve on a chilled platter. Garnish with crisp lettuce, add mayonnaise and stuffed olives.

Tuna or Salmon Loaf

1 package lemon
    gelatin
1 cup boiling
    water
¾ cup cold water
½ teaspoon salt
1 tablespoon
    lemon juice
Watkins Onion
    Seasoning
Watkins Red
    Pepper

2 teaspoons
    horse-radish
½ cup chopped
    celery
2 pimientoes,
    chopped
½ green pepper,
    chopped
2 cups tuna or
    salmon, flaked
Watkins Paprika

Stir boiling water into powdered gelatin until dissolved, add cold water and lemon juice. Pour a thin layer of liquid into a loaf pan and chill until firm. Combine pimientoes, salt, Watkins Red Pepper, Watkins Onion Seasoning, horse-radish, and spread over chilled gelatin. Cover with plain gelatin in liquid form, and chill. Add fish, another layer of plain gelatin, and chill. Add celery, green pepper, then remaining gelatin. Chill. Unmold and serve in ¾ inch slice on crisp lettuce. Add mayonnaise, Watkins Paprika, garnish with radish roses and ripe olives.

Cheese Salads

Important among the seven basic groups of food which should be included in the daily diet is milk in any form, including cheese, which has the essential nutritional qualities of milk. Cheese is an economical source of protein; and, in equal weights, contains practically as much of this essential food element as meat. It is also a nutritious, concentrated "fuel food", an excellent source of calcium, phosphorus and iron; and, when it contains milk-fat, it supplies Vitamin A.

American cheddar cheese is rich in calcium and phosphorus, and is a good source of riboflavin, or Vitamin B-2, with some thiamin and Vitamin A. Cheese provides about twice as much food-value for the money as meat, and is a more concentrated food than eggs. Swiss cheese ranks highest in protein value, one pound being equivalent to two pounds of steak. When eaten in small quantities, cheese is easily digested, and adds flavor and food value to a salad. Cream and cottage cheese are best suited to the digestion of children and invalids.

Cheese To Use In Salads

There are two distinct types of cheese, classified by the amount of moisture they contain. The first type includes the soft or unripened kinds, such as cream or cottage cheese; also the semi-hard, such as American, Swiss, Roquefort; and also the hard varieties. The second type are the cheeses developed by ripening, which are grouped as strong or mild; and those which are mold-ripened, or bacteria-ripened.

For use in salads, the following are preferred:

The cheddar and Swiss type, which may be cut into julienne strips (long, narrow pieces) and added to a salad bowl. Finely chopped chives or scallions or fresh herb leaves, such as rosemary, lemon thyme or sweet basil, may be minced and added to cream or cottage cheese.

Cottage or cream cheese should be served in mounds, on crisp lettuce, with bar le duc or a tart jam; or blend the cheese with a little whipped cream, form into balls, roll in chopped nuts, and serve with a pineapple or pear salad, or as filling for green peppers.

Full cream cheese, dairy cheese, cheddar, Old English, Swiss, and pineapple cheese, top the list for high caloric value; Roquefort, Brie and Neufchatel rate second, and cottage cheese third in order of food value.

Medium rich cheeses, with good keeping quality, are Pineapple, English Dairy, and Edam, all of which may be served with the salad course, or with crisp crackers with after-dinner coffee.

Roquefort is usually crumbled, added to a chilled green salad, and then blended with French dressing.

The rich cheeses include Roquefort, Camembert, Brie, Stilton, Gorgonzola, and Liederkranz; being highly flavored they should be used only in small quantities.

Always keep cheese closely covered from moist air, and keep in the refrigerator. To prevent cheese from drying out, rub salad oil over the cut surface. Wrap cheese in waxed paper, and place in a covered jar before storing. If cheese becomes dry and hard, it may be grated and kept in a covered jar for use over spaghetti, macaroni, a cheese omelet, or sprinkled over a mixed green salad.

Cheese Salad

2 lbs. cottage cheese
½ teaspoon salt
2 medium onions, grated or chopped
1 green pepper, chopped
6 stuffed olives, chopped
4 sweet pickles, chopped
Crisp lettuce
Watkins Paprika
Crushed pineapple

Blend cottage cheese with enough crushed pineapple to lightly moisten, then add remaining ingredients. Serve on crisp lettuce or endive and add a dash of Watkins Paprika. Grated raw carrots may be added.

Cheese and Cabbage Salad

3 cups shredded crisp cabbage
¾ teaspoon salt
⅓ teaspoon sugar
1 teaspoon Watkins Dry Mustard blended with 1 teaspoon hot water
¼ teaspoon Watkins Paprika
1 tablespoon prepared horse-radish
1 tablespoon lemon juice
¾ cup heavy cream, whipped
8 tiny cooked beets
¼ lb. American cheddar cheese

Shred crisp cabbage. Blend lemon juice, seasonings, sugar and horse-radish; fold in whipped cream. Pour over shredded cabbage and chill. When ready to serve, place cabbage mixture in lettuce lined salad bowl, arrange beets on top and add American cheese cut into strips.

Cheese and Calavo Salad

2 Calavo pears
1 3-oz. package
  cream cheese
Dash Watkins
  Celery Salt
Few drops
  lemon juice

2 teaspoons
  tomato catsup
Thousand Island
  dressing
Watkins Paprika
Shredded lettuce
Endive or romaine

Cut avocados into halves lengthwise, remove seed, and peel. Serve sections of avocado on crisp greens and add blended dressing. Arrange cheese balls on salad plate and add Watkins Paprika. Or sieve a mashed avocado, blend with the cheese, and fill center of calavos.

Cheese and Date Salad

2 packages cream
  cheese
½ cup nuts, cut
½ teaspoon salt
⅛ teaspoon Watkins Paprika

1 tablespoon
  orange juice
Grated rind
  ½ orange
1 lb. large fresh
  dates

Mash cheese, add orange juice, nuts, orange rind and chill. Remove pits from dates, stuff with cheese mixture and serve on crisp or shredded lettuce. Add French dressing.

Cheese and Ham Salad in Mold

1 envelope
  unflavored
  gelatin
¼ cup cold water
½ can condensed
  tomato soup
½ package
  cream cheese
¼ cup
  mayonnaise

1 teaspoon Watkins Prepared
  Mustard
1 tablespoon
  lemon juice
1½ cups finely
  chopped or
  ground ham
Watkins Paprika

Soften gelatin in cold water. Heat soup, add gelatin, stir until dissolved. Mash cheese, add Watkins Prepared Mustard and lemon juice, and add to gelatin mixture, stirring until smooth. When mixture begins to thicken, fold in mayonnaise and ham. Pour into individual molds. Unmold on crisp lettuce, adding a little more dressing.

Cheese Luncheon Salad with Strawberries

2 cups cottage
  cheese
4 ripe tomatoes,
  sliced
¾ cup French
  dressing

3 oranges, sliced
  thin
3 cups ripe
  strawberries
½ head lettuce
3 tablespoons
  mayonnaise

Blend cottage cheese with mayonnaise and spread between slices of tomato. On each serving plate arrange 4 orange slices and ripe berries on crisp lettuce. Add tomatoes, crisp water cress, radish roses, celery hearts and French dressing. Garnish with stuffed eggs or stuffed olives, or any fruit in season.

Cheese and Macaroni Salad

2 cups cooked
macaroni
1 cup chopped
celery
1 green pepper,
chopped
2 pimientos,
chopped

6 sweet pickles,
chopped
1 cup grated
American
cheese
French or mayon-
naise dressing

Chill and blend ingredients. Serve on crisp salad greens. Add additional mayonnaise, grated cheese and Watkins Paprika.

Cheese - Orange - Prune Salad

4 oranges peeled
and sliced
20 prunes, cooked

1 cup cottage or
cream cheese
Watkins Paprika
Crisp lettuce

Remove seeds from prunes and fill center with cheese. Chill. Arrange orange slices on crisp lettuce and add stuffed prunes. Serve with French dressing.

Cheese and Pineapple Salad

1 package lemon
gelatin
2 cups boiling
water
1 can grated
pineapple
3 cream cheese
Salt to suit taste

Watkins Paprika
⅓ cup chopped
pimiento
½ cup chopped
pecans
½ cup whipped
cream

Stir boiling water into gelatin and cool. Mash cheese until smooth add pineapple, pimiento and nuts. Stir cheese mixture into partly chilled gelatin. When mixture begins to thicken, fold in whipped cream. Chill in molds and serve on crisp lettuce. Garnish with radish roses and olives.

Cheese Salad with Tokay Grapes

1 tablespoon
granulated
gelatin soft-
ened in
1 tablespoon
cold water
2 tablespoons
boiling water
½ cup grated
American
cheese

2 packages cream
cheese
4 tablespoons
top milk
1 cup peeled
(seeded) Tokay
grapes
⅓ teaspoon salt
½ teaspoon Wat-
kins Paprika
Crisp lettuce

Soften gelatin in cold water 3 minutes, then stir in boiling water. Mash cream cheese until smooth, add top milk and blend well. Add grated American cheese, salt, Watkins Paprika and add gelatin. Fold in grapes and whipped cream. Turn into mold rinsed in cold water. Chill until firm. Serve on a slice of chilled pineapple and add a dash of mayonnaise. Add ripe strawberries as a garnish.

Cheese - Raisin Salad

On crisp heart of lettuce, place sections of grapefruit and oranges around a mound of cream cheese blended with pecans. Sprinkle raisins (soaked in grape juice) over cheese and add French dressing. Garnish with ripe olives.

Cheese-Tomato Salad

Part 1—
1 No. 2 can tomato juice
1 bouillon cube
1 teaspoon salt
1 tablespoon minced onion
1½ tablespoons plain gelatin
¼ cup cold water

Part 2—
1 cup cottage cheese
¼ cup cold water
½ cup mayonnaise
1½ tablespoons plain gelatin

Part 1—
Heat tomato juice to boiling, add bouillon cube, onion, and simmer 5 minutes. Add 1 tablespoon minced parsley, if desired. Strain. Soften 1½ tablespoons plain gelatin in cold water 5 minutes, add to hot tomato juice and stir until dissolved. Pour half the mixture into bottom of a salad mold brushed with olive oil, and chill until firm.

Part 2—
Blend cheese and mayonnaise, add gelatin softened in cold water and dissolved over hot water. Spread over the chilled tomato layer and chill. When set, add remaining tomato mixture and chill until firm. Unmold on crisp lettuce, add additional mayonnaise and garnish with stuffed olives.

Cottage Cheese in Ring Mold With Apple or Fruit Salad

2 teaspoons granulated gelatin
2 tablespoons cold milk
4 tablespoons hot milk
2 cups cottage cheese
1 teaspoon salt
1 cup cream, whipped
Watkins Paprika
Lettuce
1 cup walnut meats, cut

Soften gelatin in cold milk 5 minutes, and stir into hot milk until dissolved. Cool. Add milk to cheese, add salt and Watkins Onion Seasoning to suit taste. Add nuts. Pour into a mold rinsed in cold water and chill in the refrigerator until firm. When ready to serve, unmold on crisp lettuce and fill center with a fresh fruit or an apple and nut salad.

Cottage Cheese and Carrot Salad

1 cup cottage cheese
1 cup coarsely-grated raw carrot
1 tablespoon minced water cress
Mayonnaise or French dressing

Blend cottage cheese with grated carrot and water cress. Serve on crisp lettuce. Add dressing and a dash of Watkins Paprika.

Cottage Cheese and Cherry Salad

1½ cups cottage cheese
½ cup heavy sour cream
1 cup fresh or canned cherries, pitted and chopped
1 apple, peeled and chopped
⅓ cup sugar
¾ cup walnuts, cut
½ teaspoon salt
Watkins Paprika

Blend cheese with sour cream, adding a little at a time. Add remaining ingredients. Form into a loaf and press to remove any moisture. Chill about 3 hours. Unmold and serve on crisp lettuce. Garnish with cherries.

Cottage Cheese and Chive Salad

1 cup cottage cheese
⅓ cup chopped chives
⅓ cup sweet cream
1 teaspoon lemon juice
⅛ teaspoon salt
1 cup nuts, pecans or walnuts, chopped
Watkins Paprika

Blend all ingredients and serve on crisp lettuce. Garnish with ripe olives. Serve with any mixed green salad or as a canape on crisp crackers or potato chips.

Cottage Cheese with Grapefruit Aspic

2 cups grapefruit juice
1 envelope plain gelatin
1 teaspoon Worcestershire sauce
Drop Tabasco sauce
1 teaspoon sugar
Salt
Watkins Paprika
1 cup cottage cheese

Soften gelatin in ¼ cup cold grapefruit juice 5 minutes. Heat ½ cup fruit juice and add softened gelatin; stir until dissolved, add remaining grapefruit juice and seasonings. Place cottage cheese into individual molds and pour grapefruit aspic around cheese. Chill until firm. Serve on crisp salad greens and add mayonnaise. Garnish with pimiento strips.

Cottage Cheese and Chicken Salad

1 cup cooked meat or chicken, diced
2 cups cooked boiled potatoes, diced
½ cup chopped celery
¼ cup diced dill pickle
Salt
Watkins Paprika
Watkins Celery Salt
1 cup cottage cheese
½ cup cooked salad dressing
Salad greens
Radish roses
Pimiento olives

Add a little French dressing to meat and potatoes and chill. Blend all ingredients except cheese and chill. Just before serving, add cottage cheese and salad dressing and toss mixture together lightly, or form balls of cottage cheese, add Watkins Paprika and serve around the salad on lettuce or salad greens. Garnish with radish roses and pimiento olives, or with any fresh chilled fruit.

Cottage Cheese Salad with Grapes

½ cup heavy cream, whipped
¼ cup mayonnaise
3 cups cottage cheese
1 cup seedless grapes, peeled
½ cup fresh strawberries
½ cup canned pineapple, diced or chopped
2 tablespoons lemon juice
¼ cup nuts, cut
2 tablespoons sugar
Crisp lettuce

Add whipped cream to mayonnaise. Combine cheese, grapes, strawberries, pineapple, lemon juice, nuts and sugar. Add dressing, pack into a salad mold and chill. Serve on crisp lettuce.

Cottage Cheese and Pineapple Mold

1 package lemon or lime gelatin
1 cup boiling water
1 cup canned pineapple juice
1 cup grated pineapple
1 cup cottage cheese, put through sieve
¼ teaspoon salt
Dash Watkins Red Pepper
Strips of red and green pepper
Mayonnaise

Stir and dissolve gelatin in boiling water. Add pineapple juice. Chill until partly congealed. Add pineapple, cheese, salt and Watkins Red Pepper. Decorate individual molds with strips of red and green pepper and pour in gelatin. Chill until firm. Unmold on crisp lettuce and add mayonnaise blended with an equal quantity of cream. Garnish with stuffed olives.

Cottage Cheese and Pineapple Salad

Add sugar to sliced, ripe pineapple and chill. Arrange on crisp lettuce and add 1 heaping tablespoon cottage cheese in center of each slice. Garnish with ripe strawberry or maraschino cherry.

Cream Cheese and Grapefruit Salad

2 grapefruit
2 3-oz. packages cream cheese
1 tablespoon cream
French dressing
Watkins Paprika

Arrange chilled grapefruit sections on crisp lettuce and garnish with small balls of cheese mixed with cream and rolled in walnuts. Add French dressing and a dash of Watkins Paprika.

Molded Cheese with Melon and Pineapple

2 ounces bleu cheese
2 tablespoons cream
1 tablespoon gelatin
1 package cream cheese
½ cup chilled evaporated milk, whipped
½ teaspoon salt
¼ cup cold water
¾ cup pecans, cut
Watkins Paprika

Blend cheese and stir in cream. Soften gelatin in ¼ cup cold water 5 minutes, then stir over hot water until dissolved. Stir into cheese mixture and chill. Fold in whipped, evaporated milk and nuts. Pour into mold rinsed in cold water and chill until firm. Unmold and add chilled sliced peaches, grapefruit, or strips of honeydew melon and pineapple.

Molded Cheese and Nut Salad

2 tablespoons plain gelatin
½ cup cold water
1 cup mayonnaise
½ cup heavy cream, whip stiff
½ lb. American cheese, grated
1 green pepper (remove seeds), mince fine
1 teaspoon grated horse-radish
2 tablespoons lemon juice
Few grains salt
1 cup cut almonds or pecans
2 teaspoons Worcestershire sauce
Watkins Paprika
Crisp lettuce

Soften gelatin in cold water 5 minutes, stir over boiling water until gelatin is dissolved, then stir into mayonnaise. Cool. Whip cream and fold into mayonnaise; add remaining ingredients. Pack into refrigerator tray and chill until firm; do not freeze. Unmold on crisp lettuce and add a dash of mayonnaise or whipped cream.

Cream Cheese and Green Pepper Salad

2 green peppers	1/3 cup stuffed
2 3-oz. packages	olives, chopped
cream cheese	1/2 teaspoon salt
1/3 cup	Watkins Paprika
mayonnaise	French or Russian
	dressing

Wash large green peppers, cut off top, remove seeds and chill. Mash cream cheese, add mayonnaise or heavy cream, minced olives, seasoning, and mix well. Fill peppers with mixture and chill. Slice thin, arrange on crisp lettuce, and serve with French or Russian dressing. Sweet red peppers may be used instead of green peppers.

Cream Cheese, Pepper and Nut Salad

3 3-oz. packages	1/3 teaspoon Wat-
of cream cheese	kins Celery Salt
1/4 cup	1 green pepper,
mayonnaise	chopped
dressing	1/4 cup heavy
Watkins Paprika	cream, whipped
3/4 teaspoon	1 pimiento,
vinegar	chopped
1/3 teaspoon salt	1 cup nuts, cut

Cream cheese, fold in mayonnaise, add pepper, pimiento and seasonings. Fold in whipped cream. Chill. Serve on crisp lettuce.

Roquefort Cheese Salad

1 head lettuce	2 tomatoes
1 bunch chicory	Roquefort cheese
6 radishes	French dressing

Break or tear lettuce into pieces and arrange in a salad bowl. Slice radishes, do not peel, cut tomatoes into eighths, with skins on. Blend French dressing with crumbled cheese, about 2 tablespoons, and add to salad. Toss mixture lightly to coat lettuce.

Tomato-Cheese Salad Ring

2 packages lemon	2 packages cream
flavored gelatin	cheese
3 cups tomato	3/4 cup
juice, heated	mayonnaise
	Watkins Paprika

Dissolve gelatin in heated tomato juice then cool. Blend cheese with mayonnaise. Add 1 cup gelatin and stir until smooth. Stir in remaining gelatin mixture. Pour into a ring mold brushed with olive oil and chill in the refrigerator until firm. Unmold on crisp lettuce and fill center with chicken salad.

Egg Salads

Eggs As A Protective Food

Nutritionists recommend an egg a day for everyone; they are easily digested if properly cooked, and a valuable food for growing children and convalescents. Eggs are a good fuel food, in addition to being a good source of protein, being about equally distributed between the white and the yolk. They are also rich in calcium and phosphorus, and the yolk supplies iron in which most diets are low. Eggs are a muscle-building food and contain Vitamins A, B, D, and G, the amount depending upon the quality of the food given the hen and the exposure to sunlight. The color of the yolk is not an indication of the food value. The yolks of fresh eggs are slightly acid, while the egg white is chiefly a solution of albumen.

The composition of an egg is ¾ water, ⅛ protein, and ⅛ fat, the yolk containing all of the fat, as well as mineral salts and vitamins.

United States Standard for Eggs

The United States standard for eggs rates four classifications for clean, sound-shell, edible eggs as: U. S. Special; U. S. Extra; U. S. Standard, and U. S. Trade. In localities where eggs are graded for quality, each is graded for size into small, medium, and large, weighing respectively 17, 20½ and the largest 24 ounces per dozen.

In some sections of the United States, eggs are U. S. Government graded according to the condition of the egg, the depth of the air-cell, the size or weight of the egg, and the cleanliness and soundness of the shell.

Grade AA corresponds to U. S. Special.
Grade A eggs correspond to U. S. Extras.
Grade B eggs correspond to U. S. Standards.
Grade C, eggs below U. S. Standards.

Official U. S. Standard for Eggs
U. S. Special—Highest Grade

The shell must be clean, sound and normal.

The air cell must not exceed $\frac{1}{8}$ inch in depth and must be regular.

The yolk must be well-centered, in outline indistinct, and it must be free from visible germ development and other defects or blemishes.

The egg white must be firm and clear.

To Judge Freshness of Eggs

A fresh egg should feel heavy, sink in cold water, and when held to a bright light, show a clear round yolk. If old, part of the substance will have evaporated through the pores of the shell, leaving a space filled with air, causing the egg to float on water.

Thermo-Stabilizing Process to Keep Eggs Fresh
Used by the United States Army

According to the latest research, eggs can be kept fresh for two months at a time, if treated by a new thermo-stabilizing process in which fresh eggs, placed in a wire basket, are dipped for **five-seconds** in a boiling-water-bath. This sets the albumen in an invisible film just under the shell, thus preventing evaporation and safeguarding the eggs against the infiltration of bacteria. AA grade eggs treated by this method will remain in perfect condition, in the refrigerator, for two months. Eggs thus treated may be used the same as any eggs, except they require a longer time to whip.

Keep Eggs in the Refrigerator

Eggs are as perishable as milk and butter, and a wise shopper will buy from a grocer who keeps eggs in the cooler or the refrigerator, and not piled in a basket or box on the counter. Eggs can be kept fresh only by continuous cold. Store eggs in the refrigerator as soon as received and cover container when placed in an automatic refrigerator. Keep eggs away from highly scented food as they absorb odors and flavors. Eggs with cracked or thin defective shells should be used immediately, as eggs deteriorate rapidly. If the shells are soiled, wipe them with a rough dry cloth but do not wash the shell until ready to use; water removes the protective covering that forms a natural seal for the pores of the shell.

To Hard-Cook Eggs for a Salad

Eggs should be "cooked", not boiled, at **simmering** heat. Cook eggs at low to moderate even heat, because high temperature coagulates the protein and the egg white and yolk become tough and indigestible. Place eggs on a wire rack in enough cold water to cover and heat the water gradually to simmering, about 186 degrees F., but do not let the water boil. Cook 30 to 45 minutes in simmering water, then place the eggs into cold water, to prevent the formation of a dark ring where the egg white and yolk meet. The shell can be peeled easily from quickly cooled eggs.

Hard-Cooked Eggs as a Garnish

Slice hard-cooked eggs lengthwise, with a wire slicer, and use as a garnish for meat, fish, or a vegetable salad. Or cut the egg white in lengthwise strips as a daisy petal, pass the egg yolk through a sieve and arrange in a small mound for a daisy center. Or use hard-cooked or stuffed eggs, cut in halves, as a garnish for a meat, vegetable, or a fish salad. Scallop the edge, or serve plain, and add a dash of Watkins Paprika with a sprig of parsley or water cress.

Egg-Anchovy Salad

6 medium-sized boiled potatoes
3 hard-cooked eggs
1 tablespoon grated onion
Watkins Paprika
8 anchovy fillets, diced
Mayonnaise or Cooked dressing

Boil potatoes in jackets, peel and slice while hot, add a little French dressing and chill. Before serving, add anchovies, onion and chopped eggs. Add enough salad dressing to blend. Serve in a lettuce lined salad bowl. Stuffed eggs may be substituted if preferred.

Egg and Asparagus Salad

1½ cups diced, cooked or canned asparagus tips
½ cup sliced radishes, do not peel
3 hard-cooked eggs, quartered
Mayonnaise or cooked dressing
Watkins Paprika

Blend asparagus and radishes with dressing. Arrange on crisp lettuce, garnish with eggs and Watkins Paprika. A little French dressing added to the asparagus tips and chilled 30 minutes, will improve the flavor.

Egg and Bacon Salad

6 hard-cooked eggs
6 slices ripe tomato
1 tablespoon pickle relish
Mayonnaise
Salt
6 slices crisp, cooked bacon
Watkins Paprika

Blend mashed egg yolk with pickle relish, chopped bacon, add mayonnaise and seasoning. Place tablespoon of mixture on slice of tomato and serve on crisp salad greens.

Egg and Baked Bean Salad

Blend baked beans, chopped hard cooked eggs, diced crisp celery, diced sweet pickles and chopped chives. Add salt, Watkins Red Pepper and enough cooked salad dressing to blend. Serve on crisp lettuce.

Egg and Cheese Salad

6 hard-cooked eggs
2 tablespoons grated cheese
1 tablespoon cream
¼ cup mayonnaise
Salt
Watkins Paprika
Crisp endive

Put egg yolks through a ricer. Add cream, cheese, 1 tablespoon mayonnaise and blend mixture. Stuff egg whites, add a dash of Watkins Paprika and serve on crisp salad greens, adding a little mayonnaise. Garnish with pickled onions and radish roses.

Egg and Chicken Salad

1½ cups diced, cooked or canned asparagus tips
½ cup sliced radishes, do not peel
½ cup diced celery
1 cup chopped, cooked chicken
Cooked salad dressing
3 hard-cooked eggs
Lettuce
Watkins Paprika

Blend asparagus tips, chicken, celery and add enough French dressing to moisten, then chill. Blend all ingredients and serve on crisp lettuce. Garnish with sweet pickles or stuffed olives.

Egg Salad with Chives

Hard-cooked eggs
Green pepper
Melted butter
Chopped chives
Pimiento
Salt
Watkins Paprika
Cream mayonnaise

Put eggs, chives, pimiento and green pepper through a food grinder. Add melted butter, salt and Watkins Paprika. Cover with waxed paper and chill. Serve on crisp lettuce and add whipped cream-mayonnaise, with a dash of Watkins Paprika.

Egg Salad Club Style

4 slices buttered toast
3 tablespoons mayonnaise
4 slices ripe tomato
Water cress
4 hard-cooked eggs
1 tablespoon pickle relish
6 slices crisp bacon
Watkins Paprika

Spread hot toast with butter and a little mayonnaise. Add tomato slice, a dash of salt and the blended egg mixture. Serve on lettuce and garnish with stuffed olives and radish roses.

Egg and Cucumber Salad

Follow recipe for Stuffed Eggs and add chopped sweet cucumber pickles to the mashed egg yolk and a tablespoon chopped cucumber cubes marinated in French dressing. Blend mixture and add enough cooked dressing to moisten. Fill egg whites, serve on crisp water cress and garnish with Watkins Paprika and pimiento olives.

Egg and Ham Salad

4 hard-cooked eggs, chopped	1 teaspoon Watkins Dry Mustard
1 cup diced cooked ham	½ cup mayonnaise
2 tablespoons pickle relish	Watkins Paprika Lettuce
½ cup diced celery	

Have all ingredients cold. Blend mixture and serve on crisp lettuce.

Egg-Herring-Potato Salad

¼ lb. salt herring	2 white onions
3 medium-sized boiled potatoes	4 hard-cooked eggs
2 large tart apples, unpeeled	French dressing Crisp lettuce Sweet pickles

Cover herring with cold water and let stand several hours to remove excess salt. Drain on crumpled paper towels and remove bones. Put herring and onions through food chopper, using the largest knife. Add mixture of diced potatoes, sliced apples and toss lightly with French dressing. Chill mixture and serve on crisp lettuce. Garnish with quartered or chopped eggs, and sliced sweet pickles.

Egg Lettuce Bowl

1 head lettuce	6 radishes
4 hard-cooked eggs	⅛ teaspoon Watkins Dry Mustard
4 tomatoes	
4 spring onions	French dressing

Shred crisp lettuce into a salad bowl. Blend Watkins Dry Mustard with ½ teaspoon boiling water and add to French dressing. Sprinkle dressing over lettuce; add peeled tomatoes cut into sections, peeled and sliced onions, sliced hard-cooked eggs and sliced radishes. Toss mixture together and serve.

Egg Salad with Lemon Gelatin

1 package lemon
   gelatin dis-
   solved in 2 cups
   boiling water
6 stuffed eggs

Lettuce
Cooked salad
   dressing
Watkins Paprika

Stir boiling water into lemon gelatin or Jello, then cool. Pour gelatin to a depth of 1 inch in a salad mold or custard cup and chill until mixture begins to thicken. Place stuffed egg half (cut side down) in cup or mold and pour enough liquid gelatin around each egg to come to within ½ inch from top of eggs. Chill until firm, then pour on remaining gelatin and chill in the refrigerator. Serve on chilled salad greens, add cooked salad dressing, and Watkins Paprika. Garnish with stuffed olives.

Egg and Green Pepper Salad

½ lb. cream
   cheese
3 hard-cooked
   eggs
3 medium-sized
   peppers
½ cup pecans

1 tablespoon
   minced, sweet
   pickle
⅓ cup
   mayonnaise
Lettuce
French dressing
Watkins Paprika

Wash peppers, cut off top, remove seeds. Mash cheese with a fork until smooth. Chop eggs and nuts, add minced pickle and blend with cheese and mayonnaise. Fill peppers with mixture and chill several hours. Slice peppers crosswise and arrange 3 or 4 slices on crisp lettuce. Garnish with pieces of ripe tomato cut into eighths.

Egg and Tomato Salad

6 hard-cooked
   eggs
¼ cup stuffed
   olives, chopped
1⅓ cups celery,
   chopped
⅔ teaspoon salt

3 tablespoons
   lemon juice
¼ teaspoon Watkins Paprika
¼ teaspoon Watkins Onion Salt
6 slices tomato
1 head lettuce

Mix sliced cooked eggs, olives, celery, lemon juice and seasoning. Place mixture in center of each tomato slice and arrange on crisp lettuce. Add mayonnaise or cooked dressing and a dash of Watkins Paprika.

Egg and Vegetable Salad

1 head lettuce
1 bunch radishes
1 stalk crisp celery
1 small green
   pepper
4 hard-cooked
   eggs

6 tomatoes
1 tablespoon
   minced onion
Roquefort cheese
   dressing
Watkins Paprika

Wash, drain, chill lettuce and cut into small pieces; add sliced radishes, celery, green pepper, onion and dressing. Toss together lightly. Add quartered tomatoes and quartered hard-cooked eggs.

Egg and Tuna Salad

4 hard-cooked
  eggs
2 tablespoons
  cream cheese
2 strips crisp
  bacon, diced
1 No. 1 can
  tuna fish

1 bunch radishes,
  diced
¼ cup pimiento
  olives
Mayonnaise to
  moisten
Salt
Watkins Paprika

Cut eggs in half lengthwise, remove yolk, and chill. Put yolks through a sieve, add cream cheese, bacon, salt, Watkins Paprika and 1 tablespoon mayonnaise. Fill egg whites and arrange on crisp lettuce. Blend fish with chopped olives, radishes, moisten with mayonnaise, and arrange in center of salad plate.

Chiffonade Egg Salad

Lettuce
Romaine
Endive
Chicory

Celery
Cooked beets
  and eggs
French dressing

Chill salad greens, cut into strips and place in a chilled salad bowl. Use a wooden fork and spoon, add sliced cooked beets and hard-cooked eggs put through a ricer. Add French dressing. Toss mixture lightly and serve on chilled salad plates with Watkins Paprika.

Deviled Egg Salad

4 to 6 hard-cooked
  eggs
¼ teaspoon
  Watkins Dry
  Mustard
1 teaspoon
  vinegar

1 tablespoon
  melted butter
Watkins Red
  Pepper
Watkins Paprika
Mayonnaise or
  Cooked dressing
Salt

Cut hard cooked eggs in halves lengthwise, remove yolk, add seasoning and enough salad dressing to moisten. Refill egg whites using a spoon or force filling through a pastry tube into egg white. Add Watkins Paprika and chill. Chopped sweet pickles may be added to egg yolks. Serve on lettuce.

Stuffed Eggs in Gelatin

1 teaspoon gelatin
1 tablespoon
  cold water
1 cup mayonnaise
⅛ teaspoon salt
6 hard-cooked
  eggs

2 tablespoons
  minced cooked
  ham
1 teaspoon
  pickle relish
Watkins Paprika

Soften gelatin in cold water 5 minutes, then stir over boiling water to dissolve. Add to mayonnaise. Cut eggs into halves lengthwise, remove yolk. Mash yolks, blend with ham, chopped pickle, salt and enough mayonnaise to moisten. Fill egg white with mixture, arrange in a small loaf pan and pour gelatin mixture over eggs. Chill until firm and serve on crisp lettuce. Garnish with stuffed olives.

Stuffed Egg and Potato Salad

4 hard-cooked
  eggs
1 teaspoon
  minced chives
1 tablespoon
  mayonnaise

Cooked or canned
  asparagus tips
Potato salad
Crisp lettuce
Thousand Island
  dressing
Watkins Paprika

Cut eggs in halves lengthwise, remove yolks and mash. Add salt, mayonnaise, chives, and refill egg whites. Chill. Place a mound of potato salad on an individual salad plate, arrange asparagus tips (marinated in French dressing) on one side and half a stuffed egg on the other. Add dressing and Watkins Paprika.

Stuffed Egg Salad

Cut hard-cooked eggs in half cross-wise, remove yolk and chill. Fill centers with any of the following fillings. Arrange on water cress or other salad greens and garnish with mayonnaise dressing and a dash of Watkins Paprika.

Fillings:
Caviar with
  lemon juice
Chopped cooked
  chicken
  moistened with
  dressing
Chopped cooked
  chicken livers
Chopped nuts
  and cream
  cheese

Crisp cooked
  bacon blended
  with mashed
  egg yolk
Anchovies chopped and blended
  with dressing
Mashed egg yolk
  blended with
  chopped, sweet
  pickle and
  cooked salad
  dressing

Minced cooked
  ham and
  cooked salad
  dressing
Boneless and
  skinless
  sardine paste
Pate de foie gras
Minced pickle, pimiento, blended
  with mashed
  egg yolk

Salad Buffet

A Salad Buffet offers a delightfully informal way of entertaining because guests enjoy selecting, and tossing together, a salad combination of their own choice. Supplemented by one or two hot breads, sandwiches, hot coffee and a dessert, a very appetizing and satisfying meal can be planned.

Chicken and Vegetable Salad Buffet

Arrange one or two bowls of chilled mixed salad greens on an attractively decorated dining or buffet table. Garnish chilled chop plates, or a platter, with water cress and arrange slivered cooked chicken, turkey, ham, or tongue to be added, by the guests, to the mixed green salad. Place a well-seasoned vegetable salad in individual lettuce cups; and two different salads may be served on the plate. A fruit salad may be placed in a lettuce cup, or an individual gelatin fruit mold served on curly endive.

Bowls of French and mayonnaise dressing, for topping the salad, may be placed on cracked ice; and sprigs of crisp parsley or water cress will add a note of freshness.

As an accompaniment for the salad, have a tray with chilled raw vegetables, including celery sticks spread with cream or pimiento cheese, carrot and turnip sticks or curls, radish roses; also sliced, quartered or small stuffed tomatoes, strips of cucumbers and cauliflower flowerets, marinated in French dressing, or chilled canned hearts of palm. A tray of relishes are appetizing, with ripe, green and stuffed olives, sweet and dill pickles, pickled fruits, or canned mandarin oranges; these should be placed in bowls on cracked ice. A tray of assorted cheeses, and crisp crackers, has appetite appeal; and crisp potato chips and a bowl of salted nuts may also be served.

Popular at a buffet luncheon or supper are tiny hot buttered biscuits, or hot rolls, or sandwiches of date, raisin, nut or orange bread, spread with creamed butter and cut into long, narrow strips. Hot cheese sandwiches are delicious; open sandwiches are not favored for a buffet.

Hot coffee, served in hot cups, is the favorite beverage at a salad buffet; and any dessert may be served; but an ice cream, a sherbet, frozen peaches or strawberries with small cakes are suggested.

Each guest takes a plate and serves himself to the salad greens, then adds the various accompaniments. Use a dinner plate as a frame for the salad, as the salad should not extend over the edge of the plate.

A Fish Salad Buffet

The hostess may follow the menu suggested for a Chicken and Vegetable Salad Buffet, but substitute flaked canned or cooked tuna, shrimp, salmon, lobster, or crab meat, with an assortment of relishes and accompaniments as offered above. A casserole dish with a hot vegetable, as lima beans with canned pears, a corn pudding garnished with strips of pimiento, or fresh or frozen peas cooked with blanched almonds, may be served with the salad, which may be kept hot, with the rolls, in an electric roaster.

A Fruit Salad Buffet

Arrange bowls of crisp salad greens, and have bowls of French, mayonnaise or cooked dressing on cracked ice, and garnished with water cress.

Chilled chop plates, with crisp greens or lettuce cups, may contain assorted fruits such as grapefruit and orange sections, pineapple strips, cantaloupe and avocado slices, sliced peaches, honey dew melon, fluted banana strips dipped in pineapple juice, cherries or grapes stuffed with cream cheese and nuts and ripe strawberries.

Arrange a tray with relishes, a platter with assorted cheeses, and crisp crackers, a bowl of salted pecans and almonds, and an hors d' oeuvres platter with crisp raw vegetables. A platter of assorted cold meat with sliced chicken, baked ham, smoked tongue, corned beef, veal or chicken loaf, or gelatin turkey will add to the menu.

Serve hot rolls and sandwiches with hot coffee, and with or without a dessert.

Salad Luncheon Plate

In arranging a Salad Luncheon Plate, plan for color contrast and color harmony, avoiding such discords as orange carrots and the deep red of tomatoes. Also balance bland and highly flavored foods. A pear salad needs a highly seasoned dressing, and cream cheese can be improved by the addition of minced chives. Crisp lettuce and salad greens are made more appetizing with a piquant French dressing, or with one of Roquefort cheese, or the popular Thousand Island dressing. Select flavorful chilled raw vegetables such as tomatoes, cucumbers, celery, carrot or turnips sticks, cauliflower flowerets, shredded cabbage with pimiento, scallions, green pepper strips, raw white or purple onions cut into rings, white or red radishes, and peeled and sliced avocado.

Freshly cooked or canned vegetables may also be served as a salad, using string or lima beans, artichoke bottoms, brussels sprouts, cauliflower buds, canned hearts of palm, asparagus tips, cooked tiny beets stuffed with cream cheese and horse-radish.

Drain the cooked vegetable and add French dressing while hot, then chill. When several vegetables are used in a salad, each one should be marinated (while hot) in French dressing. For serving, the vegetables may be combined, or placed on crisp lettuce in small individual mounds.

Suggestions for Salad Plate Luncheon

Serve two different salads on a chilled luncheon plate, such as Chicken and a Fruit Salad, one in a crisp lettuce cup, the other on romaine or curly endive. With the salad, serve assorted tea sandwiches and a tray with assorted relishes. Or arrange, on crisp salad greens, sections of chilled grapefruit, orange, strips of pineapple, sliced ripe persimmons, nectarines, avocado, banana strips dipped in grapefruit or orange juice, slices of kumquats, and garnish with ripe strawberries. Pass French dressing made with lemon juice and add a dash of Watkins Paprika to top the salad.

Dates filled with cream cheese, cream cheese balls rolled in chopped nuts, fruit bread sandwiches, chicken salad sandwiches, ripe or pimiento olives, capers, small gherkin pickles, pickled beets, strips of dill or sweet pickles cut fan-shape, or India relish, may be served as appetizing accompaniments.

Or serve chicken or tuna fish loaf, with potato chips, asparagus tips with vinaigrette dressing, Watkins Paprika, with a garnish of water cress. An individual mold of fruit salad on crisp lettuce may be served. Assorted sandwiches and relishes, with a hot or iced beverage, are an important part of a salad luncheon plate.

Other suggestions are a peeled half of a ripe avocado filled with tuna fish salad on curly endive, and a fruit or vegetable salad on crisp lettuce. Or scooped out chilled tomato filled with chicken salad and served on crisp salad greens, or arrange your favorite salad on a lettuce cup; a chilled canned pear or peach, with nut bread sandwiches and relishes, with your favorite beverage, may be planned.

Or serve the white meat of turkey in a salad on crisp lettuce, with grapefruit and orange segments on curly endive and French dressing. Avocado slices on fresh mint, cheese balls with minced parsley, pimiento olives, clover leaf or orange rolls, and hot coffee, may be chosen as accompaniments. Or plan a chef salad with mixed greens and French dressing, with slivered pieces of cooked ham, smoked tongue, and chicken. Add an individual gelatin mold of fruit or cheese salad with diced pineapple on crisp lettuce. Serve with hot rolls, stuffed olives, and a chilled brandied or pickled peach. An appetizer salad of raw or cooked vegetables with French dressing and an individual mold of chicken salad on crisp lettuce, is suggested. A chilled fresh or canned peach or pear with cream cheese, with Watkins Cinnamon or pecan rolls and hot coffee, may be served.

French Dressing

The secret of a good salad is a tasty dressing. The popular salad dressing served throughout France, famous for its food, is the well-seasoned French dressing made of olive oil and vinegar, in the classic proportions of three parts olive oil and one of vinegar, with just the right seasoning. A hint of garlic is sometimes added by rubbing the salad bowl with a cut clove of garlic, then discarding, or by rubbing a piece of bread with a clove of garlic and brushing the inside of the salad bowl.

French dressing is a mere temporary emulsion which can be explained as follows: If you pour oil and water together, they will not mix; but if you shake them vigorously, little droplets of oil can be seen throughout the liquid. That is what happens in making French dressing, and the finer the droplets, the less will the oil separate. This is the reason French dressing should be shaken in a jar or bottle when made in a small quantity, and whipped in an electric mixer for a larger amount; always shake the dressing vigorously before using.

The foundation for French dressing is olive oil or a mild-flavored edible salad oil, with vinegar or lemon juice, or the combination of the two, and salt and Watkins Paprika. All variations of French dressing are made by adding other ingredients, such as Watkins Dry Mustard, Watkins Celery Salt, Watkins Red Pepper, Watkins Black Pepper, Watkins Onion Seasoning, Watkins Spice Blend, Watkins Garlic Seasoning, chili sauce, ketchup, tomato juice, tabasco or Worcestershire sauce, minced chives, or onion, or minced herbs. Various vinegars may be used such as tarragon, wine, cider, herb vinegar, or citric juices such as lemon, lime, grapefruit, or orange juice, or a combination of these ingredients. Vinegar is the acid generally used with olive or salad oils in a meat or mixed green or vegetable salad; while, in fruit salads, the juice of lemons is usually preferred.

Olive oils differ in flavor depending on the variety of the olive used, its ripeness, and on various conditions of manufacture. Olive oil is highly prized for salad dressing because of its distinctive flavor. The most delicate is the French olive oil; the heaviest flavor is the Spanish oil; between these two flavors, is the rich, golden oil of Italy, with a rich fruity flavor. In recent years vegetable oils from such sources as coconut, palm, peanut, cottonseed, and corn oil, have been used in salad dressings, as substitutes for the more expensive olive oil.

Corn oil and cottonseed oil may be used as substitutes for olive oil or olive oil may be blended with tea-seed oil, peanut oil, sesame seed oil, and with soybean oil. It is important that the salad oil be fresh and sweet; the flavor being the essential point, hence the importance of selecting quality oil. Mineral oil is not a digestible substance, and should be used in salad dressing only if recommended by a doctor. Experts claim that mineral oil, used in a salad dressing, will destroy Vitamin A.

Use French dressing for fresh, crisp, dry salad greens, on raw or cooked vegetable salads, on meat, fish and poultry salads, fruit salads, and salads with cheese. Keep salad dressing in a covered jar in the refrigerator. When left to stand, the oil will rise to the top, but this will not affect the dressing, if shaken briskly before using. Commercial French dressing often remains permanently emulsified when it contains a large amount of paprika, which acts as a stabilizer.

Different Vinegars for a Salad

The Pure Food and Drugs Act states that vinegar must contain at least 4 per cent acetic acid, and it is valued for the tart flavor which this acid imparts. The best vinegars are made from fruit juices by subjecting them first to alcoholic and then to acetic acid fermentation, including Orleans, red wine and tarragon vinegar. Cider vinegar is a good quality made from fermented apple juice, and white vinegar is made by fermenting diluted, distilled alcohol. Malt vinegar is made from fermented cereals and malt or cider vinegar may be flavored with tarragon, sweet basil or marjoram, but the results will not be as flavorful as if red wine vinegar were used. The popular vinegars used in a salad include red wine, white wine, tarragon, cider, cherry and wild blackberry.

Salad Bowl Vinegar

Salad Bowl Vinegar: A mixture with a blend of six different herbs. Use to marinate meat, to soften the fiber before cooking; chill several hours before using.

Raspberry Vinegar: Serve on chilled melon and for a fruit salad.

Mint Vinegar: Excellent for a fruit salad. Bottled herb vinegars may be added to a basic French dressing. Or use a sprinkling of minced herbs as basil, thyme, chevril or tarragon over a mixed green or a green vegetable salad.

Tarragon Vinegar: For a meat or fish salad use tarragon vinegar in making French dressing, which is considered by connoisseurs the most delicious vinegar in the world.

French Dressing

(Basic Recipe)

¾ teaspoon salt
4 tablespoons
    tarragon vine-
    gar or lemon
    juice (or com-
    bination of the
    two)

½ teaspoon
    granulated
    sugar
¾ cup olive oil
½ teaspoon Wat-
    kins Paprika

Place salt, sugar and vinegar in a bottle or small fruit jar and shake until salt is dissolved. Add olive oil, Watkins Paprika and shake or whip with a rotary beater until creamy. Keep covered in the refrigerator and shake well before using.

For A Large Quantity: Use an electric or rotary beater. Measure into a fruit jar 1½ cups olive oil, ½ cup tarragon vinegar, 2 teaspoons salt, 1 teaspoon Watkins Paprika, with sugar to suit taste. Shake vigorously to blend mixture and keep covered in the refrigerator.

French Dressing Variations

American Dressing for Fruit Salad

½ cup French dressing
    with lemon juice
1 teaspoon chopped,
    blanched almonds
1 teaspoon water cress, minced
1 teaspoon maraschino
    cherries, chopped
Blend all ingredients thoroughly. Chill.

American Cheese Dressing for Meat, Fish or Lettuce Salad

⅔ cup French dressing
¼ cup grated American cheese
Chill ingredients, beat thoroughly and serve.

Anchovy Dressing

½ cup French dressing
1 tablespoon minced onion
1 tablespoon minced parsley
2 salted anchovies or 2 tablespoons anchovy paste

Bar Le Duc

½ cup French dressing made with lemon juice and 2 table-spoons bar le duc jam. Blend, chill and serve over a cheese salad.

Bleu Cheese Dressing

½ cup French dressing
¼ lb. crumbled bleu cheese
Blend ingredients and serve with chilled mixed greens or vegetable salad, or with cooked asparagus tips or tomato salad.

Californian Dressing

½ cup French dressing
1 teaspoon Watkins
  Dry Mustard
2 tablespoons sugar
1 tablespoon chili sauce
1 tablespoon ketchup
Strained juice of 1 orange
Chill before serving.

Caper Dressing

½ cup French dressing
2 tablespoons capers, minced
2 tablespoons chopped, stuffed olives
1 teaspoon minced parsley

Chef's Salad Dressing for Lettuce, Mixed Green Salad

⅓ cup crumbled bleu cheese
1 teaspoon anchovy paste
Juice of ½ lemon
2 tablespoons vinegar
½ cup olive oil
Minced sliver of garlic
Watkins Celery Salt
Watkins Paprika
Salt
Dash Worcestershire sauce
Crumble cheese with a fork. Place all ingredients in a fruit jar, add tight cover and shake vigorously. Keep in the refrigerator and shake well before using.

Cheese and Chive Dressing for Vegetable Salad

½ cup French dressing
1 cup cottage cheese
¼ cup milk
1 tablespoon minced chives
Have all ingredients cold; blend thoroughly and add Watkins Paprika.

Chiffonade Dressing

½ cup French dressing
½ teaspoon finely minced chives
1 teaspoon chopped beets
1 teaspoon chopped hard-cooked egg white
1.teaspoon chopped hard-cooked egg yolk
1 teaspoon chopped red pepper
1 teaspoon chopped green pepper
(If too thick, add more French dressing.)

Chili Dressing

½ cup French dressing
5 tablespoons chili sauce
¼ teaspoon Watkins Dry Mustard
1 teaspoon chopped onion
¾ teaspoon Watkins Paprika
1 teaspoon Worcestershire sauce
Blend all ingredients thoroughly.

Chutney Dressing

½ cup French dressing
2 tablespoons chutney
Chill and serve.

Club Salad Dressing

½ cup French dressing
3 tablespoons minced scallions
3 tablespoons tomato juice
1 tablespoon Worcestershire sauce
1 tablespoon sugar

Colombia Dressing

½ cup French dressing made
   with lemon juice
½ teaspoon salt
½ teaspoon Watkins Prepared
   Mustard
½ tablespoon Worcestershire
   sauce

Add a chunk of ice and stir
thoroughly for 10 minutes or
until mixture thickens. Remove ice and keep the dressing
in the refrigerator until ready
to use.

Coraline Dressing

½ cup French dressing
½ teaspoon Worcestershire
   sauce
1 teaspoon finely minced
   parsley
Mashed coral from 1 cooked
   lobster

Cream French Dressings

No. 1
½ cup French dressing made
   with lemon juice
2 tablespoons heavy cream
1 tablespoon grated pineapple
1 tablespoon chopped pecans

No. 2
½ cup French dressing made
   with lemon juice
1 tablespoon heavy cream
1 tablespoon currant jelly
¼ teaspoon finely chopped
   lemon peel

No. 3
½ cup French dressing
½ teaspoon minced chives
2 tablespoons sour cream

No. 4
Fold ¼ cup French dressing
made with lemon juice into
¼ cup whipped, sweet cream.
Add 1 teaspoon powdered sugar
Excellent for fruit salad.

Cottage Cheese Dressing For Mixed Greens

1 cup cottage cheese
½ teaspoon salt
⅓ teaspoon Watkins Paprika
8 pickled onions, minced
4 tablespoons sweet vinegar
　　from pickles
7 tablespoons salad oil
Watkins Paprika
Beat cheese with a fork until soft, add seasonings, vinegar and onions. Gradually beat in salad oil. Keep in covered jar in the refrigerator.

Creole Dressing

½ cup French dressing
1 teaspoon chopped pimiento
1 teaspoon chopped
　　mushrooms
1 tablespoon chili sauce
½ teaspoon chopped chives

Creole Mint Dressing

½ cup French dressing
1 teaspoon each of fresh mint leaves, onion, pimiento, parsley and shallot, all finely chopped. Finish with a pinch of sugar and 1 tablespoon chopped hard-cooked egg-white.

Cress Dressing

½ cup French dressing
1 teaspoon Watkins Paprika
1½ teaspoons Watkins Dry
　　Mustard
¼ teaspoon Worcestershire
　　sauce
1 teaspoon chili sauce
4 tablespoons minced
　　water cress
Dash Tabasco sauce
Dash Watkins Pepper

Egg Dressing

½ cup French dressing
2 chopped hard-cooked eggs
Use on head lettuce salad.

Delmonte Dressing

¾ cup French dressing
⅛ teaspoon Watkins Dry
  Mustard
¼ teaspoon Watkins Onion
  Seasoning
2 teaspoons finely minced
  parsley
1 hard-cooked egg, finely
  chopped
Blend ingredients thoroughly.
Excellent to serve with red cabbage salad.

Fruit Salad Dressing

No. 1
½ cup salad oil
¼ cup pineapple juice
1 tablespoon lemon juice
1 tablespoon orange juice
1 teaspoon sugar
Dash salt
Watkins Paprika
Or substitute any fruit juice
for lemon juice.

No. 2
1 cup salad oil
¼ cup tarragon vinegar
¼ tablespoon Watkins
  Ground Mustard
¼ cup powdered sugar
⅛ teaspoon Watkins Paprika
1¼ teaspoon salt
½ cup orange juice
2 tablespoons lemon juice
2 tablespoons grapefruit juice
¾ teaspoon Worcestershire
  sauce

Mix together dry ingredients
and add to vinegar and oil.
Whip briskly with rotary
beater. Add fruit juice and
beat well.

Fruit Salad Dressing (Without Oil)

½ cup orange juice
3 tablespoons lemon juice
¼ teaspoon salt
¼ teaspoon Watkins Paprika

Egg and Cheese Dressing

½ cup French dressing
½ 3-oz. package cream cheese
2 hard-cooked eggs
½ teaspoon Watkins Dry
  Mustard
Mash cheese into a paste, then
beat in sieved hard-cooked
eggs. Blend all ingredients and
serve over crisp salad greens.

Garlic Vinegar Dressing

3 tablespoons salad oil
Dash salt
Dash Watkins Paprika
¼ teaspoon Watkins Dry
  Mustard
½ teaspoon dry dill
1 tablespoon garlic vinegar
(To make garlic vinegar place
2 or 3 small pieces of garlic in
a bottle of vinegar and put
aside to flavor.)

Ginger Dressing

No. 1
½ cup French dressing
½ teaspoon preserved ginger,
  chopped
½ teaspoon ginger syrup
(Serve with an apricot salad.)
No. 2
½ cup French dressing
2 tablespoons ketchup
½ to 1 tablespoon sugar
⅛ teaspoon Watkins Ginger
⅛ teaspoon Watkins Dry
  Mustard
1 clove garlic or ½ teaspoon
  chopped chives
Watkins Celery Salt
Watkins Paprika
Place all ingredients in a covered fruit jar, let stand several
hours. Remove garlic and
chives and keep covered in the
refrigerator.

Guadeloupe Salad Dressing

½ cup French dressing
2 tablespoons white rum
½ teaspoon each of finely
  chopped onion, parsley,
  chives and shallots
½ teaspoon Worcestershire
  sauce
Watkins Red Pepper
Watkins Celery Salt
Blend all ingredients.   Chill.

Herb Anchovy Dressing for Tomato, also Shrimp Salad

¼ teaspoon salad herbs
¼ teaspoon sugar
⅓ cup tarragon vinegar
¼ teaspoon garlic salt
  (if desired)
⅔ cup salad oil
2 tablespoons anchovy paste
Dissolve sugar and salt in vinegar, add herbs and steep over simmering heat for about 10 minutes, then cool.   Beat in salad oil and anchovy paste. Chill.

Honey Dressing

½ cup French dressing made
  with lemon juice
2 tablespoons honey
Blend thoroughly.

Horse-radish Dressing

½ cup French dressing
1 teaspoon prepared
  horse-radish

Ketchup Dressing

½ cup French dressing
2 tablespoons ketchup
¼ hard-cooked egg
2 tablespoons finely chopped
  water cress
A-1 Sauce, few drops
Watkins Pepper

Lorenzo Dressing

½ cup French dressing
½ teaspoon chili sauce
1 tablespoon minced
  water cress

Lime French Dressing

½ cup salad oil
¼ cup lime juice
½ teaspoon salt
⅓ teaspoon Watkins Paprika
½ teaspoon Watkins
  Dry Mustard
½ teaspoon sugar

Mint Dressing

½ cup French dressing
1 teaspoon chopped fresh mint
  or 1 tablespoon chopped mint
  jelly
Serve on combination fruit,
cheese and nut salad.

Mustard Dressing

½ cup French dressing
1 teaspoon Watkins Dry
  Mustard
Dash of Watkins Red Pepper

New Orleans Dressing

½ cup French dressing
2 tablespoons tomato ketchup
¼ teaspoon grated onion
1 tablespoon grated cucumber
½ tablespoon minced green
  pepper

Olive Dressing

½ cup French dressing
¼ cup chopped pimiento olives

Onion Dressing

½ cup French dressing
1 tablespoon onion juice
Watkins Onion Seasoning
Watkins Celery Salt
Watkins Paprika

Parmesan Cheese Dressing

¾ cup French dressing
2 tablespoons grated Parmesan
  cheese
Watkins Paprika

Piquante Dressing (for Meat or Mixed Green Salads)

½ cup French dressing
½ teaspoon Watkins Dry
  Mustard
½ teaspoon onion, minced
2 drops Tabasco sauce

Peanut Butter Dressing

½ cup French dressing
2½ tablespoons peanut butter

Poor Man's Sauce

½ cup French dressing
1 teaspoon each of parsley, young green onions, gherkins and green string beans, cut very fine.
Use with a simple vegetable salad.

Quebec Dressing

½ cup French dressing
2 chopped stuffed olives
1 chopped green onion or
1 tablespoon minced chives
½ tablespoon minced green pepper
½ teaspoon Worcestershire sauce

Roquefort Dressing

½ cup French dressing
¼ cup Roquefort cheese
Crumble the cheese (do not mash it fine) and add to the dressing. Good with an avocado pear salad.

Reducing Salad Dressing

2 tablespoons lemon juice
1 teaspoon olive oil
Or use equal amounts of lemon juice and salad oil. Orange, lemon, lime or pineapple juice may be used for a salad dressing. Mineral oil may be used instead of olive or salad oil. (See comment on mineral oil at beginning of this chapter.)

Sea Food Dressing

½ cup French dressing
¾ cup mayonnaise
¾ cup diced avocado
Watkins Paprika
Chill ingredients and blend just before serving.

Salad Bowl Dressing

6 tablespoons tarragon vinegar
¼ teaspoon Watkins Paprika
Dash Watkins Red Pepper
½ teaspoon salt
¼ teaspoon sugar, more if desired
1 cup salad oil
½ teaspoon dissolved gum arabic

Blend vinegar and seasonings, stir into oil. Add gum-arabic and shake vigorously. Keep covered in the refrigerator and shake well before using. The gum-arabic will thicken the mixture, similar to the commercial type of dressing.

Sherry Dressing

½ cup French dressing
2 generous tablespoons Sherry
1 teaspoon chervil finely chopped
Pinch of sugar to suit taste

Spanish Dressing

¾ cup French dressing
½ clove garlic
1 hard-cooked egg, sieved
1½ tablespoons Worcestershire sauce
¼ teaspoon Watkins Chili Powder
¼ teaspoon Watkins Onion Seasoning
¼ teaspoon Watkins Celery Salt
Dash Watkins Red Pepper

Vinaigrette Dressing

½ cup French dressing
½ teaspoon each green olives, capers, chives, gherkins, parsley, tarragon and chervil, all finely chopped.
(Tarragon or chervil may be omitted.)
Use for an asparagus salad
for a cantaloupe or avocado pear salad.

Tart French Dressing

Omit sugar in French dressing, add ½ teaspoon Watkins Dry Mustard and increase lemon juice in recipe to suit taste.

Tomato French Dressing

½ cup French dressing
½ can tomato soup
1 teaspoon Watkins Onion Seasoning
1 teaspoon Worcestershire sauce
Watkins Red Pepper

Aromatic Vinegar for French Dressing

1 quart best white wine vinegar
½ cup chopped shallots
¼ cup chives, chopped
¼ cup fresh mint
¼ cup sweet savory
1 teaspoon salt
2 teaspoons light brown sugar
Place in a covered jar. Leave in sun three weeks, then strain. Ready to use.

Tarragon Vinegar for French Dressing

Add a small bunch of green leaves of tarragon to the vinegar, let stand 24 hours to flavor. Do not strain.

Homemade Herb Vinegar

1 cup malt vinegar
1 teaspoon minced fresh mint leaves
¼ teaspoon dried tarragon
2 tablespoons chopped chives
¼ teaspoon dried marjoram
¼ teaspoon crushed dried chervil
Blend all ingredients in a glass jar. Seal and let stand 5 days; strain through a double cheesecloth and keep in a covered jar.

Mayonnaise Salad Dressing

Mayonnaise, French, or Cooked are the three basic salad dressings, and delicious variations of them can be made. We suggest a few good combinations which will add a distinctive flavor, and give variety to a salad, but do not hesitate to make your own special dressings. It is the homemaker with imagination who earns the reputation for creating appetizing salads. The salad dressing should be suited in flavor and consistency to the salad.

As a beginning for your experimentation, try using honey instead of sugar for sweetening, or perhaps thick fruit syrup from pickled peaches, conserves, or melted jelly. Use different flavors of vinegar; or if the vinegar is too strong, dilute with a little cold water. Olive oil has the most pronounced flavor for a salad dressing; but if it is difficult to obtain, or too expensive, use one part olive oil and two parts best quality vegetable oil.

In making any salad dressing, have all the ingredients fresh and of the first quality, and do not hurry the mixing. Use a rotary or an electric beater. In making mayonnaise, chill the salad oil, and also the bowl and beater; have the eggs at room temperature. Use a mixing-bowl with a rounded bottom, not too large. **It is important to beat the mixture constantly while adding the salad oil.** If the mayonnaise dressing should curdle, beat an egg yolk in another bowl, then gradually add the curdled dressing to the beaten egg, beating constantly.

In making mayonnaise, an egg yolk is a more efficient emulsifier than a whole egg. The addition of a small amount of previously made mayonnaise to the egg-yolk-acid mixture, facilitates emulsification. When an egg yolk is used as an emulsifier, salt stabilizes the emulsion, if added **before** the salad oil. The ideal salad oil for mayonnaise should not contain the fatty acids which solidify at the usual refrigerator temperature, about 40 degrees F. Use "wintered" salad oil from which the fatty acids have been removed. If the olive oil flavor is too pronounced in the dressing, add whipped cream to the mayonnaise just before serving.

Salad dressings made in a quantity are a great convenience; and any of the basic dressings may be kept several days in a covered container in the refrigerator. Too low a temperature will cause the emulsion to separate; if the oil in the mayonnaise comes to the top, skim it off; **do not** beat the oil into the dressing, for this may cause all the oil to separate.

Serve mayonnaise dressing on chicken, meat, fish, vegetable and gelatin salads. Blend mayonnaise with whipped cream for fruit salad. Add salad

dressing just before serving, except in making a potato, meat, fish or poultry salad, when French dressing is marinated with these ingredients and chilled one hour for better flavor.

Mayonnaise Dressing

(Basic Recipe)

Put egg yolk and seasonings into a small bowl and beat thoroughly with a rotary or electric mixer. Beat in ¼ cup of the oil gradually, a drop at a time. Slowly add 1 tablespoon of vinegar, beating constantly. Add more oil gradually as mixture thickens; then add remaining vinegar or lemon juice. **It is important to beat mixture constantly** while adding oil. If oil is added too rapidly, the mayonnaise will curdle. To remedy this, immediately beat curdled mixture gradually into a second egg yolk and continue as above. Keep dressing in a covered jar, farthest away from the freezing unit. For a more stiff dressing, add more olive oil and blend thoroughly; for a thinner dressing, add a half tablespoon or more of vinegar, a little at a time, until the right consistency.

1 egg yolk
¾ teaspoon salt
½ teaspoon Watkins Dry Mustard
½ teaspoon Watkins Paprika
Dash Watkins Red Pepper

2 tablespoons vinegar or lemon juice or combination of the two
1 cup olive oil
Will make 1¼ cups

Mayonnaise Dressing

(That will not curdle)

1 teaspoon Watkins Dry Mustard
1 teaspoon Watkins Paprika
1 teaspoon salt
2 egg yolks

1 tablespoon boiling water
1 cup olive oil
1 tablespoon lemon juice
1 tablespoon vinegar

Blend Watkins Paprika, salt and Watkins Dry Mustard. Use a rotary beater, whip egg yolks and beat in dry ingredients. Whip mixture and gradually add boiling water. Add olive oil, a tablespoon at a time, beating constantly (until ½ cup is used, then add oil a little faster). Gradually add lemon juice and mix well, then add vinegar last. Blend mixture thoroughly and keep in a covered jar in the refrigerator.

Mayonnaise Dressing Variations

Almond Cucumber Dressing

1 cup mayonnaise
¼ cup chopped cucumbers
2 tablespoons chopped almonds

Anchovy Mayonnaise

½ cup mayonnaise
1 tablespoon chopped anchovies
  or anchovy paste
1 tablespoon chopped gherkins

Aspic Dressing

1 cup mayonnaise ½ cup aspic

Slowly add the aspic which has been slightly melted, beating constantly. Chill thoroughly to stiffen. Use to garnish elaborate salads.

Banana Mayonnaise

Add pulp of 3 bananas and 2 cups whipped cream.

Bombay Mayonnaise

⅓ cup mustard with horseradish
1 tablespoon chutney, chopped

⅔ cup mayonnaise
1 tablespoon lemon juice
Dash curry powder

Blend well. Serve with chopped chicken or turkey, celery and apples. Garnish with sprigs of parsley.

Calavo Mayonnaise

1 calavo
1 tablespoon lemon juice
Salt
Mayonnaise

Dash of Watkins Onion Seasoning
Worcestershire sauce

Mash the calavo with a fork and whip or beat it until smooth. Add lemon juice, salt and other ingredients to suit taste, and enough mayonnaise to make a good consistency. Whip until smooth and fluffy. Serve on a salad of head lettuce and tomato.

Chantilly Dressing

1 cup mayonnaise
3 tablespoons whipped cream
2 tablespoons bar le duc or currant jelly

Chantilly Dressing

1 cup mayonnaise
½ cup whipped cream
1½ tablespoons grated horse-radish
1 teaspoon grated onion
Serve on asparagus tip salad.

Cheese Mayonnaise

¾ cup mayonnaise
2 tablespoons thin cream
½ cup grated American cheese
Salt to taste
½ teaspoon Watkins Paprika
Serve with fruit salad.

Chiffonade Dressing

1 cup mayonnaise
1 tablespoon minced green pepper
1 tablespoon minced chives
3 tablespoons chopped, cooked beets
1 hard-cooked egg, chopped fine

Serve on crisp hearts of lettuce, romaine or endive.

Collegiate Dressing

2 tablespoons mayonnaise
1 tablespoon orange or pineapple juice
2 tablespoons whipped cream
2 teaspoons malted milk powder

Fold cream into mayonnaise, add the malted milk blended smoothly with orange juice. Use for fruit salad.

Cooked Mayonnaise

2 tablespoons salad oil
2 tablespoons flour
2 tablespoons lemon juice
Boiling water
1 egg yolk, beaten
1 cup salad oil
1 teaspoon salt
⅛ teaspoon Watkins Paprika
¼ teaspoon Watkins Dry Mustard
1 egg white, beaten

Blend the first three ingredients in a measuring cup, fill cup with boiling water. Cook in double boiler, stirring constantly, until mixture thickens. Add beaten egg yolk and cool. Gradually beat in oil, add seasonings, and fold in stiffly-beaten egg white.

Mayonnaise with Cottage Cheese

To a thick mayonnaise dressing made with eggs and olive oil, beat in ½ cup fine grained, sieved cottage cheese. Chill and serve.

Cottage Cheese Mayonnaise

Prepare just
before serving
1 cup cottage
cheese
1 tablespoon
sugar

½ teaspoon
Watkins Dry
Mustard
⅓ teaspoon salt
½ teaspoon Wat-
kins Paprika
½ cup olive oil

Mix together the first five ingredients, gradually beat in olive oil and blend well. Use this dressing promptly.

Cream Cheese Dressing

4 tablespoons mayonnaise
1 3-oz. package cream cheese
1 teaspoon Watkins Prepared
Mustard
Dash Watkins Garlic Seasoning

Cream Mayonnaise for Fruit Salads

Blend and whip together 2 parts mayonnaise and 1 part whipped cream. Or follow your favorite recipe for mayonnaise and add ¼ cup of thick sour cream and blend thoroughly.

Crisp Mayonnaise

¼ cup finely chopped celery
¼ cup finely chopped
cucumber
¾ cup mayonnaise
2 tablespoons sour or
thick cream
2 tablespoons shredded
pimiento

Curry Mayonnaise

½ teaspoon curry powder
1 cup mayonnaise
Use for shellfish salad.

East Indian Mayonnaise

½ teaspoon salt
½ teaspoon
curry powder
½ clove garlic
chopped very
fine
1 egg

Few grains Wat-
kins Red Pepper
1 tablespoon
vinegar
1 tablespoon
lime juice
1 egg yolk
1½ cups olive oil

Mix garlic and dry ingredients, add egg and extra yolk, beat all with rotary beater until thick and lighter in color. Slowly add vinegar and oil, beating vigorously. When all oil has been used, add lime juice. Chill before using.

Economy Mayonnaise

2 tablespoons salad oil	1 egg yolk, beaten
2 tablespoons flour	1 cup salad oil
2 tablespoons lemon juice	1 teaspoon salt
Boiling water	¼ teaspoon Watkins Dry Mustard
	1 egg white

Blend the two tablespoons salad oil, flour and lemon juice in a measuring cup, fill cup with boiling water and pour into top of a double boiler. Stir constantly and cook over hot water until mixture thickens. Remove from fire and beat into egg yolk and cool. Gradually beat in the salad oil, seasonings, and stir in beaten egg white. Keep in a covered jar in the refrigerator. Whip mixture before using.

Escoffier Dressing

¼ cup imported Escoffier sauce (purchase in bottle)
¾ cup chili sauce
1 cup mayonnaise
Juice ½ lemon
Minced chives
Salt
Watkins Pepper
Watkins Paprika
Chill, blend mixture and serve on crisp lettuce.

Evaporated Milk Mayonnaise

¼ cup undiluted evaporated milk, chilled	½ teaspoon salt
¼ teaspoon Watkins Paprika	⅓ teaspoon Watkins Dry Mustard
1 teaspoon powdered sugar	3 tablespoons vinegar
	¾ cup olive oil

Blend seasonings in a chilled bowl, stir in chilled evaporated milk. Use a rotary beater and whip mixture, adding a teaspoon of oil at a time. Lastly, beat in vinegar, then add a half tablespoon of boiling water and whip thoroughly. Keep in a covered jar in the refrigerator.

Frozen Mayonnaise

½ cup mayonnaise	¼ cup whipping cream
Juice of ½ lemon	

Whip cream until it holds its shape. Fold in the mayonnaise, add lemon juice, and freeze in small molds or tiny paper cups.

Herb Dressing

1 cup mayonnaise
1 teaspoon each of minced parsley, tarragon, water cress, chervil, chives and basil.

Honey-Cream Dressing

½ cup mayonnaise
¼ teaspoon Watkins
   Dry Mustard
1 tablespoon mild flavored
   honey
½ teaspoon lemon juice
½ cup whipped cream
Add whipped cream just before
serving.

Horse-radish Mayonnaise with Cold Boiled Fish or Corned Beef Salad

1 cup mayonnaise
1 tablespoon horse-radish
1 tablespoon Worcestershire
   sauce
¼ cup tomato ketchup

Lorenzo Dressing

1 cup mayonnaise
1 tablespoon finely chopped
   celery
1 tablespoon pineapple, grated
1 tablespoon chopped water
   cress

Mayonnaise with Condensed Milk

¼ cup vinegar or
   lemon juice
¼ cup salad oil
⅔ cup evaporated
   condensed milk
1 egg yolk

½ teaspoon salt
1 teaspoon
   Watkins Dry
   Mustard
Watkins Red
   Pepper

Blend dry ingredients with beaten
egg yolk. Beat in oil and vinegar
slowly. Lastly, add condensed
milk.

Mayonnaise Without Salad Oil

Yolks of 2 hard-
   cooked eggs
Yolks of 2 raw
   eggs
2 tablespoons
   heavy cream
¼ teaspoon salt

½ teaspoon
   lemon juice
Watkins Paprika
Dash Watkins
   Red Pepper
1 teaspoon
   minced chives

Mash egg yolks fine and blend
with beaten raw yolks. Mix to a
smooth paste adding remaining ingredients. Will make about one-
half cup.

Red Mayonnaise

1 cup mayonnaise
2 tablespoons lobster coral, or tomato paste,

or a few drops Watkins Red Color Mixture

Put lobster coral through a sieve and add to mayonnaise. Tomato paste, or a tablespoon beet juice or Watkins Red Coloring may be substituted. Use for a fish salad.

Remoulade Dressing

1 cup mayonnaise
1 tablespoon chopped capers
1 tablespoon chopped chives or parsley

Russian Dressing

½ cup mayonnaise
2 tablespoons thick chili sauce
1 teaspoon Worcestershire sauce
2 tablespoons lemon juice
Serve on mixed salad greens or simple vegetable salads, as sliced tomatoes.

Russian Dressing Variations

No. 1
1 cup mayonnaise
⅓ cup chili sauce
1 hard-cooked egg, chopped
1 tablespoon chopped green pepper
1 tablespoon chopped pimiento
1 tablespoon chopped chives

No. 2
1 cup mayonnaise
½ cup chili sauce
1 tablespoon minced green pepper
⅓ cup minced stuffed olives

No. 3
1 cup mayonnaise
½ cup chili sauce
2 tablespoons finely chopped celery, pickle and pimiento
Watkins Paprika
1 tablespoon lemon juice
1 teaspoon Worcestershire sauce

Ravigote Mayonnaise

1 cup mayonnaise
2 tablespoons
  puree cooked
  spinach
1 tablespoon
  minced capers

3 chopped
  anchovies
½ cup minced
  parsley and
  water cress

Drain off water from spinach. Blend all ingredients and serve with sea food salad.

Sherry Mayonnaise

1 tablespoon
  sherry

1 cup mayonnaise

Blend well. Serve with fruit salad. Grenadine may be substituted for sherry.

Stiff Mayonnaise for Decorating a Salad

To a pint of plain mayonnaise, add 1 teaspoon gelatin softened in 1 teaspoon cold water stirred over hot water until melted. For a very stiff mayonnaise, double the amount of gelatin.

Surprise Dressing

1 cup thick
  mayonnaise
1 tablespoon
  chili sauce
2 tablespoons
  vinegar

1 tablespoon
  grated cheese
2 olives, chopped
  fine
1 egg white,
  beaten stiff

Mix all ingredients and beat well to insure smoothness. Keep in the refrigerator in a covered jar.

Tartare Dressing for Fish Salad

1 cup mayonnaise
2 tablespoons chopped,
  sweet pickle
1 tablespoon minced parsley
1 tablespoon minced chives
1 tablespoon chopped capers

Tomato Dressing

¼ cup mayonnaise
¼ cup thick tomato soup
Dash Worcestershire sauce
¼ teaspoon onion, grated
½ teaspoon parsley, minced
Serve on baked bean salad.

Thousand Island Dressing on Crisp Lettuce

No. 1

1 cup mayonnaise
4 tablespoons chili sauce
3 tablespoons ketchup
1 tablespoon tarragon vinegar
1 tablespoon minced
    green peppers
3 tablespoons minced,
    red peppers
1 teaspoon Watkins Paprika
1 tablespoon minced chives
2 tablespoons each of chopped,
    ripe and green olives

No. 2

1 cup mayonnaise
2 hard-cooked eggs
2 tablespoons tomato ketchup
1 teaspoon onion juice
3 tablespoons French dressing
2 tablespoons chili sauce
2 tablespoons finely chopped
    pickle

No. 3

1 cup mayonnaise
⅓ cup chili sauce
¼ cup cream, whipped
2 tablespoons chopped pickle
1 tablespoon chopped pimiento
Watkins Paprika

Virginia Dressing

1½ cup mayonnaise
⅔ cup chili sauce
½ teaspoon Worcestershire
    sauce
1 tablespoon lemon juice
Salt
Watkins Pepper
1¼ cups finely minced water
    cress

White Wine Dressing

¼ cup fresh strawberries
    or raspberries
2 tablespoons fruit juice
2 tablespoons white wine
1 cup mayonnaise

Cooked Salad Dressing

A Cooked Salad Dressing is composed of eggs, seasoning, vinegar, and some liquid, such as milk, cream, or water. When milk is used, flour is generally added for thickening, which lessens the tendency for the mixture to curdle. Sweet, sour, evaporated milk, cream, or water will make a smooth, creamy dressing. Butter or margarine is used in place of salad oil, and may be added as the basic sauce is made, or after the other ingredients are blended.

Plain, cooked dressing, because of its tartness, is especially adapted to use on potato, meat, vegetable, and many fruit salads. Cooked dressing may be thinned with cream, but the dressing should be highly seasoned to be appetizing. Cooked dressings, particularly those made from water and milk, have a lower calorie value than a French or a mayonnaise dressing. Keep cooked dressing in a covered jar in the refrigerator.

Plain Cooked Salad Dressing

¾ cup milk	Dash Watkins
2 tablespoons	Red Pepper
flour	2 egg yolks
1 tablespoon	2 tablespoons
sugar	butter
1 teaspoon salt	¼ cup mild
1 teaspoon	vinegar
Watkins Dry	Watkins Paprika
Mustard	

Scald milk in top of a double boiler. Blend flour, sugar, salt and seasonings in a small mixing bowl. Stir and gradually add hot milk to dry ingredients. Return mixture to double boiler, stir constantly and cook over boiling water until mixture thickens. Stir and cook 10 minutes longer to thoroughly cook flour. Beat egg yolks then stir hot mixture slowly into beaten eggs. Then return mixture to double boiler and stir and cook 2 minutes longer. Stir in butter, a little at a time, and blend well. Slowly stir in vinegar. If vinegar is added too quickly the mixture will curdle. Remove from stove immediately, turn into a bowl and cool. When cold, keep covered in the refrigerator. Just before using, the dressing may be thinned with sweet, sour, or whipped cream. Add Watkins Paprika.

Cooked Salad Dressing Variations

To lend variety to cooked dressing, add one of the following combinations to the foundation recipe:

Curry Dressing

Slightly cool dressing after removing from fire and add ¼ teaspoon curry powder and ¼ cup minced pickle relish.

Chutney Dressing

Add 1 tablespoon each of chopped chutney, chopped pimiento and minced parsley.

Chili Sauce Dressing

Add ⅓ cup chili sauce and 1 tablespoon minced green pepper with Watkins Paprika.

Fluffy Dressing

When preparing foundation recipe, separate the egg, using the yolk. When dressing is cool, fold in the stiffly beaten egg white.

Horse-radish Dressing

After removing dressing from fire, stir in 1 tablespoon horse-radish.

Peanut Dressing for Fruit Salad

Add ¼ cup peanut butter to hot, cooked dressing.

Whipped Fruit Dressing

Fold ⅓ cup cooked salad dressing into ⅓ cup whipped cream. Add 2½ tablespoons confectioner's sugar and 2 tablespoons orange or grapefruit juice.

Cooked Dressing with Salad Oil

1½ teaspoon Watkins Dry Mustard	2 eggs, beaten
1 teaspoon salt	2 tablespoons salad oil
1¼ teaspoons powdered sugar	⅓ cup vinegar, add enough cold water to make ½ cup
Few grains Watkins Red Pepper	Watkins Paprika

Combine dry ingredients in top of a double boiler. Stir constantly and slowly add beaten eggs, salad oil, then gradually the diluted vinegar last. Stir and cook over boiling water until mixture begins to thicken. Strain, cool, and keep in a covered jar in the refrigerator.

Cooked Fruit Juice Dressing

2 eggs	⅓ cup orange juice
2 tablespoons flour	¼ cup sugar
1 cup canned pineapple juice	Watkins Paprika
3 tablespoons lemon juice	½ cup heavy cream

Beat eggs, then beat in flour and sugar. Stir in fruit juices and cook over hot water until mixture thickens, stirring constantly. Chill. Just before serving, fold in whipped cream.

Cooked Dressing with Cheese

4 egg yolks
¼ cup vinegar
1 tablespoon butter
5 tablespoons cream cheese
½ teaspoon salt
2 tablespoons cream

½ teaspoon sugar
¼ teaspoon Watkins Dry Mustard
⅛ teaspoon Watkins Paprika
Few drops tobasco sauce
⅛ teaspoon Watkins Celery Salt

Use top of double boiler. Beat egg yolks, beat in vinegar. Cook mixture over hot water until thickened, stirring constantly. Remove from heat, add butter, then cream cheese and stir until smooth. When cool stir in seasonings. One-half to 1 cup heavy cream, whipped, may be folded into chilled dressing before using.

Cooked Dressing With Cream

¼ teaspoon Watkins Dry Mustard
½ teaspoon salt
¼ teaspoon Watkins Paprika
3 egg yolks
2 tablespoons melted butter

2 tablespoons vinegar
1 tablespoon lemon juice
1 tablespoon sugar
½ cup thick cream

Mix dry ingredients and add to beaten egg yolks and cream. Stir and cook mixture in top of double boiler over hot water, whipping until thick. Remove from fire, stir in vinegar and lemon juice. Beat well. Add butter. Keep in a covered jar in the refrigerator. Add a little plain or whipped cream, if desired, before serving.

Cooked Mayonnaise Type Dressing

(For Cabbage, Potato Salad)

3 tablespoons salad oil
2 tablespoons flour
2 tablespoons sugar
1¼ teaspoons salt
1 teaspoon Watkins Dry Mustard

Dash Watkins Red Pepper
1 cup milk
6 tablespoons lemon juice or vinegar
2 eggs, slightly beaten
Watkins Paprika

Blend dry ingredients, stir in salad oil, then milk. Cook over boiling water, stirring constantly. Add lemon juice and eggs. Cook until mixture thickens. Add whipped cream just before serving.

Cooked Sour Milk Dressing

4 tablespoons
flour
1 tablespoon salt
3 eggs, beaten
1½ cups sour
milk
2 tablespoons
butter

½ cup vinegar
1 tablespoon
Watkins Dry
Mustard
2 tablespoons
sugar
Watkins Paprika

Blend flour, salt, Watkins Dry Mustard, sugar, Watkins Paprika in top of a double boiler. Stir in beaten eggs, gradually add milk, then vinegar. Stir constantly and cook over hot water until mixture thickens. Remove from fire and beat in butter. Keep in covered jar in refrigerator.

Cooked Dressing for Fruit Salad

4 egg yolks
¼ cup vinegar
1 cup sour cream
½ tablespoon
sugar
½ teaspoon salt

¼ teaspoon
Watkins Dry
Mustard
⅛ teaspoon Watkins Paprika

Beat egg yolks with a rotary whip, beat in all ingredients. Stir constantly and cook over hot water until mixture thickens. Remove from fire, beat, cool, and keep tightly covered in the refrigerator.

Cooked Salad Dressing (Scant Table Fat)

2 eggs
3 tablespoons
vinegar
⅓ cup milk
1 tablespoon
butter or
margarine
½ teaspoon salt

½ teaspoon sugar
½ teaspoon
Watkins Dry
Mustard
Watkins Celery
Salt
Watkins Paprika

Use a rotary whip and beat eggs; gradually add vinegar and blend thoroughly. Add other ingredients, stir constantly, and cook over hot water until mixture is slightly thickened, then cool. Keep in a covered jar in the refrigerator.

Cooked Salad Dressing With Evaporated Milk

1 teaspoon
Watkins Dry
Mustard
1 teaspoon salt
2 tablespoons
flour
1 egg

2 tablespoons
sugar
1 cup evaporated
milk
4 tablespoons
vinegar
Watkins Paprika

Blend Watkins Dry Mustard, salt, flour and sugar. Add beaten egg, then stir in milk. Stir constantly and cook over boiling water until mixture thickens. Cool. Gradually stir in vinegar. Add Watkins Paprika. Keep in a covered jar in the refrigerator.

Cooked Sour Cream Dressing (for Meat and Poultry Salad)

1 teaspoon
  Watkins Dry
  Mustard
1 teaspoon salt
Dash Watkins
  Red Pepper
1 cup sour cream

1 tablespoon
  sugar
2 egg yolks,
  beaten
2 tablespoons
  vinegar
Watkins Paprika

Mix dry ingredients in top of a double boiler. Stir in egg yolks, then sour cream, stir and cook until mixture thickens. Remove from fire, cool, then gradually stir in vinegar.

Cream Dressing for Cole Slaw

3 tablespoons
  butter
½ teaspoon
  Watkins Dry
  Mustard
⅓ teaspoon salt
½ tablespoon
  sugar

1 tablespoon flour
1 egg
¾ cup light
  cream, sweet
  or sour
¼ cup vinegar
Watkins Paprika

Melt butter in top of double boiler, stir in seasonings and flour and blend. Add beaten egg and cream. Stir and cook over hot water until mixture thickens, then gradually add vinegar. Remove from fire and beat until smooth.

Dressing for Chicken Salad

½ cup rich
  chicken stock
½ cup vinegar
5 egg yolks,
  beaten
1 tablespoon
  Watkins Dry
  Mustard
1 teaspoon salt

½ teaspoon Wat-
  kins Paprika
Dash Watkins
  Red Pepper
⅓ cup melted
  butter
½ cup heavy
  cream

Obtain stock by cooking and reducing liquid in which fowl was cooked to ½ cup. Add vinegar, egg yolks and seasonings to stock. Stir constantly and cook mixture in top of a double boiler until thickened. Strain, add butter and cream. Cool.

Orange Dressing

2 tablespoons
  sugar
1 tablespoon flour
½ teaspoon
  Watkins Dry
  Mustard
¼ teaspoon Wat-
  kins Paprika

½ teaspoon salt
1 cup orange juice
¼ cup lemon
  juice
1 egg, slightly
  beaten
2 tablespoons
  butter

Combine sugar, flour and seasonings. Add juices, stir until smooth, cook over hot water or over low heat until thickened. Stir small amount into egg, then add to remaining dressing and blend. Cook 2 minutes longer, stirring well. Add butter and beat mixture until smooth.

Cooked Dressing for Meat and Vegetable Salads

4 egg yolks	½ teaspoon salt
¼ cup vinegar	¼ teaspoon
2 tablespoons butter	Watkins Dry Mustard
5 tablespoons cream cheese	⅛ teaspoon Watkins Paprika
2 tablespoons cream	⅛ teaspoon Watkins Celery
½ teaspoon sugar	Salt

Beat egg yolks, gradually beat in vinegar. Stir and cook mixture in top of a double boiler over hot water. When mixture begins to thicken, remove from heat, add butter, cream cheese, and blend well. Add cream and seasonings. All cream may be added and omit the cheese.

Pineapple Dressing

1 tablespoon sugar	1 egg
1 teaspoon cornstarch	Juice of 1 lemon
1 cup pineapple juice	½ cup cream, whipped
	Watkins Paprika

Mix sugar and cornstarch, add slightly beaten egg with fruit juices and cook in double boiler until thick. Remove from fire and when cold, fold in whipped cream.

Rich Salad Dressing

2 egg yolks	2 tablespoons sugar
2 tablespoons flour	⅓ cup mild vinegar
2 tablespoons olive oil or butter	1¼ cups top milk or undiluted evaporated milk
1½ teaspoons salt	
¾ teaspoon Watkins Dry Mustard	¼ teaspoon Watkins Paprika

Blend dry ingredients in top of a double boiler over hot water. Stir in beaten egg yolks, add olive oil or butter, then milk. Stir constantly and cook until mixture begins to thicken, then gradually stir in vinegar. When mixture thickens, remove from heat and cool. Keep in a covered jar in the refrigerator.

Tart Cooked Dressing

4 tablespoons melted butter	½ cup mild vinegar
1 tablespoon flour	1 teaspoon
1 tablespoon sugar	Watkins Dry Mustard
½ cup water or milk	Dash Watkins Red Pepper
1 teaspoon salt	2 eggs

Stir butter and flour together in top of a double boiler; add water slowly and stir and cook mixture until thickened. Beat egg yolks slightly, add salt, Watkins Red Pepper, sugar, Watkins Dry Mustard and vinegar; then stir into the flour mixture and cook until quite thick. Remove from heat and stir briskly into the beaten egg whites.

Miscellaneous Salad Dressings

Salad dressings to be successful must have a personal taste appeal; and this is secured by the use of Watkins flavorful seasonings, in any basic salad dressing. With quality olive oil, good vinegar, the seasoning is one of individual taste.

The calorie value of all salads varies with the type and quantity of the dressing used; the amount of fat, in the form of salad oil or cream, is the chief factor that determines the calorie content of a dressing. The amount of dressing used should be sufficient to flavor the ingredients, but should not be used in excess.

Avocado Salad Dressing

½ cup orange juice
1 tablespoon lemon juice
1 teaspoon honey
½ teaspoon salt
1 ripe avocado, cut fine
Watkins Paprika

Blend fruit juices and seasonings, add mashed avocado and stir until well blended, or use an electric beater. Add Watkins Paprika.

Avocado Cream Dressing For Fruit Salads

1 cup ripe avocado pulp
1 cup whipping cream
2 tablespoons honey
Watkins Paprika

Put avocado through a sieve, add honey and chill. Whip cream and fold in avocado mixture. Add Watkins Paprika.

Bacon Dressing

Bacon salad dressing may be made by combining hot bacon fat with one-third as much vinegar; add salt, Watkins Paprika, and a little sugar, to suit taste.

Beet Salad Dressing

2 cups sour cream
1 teaspoon salt
3 tablespoons
   minced chives
1 cup minced,
   uncooked beets
Watkins Paprika

Blend ingredients in order given and mix thoroughly. Chill. Will make 3 cups dressing.

Cottage Cheese Dressing
For Vegetable Salad

½ lb. cottage
   cheese, put
   through ricer
¼ cup sour cream
1 tablespoon
   honey
1 teaspoon salt
½ cup orange
   juice
2 tablespoons
   lemon juice
Watkins Paprika

Whip cheese until smooth, add seasonings. Stir in sour cream and fruit juice gradually; mix well. Chill. Serve with a mixed green salad.

Cream Dressing

1 cup cream
2 tablespoons
   lemon juice
2 tablespoons
   vinegar
1 tablespoon
   sugar
1 teaspoon salt
¼ teaspoon Wat-
   kins Paprika
1 teaspoon
   Watkins Dry
   Mustard

Beat cream; mix remaining ingredients and add gradually to cream, beating constantly. Sweet or sour cream may be used.

Cream Cheese Dressing

Whip a package of cream cheese with unsweetened pineapple juice until smooth and creamy. Use as a dressing over mixed green salad or a fruit salad.

Cucumber Cream Dressing
For Meat Salad

2 tablespoons
   vinegar
2 tablespoons
   sugar
1 cup peeled,
   diced cucumber
1 cup whipped
   cream
Watkins Paprika

Soak cucumber in iced, salted water. Drain and dice. Add vinegar and sugar. Just before serving, add whipped cream.

Creamed Roquefort Dressing

9 ounces Roquefort cheese
4 3-oz. cakes of cream cheese

Juice of 2 lemons, strained
1 pint sweet cream
Watkins Paprika
Salt to suit taste

Mash Roquefort and cream cheese with a fork, blend in lemon juice and cream and mix well until smooth. Add salt and Watkins Paprika. Keep in a covered glass jar in the refrigerator. This makes about 1 quart of dressing.

Health Fruit Juice Dressing

Blend 2 tablespoons each of grapefruit, orange and pineapple juice, 1 tablespoon lemon juice, and Watkins Paprika. Chill.

Honey Cream Dressing

2 tablespoons honey
5 tablespoons cream

5 tablespoons lemon juice

Chill, mix well and serve.

Hot Oil Dressing with Sliced Cucumbers

1 teaspoon Watkins Dry Mustard
1 tablespoon sugar

1 teaspoon salt
⅓ cup vinegar
2 tablespoons salad oil

Blend seasonings, stir into vinegar and oil and heat to boiling. Pour over chilled prepared cucumbers, add Watkins Paprika and serve.

Horse-radish Cream Dressing With Mixed Green Salad

1 teaspoon salt
½ teaspoon sugar
½ teaspoon Watkins Dry Mustard
¼ teaspoon Watkins Paprika
1 tablespoon wine vinegar

3 tablespoons grated horse-radish
1 tablespoon tarragon vinegar
1 tablespoon lemon juice
Watkins Paprika

Blend all ingredients. Just before serving beat in one cup whipped cream. Add Watkins Paprika.

Lemon Sherry Dressing
For Melon Salad

½ cup lemon juice
¼ teaspoon salt
½ cup sugar
¼ cup sherry wine

Blend lemon juice and salt. Gradually stir in sugar until dissolved. Add sherry and shake well. Chill and serve.

Mustard Dressing with Cream
For Beetroot Salad

1 tablespoon Watkins Dry Mustard
Juice of 1 lemon
⅓ pint sweet cream
Salt
Watkins Paprika

Blend seasoning with lemon juice, add gradually to cream.

New York Salad Dressing

4 hard-cooked eggs
2 level teaspoons Watkins Paprika
2 level teaspoons Watkins Celery Salt
2 teaspoons powdered sugar
2 green peppers, minced
10 small young onion tops or chives, minced
Juice of 1 lemon, strained
½ cup olive oil
1½ cups mayonnaise

Mash yolks of hard-cooked eggs and blend with a little vinegar; chop the whites of eggs fine. Blend all ingredients and whip with an egg beater. Keep tightly covered in a glass jar in the refrigerator. This makes about 1 quart of dressing.

Roquefort Dressing

4 tablespoons mayonnaise
3 tablespoons French dressing
3 tablespoons grated Roquefort cheese
½ teaspoon Worcestershire sauce
Watkins Paprika

Sour Cream Dressing

1 cup sour cream
¼ cup brown sugar
¼ teaspoon salt
2 tablespoons vinegar
Watkins Paprika

Stir dry ingredients into cream, gradually add vinegar and stir constantly to blend. Add Watkins Paprika.

Quick Sour Cream Dressing With Vegetable Salad

¾ cup sour cream
3 tablespoons vinegar
½ teaspoon salt

3 tablespoons sugar
¼ teaspoon Watkins Paprika

Whip cream, vinegar, seasonings until mixture thickens using a rotary beater. Chill and serve. No cooking.

Sour Cream Dressing for Cucumbers and Cucumber Salad

1 cup (mild) sour cream, chilled
½ teaspoon salt

2 tablespoons lemon juice
Watkins Paprika

Beat cream, but not until stiff. Stir in salt, Watkins Paprika, and lemon juice.

Sour Cream Dressing for Cucumbers or Cole Slaw

1 cup sour cream
2 tablespoons vinegar
1 tablespoon lemon juice
1 teaspoon sugar
1 teaspoon salt

Watkins Pepper
Watkins Paprika
Watkins Mustard
1 canned pimiento
Celery seeds

Beat cream until stiff, add vinegar, lemon juice, sugar, salt, Watkins Pepper, Paprika and Mustard to suit taste. Beat all together until very thick. Add a few celery seeds and the pimiento cut in small pieces.

Sour Cream Dressing with Evaporated Milk

1 tablespoon sugar
¼ teaspoon salt
Watkins Paprika

½ cup evaporated milk, chilled
2 tablespoons vinegar

Add seasonings to milk and stir until blended. Gradually stir in vinegar and mix well.

Whipped Sour Cream Dressing

1 egg
½ teaspoon Watkins Dry Mustard
¼ teaspoon salt

Watkins Paprika
1 tablespoon lemon juice
1 cup thick sour cream, whipped

Use a rotary beater and whip egg with seasonings until thick. Beat in lemon juice and fold mixture into the whipped cream. Add Watkins Paprika. Will make 1 cup dressing.

Sandwiches

Any of the following sandwiches may be served with a salad:

Paper thin sandwiches of white bread spread with creamed butter and minced water cress, or serve thin brown bread sandwiches with creamed butter and minced cucumbers, marinated in French dressing.

Brown or Graham bread sandwiches spread with creamed butter and cream cheese and Watkins Paprika. Cut into narrow strips and serve with a fruit or a mixed green salad.

Melba toast with a green salad: Cut dry bread in $\frac{1}{8}$ inch slices, place on a baking sheet and brown in a slow oven at 300 degrees F. Turn bread several times during toasting, until evenly browned and crisp.

Slender strips of white bread may be buttered and sprinkled with grated cheese, Watkins Paprika and toasted.

Or spread squares of buttered toast with a mixture of equal parts chopped pimiento, chopped green pepper, a dash of salt, and a little mayonnaise.

Tiny hot baking-powder biscuits spread with creamed butter are a popular accompaniment with a mixed green or vegetable salad. Caraway seeds or grated cheese may be added to the dough if desired.

Pie crust cheese straws made with sharply flavored cheese, a little Watkins Red Pepper, enough to give a ruddy tinge, may be rolled into the dough then cut into thin strips, baked and served as cheese straws.

Cut French bread on the bias, in two-inch strips, spread with soft butter and toast. Or brush two-inch slices of French bread with melted butter in which a clove of garlic has been crushed, then toast in the oven and serve hot.

Serve crackers crisp. Spread crackers on a baking sheet, and place in a medium hot oven to dry out the moisture. Or spread the crackers with butter and add Watkins Paprika, then heat under the broiler flame. Or add a sprinkling of sesame seeds to buttered crackers and brown lightly under the broiler.

Wafflettes may be served with a salad, or for afternoon tea. Use a plain waffle batter and add chopped candied ginger. Drop a half teaspoonful of batter on a hot waffle iron, and make eight small waffles at a time. Serve hot with a variety of toppings, such as a chicken or cheese spread and a dash of Watkins Paprika.

Serve thin sandwiches in plain or fancy shapes, made with any of the following suggested fillings and spreads:

Sandwich Hints

Sandwiches to be served with salad should be cut very thin, with crust removed. Cut bread in different shapes, and use any one of several kinds of bread. Select white, whole wheat, Graham, Boston-brown, raisin, bran, rye, or pumpernickel bread, or use nut bread, orange or fruit bread. Packaged crackers may also be used in making sandwiches.

The bread should not be too fresh. Use a sharp knife with a sawing motion to slice bread thin, and a dull knife for spreading. Butter should be creamed until it is soft, and spread on the cut-end of the loaf before slicing. This will aid in making thin slices with an unbroken surface.

Let butter stand at room temperature to slightly soften, then beat with a fork until creamed. For a larger quantity, whip with a rotary beater until the butter is like cream in consistency. Spread the creamed butter over the entire surface of the loaf evenly, right to the edge, to prevent the filling from soaking into the bread. If sandwiches are not to be used immediately, a lettuce leaf placed on each slice, will keep moist fillings from soaking into the bread. Wrap sandwiches singly or in small stacks, in waxed paper, parchment paper, or transparent cellulose sheeting, and keep in the refrigerator in a covered container until ready to serve. Or cover with a dry napkin, then with a napkin wrung out in hot water; place each type of sandwich on a separate plate to prevent mixing.

When making a number of sandwiches in fancy shapes, use sandwich bread and slice the long way of the loaf. Trim the crust from the loaf, spread one side with creamed butter, cut off a thin slice, spread with filling, add the top slice, and cut in desired shapes. Keep fillings moist by adding a little cream to the filling, or by adding salad dressing, or a moist relish. Save the crusts for bread pudding, or dry the crust and keep in a covered fruit jar and use for crumbs.

Pinwheel sandwiches may be made by slicing the bread the long way of the loaf. Spread the bread with creamed butter, cut off a thin slice, add filling, and roll. Wrap tightly in a damp cloth and chill in the refrigerator. Before serving, cut into slices. The bread must be very fresh in making rolled sandwiches.

To make ribbon sandwiches, cut crusts from both a white and a dark loaf of bread, then cut each loaf in lengthwise slices, one-half to three-fourths inch thick. Fit slices together, alternating a white and a dark slice, trim edges evenly. Spread with your favorite filling, fit slices together tightly and wrap loaf in a dampened cloth. Just before serving, cut in thin slices.

Checkerboard sandwiches are made by cutting dark and white bread in long slices. Place three slices together, a dark one on top and bottom. Put together another three slices, white ones on top and bottom. Spread slices with creamed butter or any desired butter spread, or use a cheese spread. Place slices together firmly. Cut each loaf into three parts, lengthwise, and fit slices of the two loaves together, to form checkerboard loaves. Spread sides with creamed butter and fit together. Wrap in a dampened cloth and let stand until firm. Just before serving, cut in slices.

Butter Spreads for Salad Sandwiches

Anchovy Butter: Blend ¼ cup creamed butter with 1 tablespoon anchovy paste, ½ teaspoon lemon juice and a dash of Watkins Paprika.

Cheese Butter: Blend equal parts of soft snappy cheese and creamed butter, or 2 parts creamed butter to 1 part Parmesan cheese.

Chive Butter: Blend ¼ cup creamed butter with 1 tablespoon finely minced chives, and 1 teaspoon lemon juice.

Chutney Butter: Mix ¼ cup creamed butter with 1 tablespoon chutney.

Horse-radish Butter: Mix ¼ cup butter with 2 tablespoons horse-radish.

Lemon Butter: Combine ¼ cup creamed butter with 2 teaspoons lemon juice and a little grated lemon rind.

Mustard Butter: Blend ¼ cup creamed butter with 1 tablespoon prepared mustard.

Olive Butter: Blend ¼ cup creamed butter with 1 tablespoon olive paste and ¼ teaspoon lemon juice.

Onion Butter: Blend ¼ cup creamed butter with 1 teaspoon onion juice, or minced onion.

Orange Butter: Blend ¼ cup creamed butter with 2 teaspoons orange juice and a little grated orange rind.

Parsley Butter: Blend ¼ cup creamed butter with 2 tablespoons minced parsley and 1 teaspoon lemon juice.

Pimiento Butter: Blend ¼ cup creamed butter with 2 tablespoons mashed pimiento and 1 teaspoon minced sweet pickle.

Shrimp Butter: Blend ¼ cup creamed butter with ¼ cup minced cooked shrimp and 1 teaspoon lemon juice.

Water Cress Butter: Blend ¼ cup creamed butter with 2 tablespoons minced water cress, 1 teaspoon lemon juice, and a few drops of Worcester-shire sauce.

Economical Butter Spread for Sandwiches

½ lb. butter
1 cup milk
½ teaspoon salt
1½ teaspoon gelatin, soften in ¼ cup cold water 5 minutes

Variation:
¼ cup cold water and ¾ cup evaporated milk may be substituted for fresh milk

Let butter stand at room temperature to soften; cream with wooden spoon. Gradually blend ¼ cup milk, salt and gelatin in top of a double boiler and heat over boiling water to dissolve gelatin; add remaining milk and heat to lukewarm. When slightly cooled, stir into softened butter, a little at a time, and whip with a rotary beater after each addition. Blend thoroughly, pack into a butter-dish, cover tightly and keep in the refrigerator.

Economical Sandwich Spread

1 tablespoon gelatin
1 tablespoon cold water
3 tablespoons boiling water
½ teaspoon salt

½ cup fresh or evaporated milk
½ cup mayonnaise
½ lb. fortified margarine

Soften gelatin in cold water 5 minutes, then add boiling water and stir until gelatin is dissolved. Add milk and mayonnaise. Cool. Soften margarine at room temperature (do not melt). Add mayonnaise mixture, a little at a time, and whip with a rotary beater. Store in covered dish in the refrigerator.

Sandwich Spread to Save Butter

½ lb. butter
1 lb. vitaminized margarine

½ can evaporated milk

Soften butter and margarine at room temperature (do not heat), then blend, using a wooden spoon. Add 1 teaspoon salt and tablet of coloring that comes with margarine. Add milk gradually and mix well. Pack into a loaf pyrex dish, cover securely with waxed paper, and store in the refrigerator. Will make 2 pounds of butter spread.

Crab Meat Spread

1 6-oz. can crab meat, flaked
¼ cup minced canned pimiento
⅛ teaspoon salt

½ cup minced celery
⅛ teaspoon Watkins Paprika
¼ cup mayonnaise

Blend all ingredients and use as a spread on plain buttered, toasted bread, or crisp crackers.

Cheese Spread

2 3-oz. packages
    cream cheese
1 teaspoon
    minced chives

2 tablespoons
    bottled mush-
    room sauce
Watkins Paprika

Cream cheese well, add mushroom sauce, chives and Watkins Paprika. Use as a spread on crisp crackers.

Chicken Liver Pate De Foie Gras Sandwich Spread

¼ lb. chicken
    livers
1 teaspoon
    Worcestershire
    sauce
½ teaspoon
    Watkins Dry
    Mustard

¼ cup soft butter
½ teaspoon salt
Watkins Onion
    Seasoning
Watkins Celery
    Salt
Dash Watkins
    Red Pepper

Simmer chicken livers in boiling salted water to cover for 20 minutes, or until tender. Drain, put through food chopper, using a fine blade. Blend all ingredients and chill. Use as a spread on buttered bread, toast, or crisp crackers.

Fruit Spreads for Sandwiches

Fruits such as raisins, dates, dried apricots, drained canned pineapple, chopped drained cherries, etc., may be made into a paste by putting through a food chopper. Add chopped nuts and moisten with cream or lemon juice. Cream cheese may be blended with the chopped fruit.

Ham and Olive Spread

⅔ cup minced
    cooked ham
½ cup minced
    stuffed olives
2 tablespoons
    minced parsley

1 tablespoon
    Worcestershire
    sauce
¼ cup
    mayonnaise
Watkins Paprika

Blend all ingredients and use as a spread on buttered, toasted bread, or crackers.

Sardine-Cucumber Spread

Drain 1 small can boneless and skinless sardines and mash. Add 1 medium-sized chopped cucumber (remove seeds). Blend mixture and use as a spread with buttered white bread.

Liver and Crisp Bacon Spread

(Will make 1½ cups)

½ lb. calves liver
1½ teaspoons
  salt
2 cups boiling
  water
10 slices crisp
  bacon
½ cup light sour
  cream

2 tablespoons
  Watkins
  Prepared
  Mustard
Watkins Onion
  Seasoning
Watkins Paprika
  or Red Pepper

Simmer liver in boiling water with 1 teaspoon salt until tender, about 45 minutes. Cool. Put through medium blade of food chopper with cooked crisp bacon. Blend all ingredients. Fill small cheese jars and chill in the refrigerator. Serve as a spread on crisp crackers or Melba toast.

Lobster Spread

1 6-oz. can lobster
  meat, or 1¼
  cups flaked
  lobster
1 tablespoon
  lemon juice

2 tablespoons
  mayonnaise
1 tablespoon
  French dressing
Watkins Paprika

Blend all ingredients and use as a spread on buttered or toasted bread, or crisp crackers.

Mock Pate De Foie Gras
Spread

(Substitute For Pate De Foie Gras)

⅛ lb. liverwurst
Watkins Onion
  Seasoning
1 tablespoon
  minced parsley

1 tablespoon
  mayonnaise
Watkins Celery
  Salt

Buy liverwurst in one piece, remove casing and mash. Blend all ingredients and use as a spread on buttered white bread, or crisp crackers.

Sherry Cheese Spread

(Will make 4 cups)

2 lbs. sharp
  cheese
2 tablespoons
  butter, creamed
1½ teaspoon salt
¾ cup sherry

2 teaspoons
  granulated
  sugar
Dash Watkins
  Red Pepper

Put cheese through food chopper, using fine blade. Add butter, sugar, Watkins Red Pepper and salt. Blend mixture with a fork. Gradually add sherry and blend thoroughly. Fill cheese jars and press down well. Seal with suet, as follows: melt suet over low heat; strain, cool, and pour over cheese. Let harden and cover tightly. Keep in a cool place. Use as a spread for crisp crackers, Melba toast, etc.

Fillings for Plain or Fancy Sandwiches

Combine 2 parts chopped cooked tongue or ham, with 1 part minced pickle, and add mayonnaise to moisten.

Blend lobster paste and minced celery with a little mayonnaise and use as filling for white or nut bread.

Blend equal parts of peanut butter and minced candied ginger and spread on white bread with creamed butter.

Combine equal parts of minced, cooked chicken and ham and blend with a little mayonnaise and minced pickle.

Blend 1 cup cream cheese softened with a little cream and 1½ cups minced salted almonds.

Combine ½ cup crisp chopped bacon with an equal amount of cream cheese and a little cooked salad dressing. Add Watkins Paprika.

Blend ½ cup cream cheese, ½ cup chopped nuts, 2 tablespoons orange juice, ⅛ teaspoon salt, 1 tablespoon creamed butter, ¼ cup minced pimiento. Blend entire mixture, chill and use as a filling with white bread, spread with creamed butter.

Make a filling of ½ cup chopped dates, ½ cup chopped, blanched almonds, ¼ cup whipped cream, and ⅛ teaspoon salt. Spread on thin slices of buttered white, brown or nut bread.

Combine tuna fish, chopped celery, chopped nuts and a little mayonnaise, as a substitute for chicken salad sandwiches. Vary proportions according to taste. Add Watkins Paprika.

Make a paste of 1 cup chopped, raw prunes and ½ cup cream cheese, a tablespoon heavy cream and a dash of salt. Spread on buttered whole wheat or Graham bread.

Blend pimiento cheese with a little cream and add chopped nuts.

Grate American cheese and blend with chopped sweet pickle, or minced olives, pimiento, or minced green pepper.

Chop cooked chicken, veal, ham or tuna fish fine and blend with minced water cress and a little mayonnaise dressing.

Combine chopped seeded raisins, orange marmalade, and a little mayonnaise.

Blend cream cheese, chopped candied ginger, and chopped walnuts.

Combine mashed apricots, chopped nuts, and cream cheese.

Mashed sardines, chopped cucumber, lemon juice and mayonnaise.

Flaked salmon, chopped crisp celery, and mayonnaise.

Grated cheese, chopped green pepper, minced chives, and a little mayonnaise.

Mashed baked beans, minced onion, salt, Watkins Paprika, and mayonnaise.

Mix together cream cheese, a little cream and guava jelly.

Blend cream cheese with chopped green, ripe or stuffed olives.

Cream cheese with chopped roasted peanuts—add a little cream to moisten.

Cream cheese, cut nut-meats, seedless raisins with a little cream.

Cream cheese with currant jelly, or marmalade.

Cream cheese, pecan meats, quince jelly and a little cream.

Fillings—(Continued)

Potted or minced cooked ham, chopped celery and mayonnaise.

Chopped cooked crisp bacon, minced water cress, and mayonnaise.

Chopped cooked ham, hard-cooked egg, Watkins Paprika, a little mustard and mayonnaise.

Cream or cottage cheese mixed with either minced olives or pickles, pimiento, green pepper, parsley and chives.

Grind stuffed or ripe olives and mix with mayonnaise.

Chop equal parts of cooked chicken and nuts, moisten with a little mayonnaise.

Combine chopped dates, nuts and cream cheese, and blend with a little cream.

Blend cream cheese with currant jam and chopped walnuts.

Mix peanut butter with chopped raisins, dates or mashed ripe bananas, and a little cooked dressing.

Blend chopped fresh or drained canned cherries, cream cheese and a little cherry juice to a smooth paste.

Add 2 tablespoons lemon juice to 1 cup chopped blanched or toasted almonds.

Mix equal parts of peanut butter, mashed ripe bananas with a little cream, and just enough lemon juice for flavor.

Spread one slice of buttered bread with cream cheese and a little cream; spread other slice with orange marmalade and press slices together.

Mix ground cooked ham with minced olives, sweet pickles or nuts.

Blend ½ cup cottage cheese and ¼ cup chopped pimiento olives.

For afternoon tea sandwiches, blend cream cheese with chopped dried figs, apricots or dates; or with crisp minced bacon, or with bar le duc or marmalade.

Split and butter tiny biscuits while hot, and spread with blended honey and chopped blanched almonds, or cream cheese and bar le duc, or chopped nuts and orange maramalade, or peach jam and chopped almonds.

Keep a selection of your favorite commercial sandwich and cheese spreads ready for making sandwiches quickly.

Blend ¼ cup peanut butter, ½ cup apple sauce and add a dash of Watkins Nutmeg.

Cream together one 3-oz. package cream cheese, ¼ cup peanut butter, and ½ cup cherry preserves.

Blend ½ cup cooked chopped prunes, ¼ cup orange juice, 1 tablespoon grated orange rind, and a dash of salt.

Blend ½ cup chopped dates, ½ cup chopped nuts, 1 tablespoon mayonnaise, and 1 teaspoon lemon juice. Add dash of salt.

Combine ½ cup peanut butter and ⅓ cup orange marmalade.

Mix ½ cup apple butter, ⅓ cup nuts, and a dash of Watkins Nutmeg.

Mash one 3-oz. package cream cheese, add a little cream and a dash of Watkins Ginger.

Blend ½ cup peanut butter and 2 tablespoons molasses, 1 cup ground peanuts.

Blend one 3-oz. package cream cheese with ⅓ cup peach or apricot jam, 1 teaspoon lemon juice and a dash of salt.

Fillings—(Continued)

Mix 1 cup chopped cold boiled ham with ½ cup pepper relish. Use as a filling for buttered white bread.

Combine 1 cup minced cooked ham, ½ cup minced sweet pickles, ⅓ cup chopped pimiento olives and add mayonnaise or cooked salad dressing.

Mix 1 cup chopped cooked ham, ½ cup walnuts, ½ cup chopped olives, and add a little cooked dressing to moisten.

Blend ⅓ cup minced cooked ham, ⅓ cup grated American cheese, 3 tablespoons grated or crushed pineapple, a dash of Watkins Cinnamon and a tablespoon of pickle relish.

Combine 1 cup minced corned beef, ⅓ cup chow chow, 1 teaspoon Worcestershire sauce, Watkins Red Pepper, and a little mayonnaise.

Chopped cooked ham, chicken or veal, Watkins Onion Seasoning, Watkins Paprika, minced celery and minced chives, blended with mayonnaise.

Combine equal amounts of peanut butter, finely chopped dates and currant jelly.

Serve fruit, cheese, nut sandwich fillings for afternoon tea, open or closed sandwiches. Add a sprig of water cress. Use a cooky press to pipe decorative fluting or rosette of cream cheese.

Almond Sandwich

1¼ cups blanched or toasted almonds
½ teaspoon salt
3 tablespoons lemon juice
Watkins Paprika

Chop almonds fine, blend with salt and lemon juice and use as a filling with slices of buttered bread. Press a blanched almond in the center of the sandwich.

Almond and Olive Sandwiches

1 cup chopped salted almonds
¼ cup minced
stuffed olives
2 tablespoons mayonnaise

Blend almonds, olives and mayonnaise and use as a filling between buttered slices of bread. Cream cheese may be added if desired.

Toasted Apricot Sandwich

Wash dried apricots and soak in warm water overnight. Cook in same water slowly until soft and put through a food chopper. Add corn syrup or sugar and cook to a jam. Chill. Spread between thin slices of buttered bread and sprinkle with a little Watkins Cinnamon. Toast and serve hot.

Apricot and Nut Sandwiches

1 cup stewed
   dried apricots
¾ cup chopped
   nuts

2 tablespoons
   cream

Drain apricots and mash. Add nuts, cream and blend mixture. Use as a filling between slices of buttered white bread. Cut into long narrow strips.

Hot Bacon Sandwich

Cook bacon crisp. Butter slices of enriched white bread, spread with mayonnaise. Add crisp bacon, top with another slice of bread spread with creamed butter, then toast in the oven. Cut into four triangles and serve on crisp lettuce.

Bacon, Camembert Sandwiches

6 slices crisp
   bacon
Creamed butter

6 tablespoons
   cheese

Cook bacon until crisp, drain and chop fine. Blend bacon with cheese and use as a filling between buttered slices of bread.

Bacon and Cheese Pinwheels

Remove crust from white bread and cut in lengthwise slices. Cream butter, add chili sauce and blend well. Spread each slice of bread with chili sauce butter, then with blended cheese and minced cooked bacon. Roll as for a jelly roll. Wrap in waxed paper and chill. Slice just before serving and garnish with crisp water cress.

Broiled Bacon and Cheese Sandwiches

Wrap half a piece of very thin sliced bacon around one-inch cubes of American cheese, and fasten with a toothpick. Toast under a broiler until bacon is crisp and cheese slightly melted. Place in rolls spread with creamed butter, adding a little Watkins Mustard if desired.

Glazed Banana Sandwich

Heat and mash 1 cup cooked apricots with ¼ cup sugar and beat until smooth. Chill. Arrange slices of ripe banana on buttered nut bread and spread with apricot glaze.

Barbecue Sandwiches

Put thin slices of hot baked ham, roast beef, or broiled steak or hamburgers on buttered bread. Spread with barbecue sauce and cover with a slice of buttered bread.

Barbecue Sauce

¼ cup butter
2 tablespoons Worcestershire sauce
1 tablespoon lemon juice
1 tablespoon granulated sugar
Dash Watkins Red Pepper
⅛ teaspoon Watkins Paprika

Melt butter in a saucepan, stir in remaining ingredients and heat mixture. Will make ½ cup sauce.

Beef Sandwich

1 lb. ground beef
1 teaspoon Watkins Prepared Mustard
1 teaspoon horse-radish
1 teaspoon minced onion
¾ teaspoon salt
1½ teaspoons Worcestershire sauce

Cook beef in hot fat, add seasoning and use as filling with buttered, white bread. Place under broiler to brown.

Campfire Sandwich

Slice sweet or dill pickles into quarters, lengthwise. Wrap two pieces in a slice of American cheese. Place in a buttered roll, skewer with a toasting fork and heat to melt cheese.

Caviar Sandwiches

Blend ½ cup caviar, 2 teaspoons lemon juice, Watkins Paprika, and spread on buttered slices of bread.

Cheese and Anchovy Rolls

1 3-oz. package cream cheese
1 tablespoon anchovy paste
1 tablespoon heavy cream
Watkins Paprika

Cream cheese, add anchovy paste, cream and mix well. Slice fresh sandwich bread thin, place slices of bread on a clean damp cloth, trim off crust, and spread with filling. Roll tightly, fasten with toothpicks, cover with waxed paper and chill in the refrigerator. When ready to serve, place under broiler to brown, cut in half crosswise, and serve at once. Garnish with crisp water cress.

Rolled Asparagus Sandwich

Marinate drained canned asparagus in French dressing for added flavor. Cut fresh white bread in thin slices, remove crust and place between clean dampened towels so the bread will roll. Chill.

Spread slices of bread with creamed butter. Dip drained stalks of canned asparagus in a little mayonnaise, place on slice of bread, add a thin strip of pimiento and roll bread with tip of asparagus extending over edge of bread. Cover with damp cloth until ready to serve.

Variation: Instead of asparagus tips use tender inside stalks of celery spread with Roquefort or cream cheese and nuts. Chilled water cress and cream cheese may be used as filling.

Chicken Sandwich Loaf

Remove crusts from a loaf of sandwich bread and cut in fourths, lengthwise. Spread each slice with creamed butter. Spread first slice with a well-seasoned chicken filling. Cover with second slice of bread and spread with your favorite vegetable mixture; chopped cucumbers and sliced almonds is a good combination with chicken filling. Spread the third slice with more of the chicken filling. Cover with the fourth slice, buttered side down. Press loaf together firmly and trim off edges.

Spread the entire loaf with cream cheese moistened with a little cream (it will take four cakes of cream cheese for a large sandwich loaf). Spread cheese in a thick layer and make swirls as you spread the cheese. Garnish with slices of stuffed olives. Cover with waxed paper and chill before serving.

Club Sandwich

Toast 3 slices of bread and cut in triangles. Spread with creamed butter. Place triangles side by side to form the bottom slice, and cover with lettuce leaf. Spread lettuce with mayonnaise, and add slices of white meat of chicken. Cover with toast triangles, buttered. On these place several slices of crisp bacon and another lettuce leaf. Cover with the last toast triangle and add a slice of ripe tomato topped with a little mayonnaise. Place ripe olives and small pickles on the salad plate to garnish.

Hot Cheese Sandwich

Melt American cheese over low heat, add Worcestershire sauce to suit taste, and spread over hot toast.

Or toast one side of bread, place a slice of American cheese on the other side, place under the broiler until cheese is melted. Add a dash of Watkins Paprika.

Or toast bread, spread one side with creamed butter and sprinkle with a layer of grated cheese, adding a pinch of salt and a dash of Watkins Red Pepper. Place in a shallow pan and heat in oven or broiler to melt cheese.

Toasted Cheese Rolls

Chill thin sliced bread for several hours. Butter each slice, and spread with a soft yellow cheese. Add a dash of Watkins Paprika, roll and toast under low broiler heat. Turn to lightly brown on all sides.

Toasted Cheese-Walnut Sandwich with a Salad

2 tablespoons olive oil
1 tablespoon vinegar
⅛ teaspoon salt
⅛ teaspoon Watkins Paprika
½ cup cream cheese

Blend all ingredients and spread on quarter-inch slices of Graham bread. Sprinkle with chopped nuts and cover with buttered slice of bread. Cut in finger-shaped pieces, and toast. Serve hot.

Chicken or Fish Salad Sandwiches

1¼ cups chopped cooked chicken or tuna fish
2 teaspoons minced green pepper
⅛ teaspoon salt
½ cup finely chopped celery
1 tablespoon lemon juice
3 tablespoons mayonnaise
Crisp lettuce

Spread chilled salad mixture between buttered slices of bread, placing a crisp leaf of lettuce in each sandwich. Chopped stuffed olives may be used instead of the green pepper.

Hot Chicken Sandwiches

1 cup chopped cooked or canned chicken
1 teaspoon chopped sweet pickle or chives
⅓ cup minced celery
1 teaspoon bottled horse-radish
1 egg
½ cup evaporated milk
Salt
Watkins Paprika

Mix chicken, chives, horse-radish and celery with a little mayonnaise and spread between slices of buttered bread. Beat egg slightly, add milk, salt and Watkins Paprika. Dip sandwiches in egg mixture and brown on both sides in butter or margarine. Chopped cooked beef or veal may be substituted for chicken.

Chicken and Pineapple Sandwich

Blend 2 cups cooked, chopped chicken, preferably all white meat, with ⅔ cup crushed pineapple and 2 tablespoons mayonnaise. Use as a filling between buttered white bread or small hot biscuits.

Chicken, Pineapple and Nut Sandwich

1 can (8 oz.)
  crushed
  pineapple
1 cup cooked
  chopped
  chicken

2 cups chopped
  walnuts
½ cup cooked
  salad dressing
Watkins Paprika

Blend crushed pineapple, chicken, walnuts and salad dressing. Add Watkins Paprika. Use as a filling between buttered slices of white bread.

Chicken Salad Open Sandwich

Place chicken salad on lettuce leaf on one slice of toast. Place slices of tomato on lettuce on other piece of toast; add strips of crisp bacon. Leave the sandwich open. Garnish with dill pickle cut fan shape, and crisp parsley.

Combination Open Sandwich

For each sand-
wich:
2 slices plain or
  toasted bread,
  cut ½ inch
  thick
2 heart leaves of
  lettuce
½ dill pickle

1 thin slice
  baked ham
2 slices white
  meat of chicken
1 cup creamed
  slaw
2 thin strips
  green pepper
Crisp parsley

Place ham on buttered bread and slices of chicken on top of ham. Place creamed slaw in lettuce leaf on other piece of toast and add a dash of Watkins Paprika. Garnish with pickle and parsley.

Corned Beef-Pickle Relish Sandwich

½ cup seedless
  raisins
1 cup ground
  canned corned
  beef

½ cup sweet
  pickle relish
½ cup
  mayonnaise

Pour ½ cup boiling water over raisins, let stand 10 minutes, drain and chop. Blend cooked corned beef with all ingredients and spread between buttered slices of bread. Two tablespoons chopped canned pimiento may be added.

Corned Beef Sandwich

Arrange sliced cooked corned beef on buttered bread, add a little Watkins Mustard, top with buttered bread and cut diagonally into halves or quarters.

Corned Beef Salad Sandwich

1 No. 1 can corned
  beef, chill
¾ cup finely
  chopped celery
3 hard cooked
  eggs, chopped
  fine
⅓ teaspoon salt

¼ cup minced
  stuffed olives
½ cup
  mayonnaise
1 tablespoon
  lemon juice

Blend salad ingredients and use as a filling between buttered slices of bread. Place a crisp leaf of lettuce in each sandwich, if served promptly.

Cottage Cheese, Dill Pickle Sandwiches

¾ cup cottage
  cheese
⅓ cup minced
  dill pickle

¼ teaspoon
  minced
  pimiento

Spread loaf of brown bread with creamed butter, cut bread, and spread with filling of cheese, pickle and pimiento.

Cottage Cheese and Glace Fruit Sandwiches

½ cup chopped
  glace fruit
1 tablespoon
  lemon juice

1 cup cottage or
  cream cheese

Blend fruit with lemon juice and add cheese. Use as a filling for buttered slices of white bread.

Cottage Cheese and Ripe Olive Sandwiches

1 cup black ripe
  olives
⅓ cup cottage
  cheese

Salt
Watkins Paprika
1 teaspoon
  lemon juice

Remove pits from olives and chop meat fine. Blend all ingredients and use as a spread between thin slices of buttered bread.

Cream Cheese and Guava Jelly Sandwich

¾ cup cream
  cheese
¼ cup almonds

2 tablespoons
  cream
Guava jelly

Soften cheese with cream and mix until smooth. Add chopped almonds. Spread white bread with creamed butter, then with Guava jelly, and cover with cheese mixture. Cut into fancy shapes.

Cream Cheese and Horse-radish Sandwich

2 cream cheeses
½ cup cream
2 tablespoons
   horse-radish
¾ teaspoon salt

Juice 1 lemon
(2 tablespoons
   minced onion
   if desired)
Watkins Paprika

Blend all ingredients and use as a filling between slices of buttered whole wheat bread.

Cream Cheese and Olive Sandwiches

1 3-oz. package
   cream cheese
⅓ cup stuffed
   olives, chopped

1 tablespoon
   French dressing

Blend cheese, minced olives and dressing and use as a spread between buttered slices of bread.

Cream Cheese and Peanut Sandwich

1 3-oz. package
   cream cheese
Mayonnaise

½ cup chopped
   roasted peanuts

Cream butter and spread on loaf, then cut bread thin. Spread with mixture of cream cheese and peanuts.

Cream Cheese and Pineapple Sandwich

Mix equal portions of cream cheese and chopped drained canned pineapple. Add half the quantity of chopped blanched almonds, a little salt, Watkins Paprika and Watkins Red Pepper. Use as a filling between thin slices of buttered bread; cut into fancy shapes, or use as a filling in a rolled sandwich. Marmalade may be substituted for the pineapple.

Cucumber Sandwiches

Soak thin slices of peeled cucumber one hour in white vinegar, salt and Watkins Paprika. Chill. Drain and use between thin buttered slices of brown or white bread.

Date-Nut Sandwich

Combine 1 cup chopped dates with 3 tablespoons orange juice, 1 tablespoon lemon juice and ½ cup chopped nuts. Spread between slices of whole wheat or white buttered bread.

Date Sandwich Loaf

Fruit Filling:
1 cup pitted dates
1 cup nuts
3 tablespoons orange juice
Put dates and nuts through food chopper and moisten with orange juice.
Cheese Filling:
1 3-oz. package cream cheese
⅛ cup chopped nuts
2 tablespoons cream or mayonnaise
Topping:
4 3-oz. packages cream cheese
Juice of orange or lemon
Blend mixture thoroughly.

Cut crusts from one loaf of white bread and one loaf of whole wheat. Cut lengthwise in ¼ inch slices and spread each with creamed butter. Spread one slice of white bread with fruit filling, cover with dark bread. Spread the dark slice with cream cheese filling and cover with white slice spread with orange marmalade and minced candied ginger. Alternate until fillings are used. Spread entire outer surface with whipped cream cheese topping and chill at least one hour. Slice and serve.

Egg and Olive Sandwich

1 hard cooked egg yolk	1 tablespoon chopped peanuts
½ cup chopped olives	Cooked salad dressing
¼ cup chopped celery	

Put egg yolk through sieve. Blend yolk, olives, celery, peanuts and enough dressing to moisten. Spread filling on thin slices of bread covered with creamed butter. Cut into fancy shapes.

French Sandwich (Hot)

Partly cook ground raw round steak in a little butter, season with Watkins Onion Seasoning, salt, Watkins Pepper, and spread between slices of buttered white bread. Press together and cut in half. Dip sandwich into beaten egg and milk mixture (1 egg to ½ cup milk), and brown both sides in hot fat. Serve hot. Garnish with stuffed olives and crisp water cress.

Frankfurters Wrapped in Bacon

Fasten a thin slice of bacon around a frankfurter. Broil until bacon is crisp. Serve in a buttered roll.

Fruit Sandwiches

Thin slices   Thick apricot
   pineapple   puree
Chopped pecans

Blend apricot puree and chopped nuts. Spread thin slices of white bread with creamed butter, add pineapple and top with nut mixture. Top with slice of buttered bread and cut into fancy shapes. Keep covered with waxed paper until ready to serve.

Open Minced Ham and Bean Sandwich

½ lb. raw, cured   1 medium can
   ham   baked beans
2 tablespoons fat   Sandwich buns
¼ cup ketchup   India relish

Grind ham and brown slowly in hot fat. Add beans and cook about 5 minutes. Add ketchup. Cut buns in half, hollow out slightly, then toast. Spread each half with creamed butter and fill with ham and bean mixture. Add a topping of relish and serve on a lettuce leaf.

Ham and Chicken Sandwich

½ cup minced   ¼ cup
   cooked ham   mayonnaise
½ cup minced   ⅓ cup chopped
   cooked chicken   celery

Blend ham, chicken, celery and mayonnaise. Use as a filling with buttered white bread. Place a crisp leaf of lettuce over filling.

Ham, Egg and Cheese Sandwich Loaf

Red Filling:
4 slices of boiled ham (remove all fat) and 1 pimiento put through meat grinder. Add enough mayonnaise or cooked dressing to blend.
Yellow Filling:
3 hard cooked eggs put through a sieve; add mayonnaise to blend.
Green Filling:
Combine 1 package of cream cheese with 2 tablespoons minced green pepper and chopped nuts

Cut crust from a loaf of sandwich bread and slice into four pieces, the long way of the loaf. Spread top of each slice with creamed butter, then spread each with the following fillings, in the order given. Soften 2 3-oz. packages of cream cheese with a little cream, add ⅓ teaspoon salt and spread on the outside of the loaf. Cover with waxed paper and chill several hours before serving. Garnish with crisp water cress and pimiento olives.

Ham and Chutney Sandwiches

½ cup minced
  cooked ham
¼ cup chopped
  chutney

¼ cup soft
  American
  cheese spread

Blend ham with chutney. Spread soft cheese on one slice of buttered bread, add filling and cover with slice of buttered bread.

Ham Salad Sandwich

¾ cup crisp
  cabbage
¾ cup crisp
  cucumber
1 cup cooked ham

2 tablespoons
  pimiento
2 tablespoons
  green pepper
Mayonnaise

Chop all ingredients and add enough mayonnaise to make a spread. Use as a filling between thin slices of buttered bread. Wrap in waxed paper until ready to serve.

Kanobs

Have cubes of lamb, little sausages, cubes of steak, or inch square slices of thin bacon and alternate on a long, sharp stick skewer or picnic fork. Broil over hot coals or under broiler, turning to cook all sides. Serve between a buttered roll.

Lobster Club Sandwich

1 lb. lobster
  meat, canned
2 tablespoons
  butter
2 tablespoons
  sherry
⅛ teaspoon salt
Mayonnaise

Dash Watkins
  Paprika
6 slices crisp
  bacon
3 ripe tomatoes,
  sliced
12 slices hot
  buttered toast

Cut lobster meat into small pieces and cook in butter, stirring constantly. Remove from fire and stir in sherry. Add salt and Watkins Paprika. Cook bacon until crisp. Arrange a leaf of crisp lettuce on a slice of buttered toast and spread lettuce with mayonnaise. Add crisp bacon, lobster, then a thin tomato slice and another layer of lobster. Cover with a slice of hot buttered toast. Hold sandwich together with skewers and cut diagonally into triangles. Serve hot and garnish with crisp water cress and pimiento olives.

Mock Lobster Sandwich

½ lb. cooked
  halibut, chilled
Mayonnaise

1 tablespoon
  chopped
  pimiento

Chop fish coarsely, add pimiento, moisten with a little mayonnaise and use as a filling for white bread, spread with creamed butter.

Lobster Salad Sandwich

Use equal parts of cooked lobster meat and celery chopped fine. Add salt and Watkins Paprika, and enough mayonnaise to moisten. Use as filling on buttered white bread. Chicken or crab meat may be used instead of lobster.

Toasted Left-Over Sandwiches

Wrap left-over sandwiches in waxed paper and store in the refrigerator. Just before serving spread the outside of the sandwich with melted butter and toast in the broiler-oven. Or use a heavy iron skillet and brown the sandwiches on both sides in butter or margarine, turning once.

Men's Favorite

Rye bread
Creamed butter
Baked ham
Swiss cheese
Watkins Prepared Mustard
Crisp lettuce

Spread rye bread with creamed butter. Place slice of ham then a slice of cheese on buttered bread. Spread a little Watkins Mustard over cheese, top with lettuce, then a slice of buttered bread. Cut into halves and serve with dill pickles.

Hot Mushroom Sandwiches

2 tablespoons butter
1 No. 2 can cream of mushroom soup
3 tablespoons flour
Thin slices baked ham or chicken

Melt butter, stir in flour, and gradually add mushroom soup; cook until mixture thickens, stirring constantly.
Toast bread on one side; place meat on untoasted side spread with creamed butter. Top with hot mushroom sauce. Serve with a thick slice of chilled tomato and pimiento olives.

Onion Sandwich

2 tablespoons minced green pepper
1 3-oz. package cream cheese
Crisp bacon
Mayonnaise
2 Bermuda onions, sliced
½ cup cucumber, diced

Blend pepper with cheese and add enough mayonnaise to make a spread. Place 2 thin slices of onion on buttered white bread, spread with cheese mixture, then a little chopped cucumber over top. Add crumbled crisp bacon and top with slice of buttered bread.

Onion Sandwich

Place thin slices of a peeled onion in salted ice water and let stand to extract the strong flavor of onion. Drain, dip in French dressing and use between buttered slices of bread, adding Watkins Paprika.

Onion Club Sandwich

Peel and cut Bermuda onions into thin slices. For an individual sandwich-filling, use two slices of onion marinated in a little French dressing, some finely diced cucumber, a thin layer of cream cheese blended with chopped nuts, and minced cooked crisp bacon with lettuce and mayonnaise dressing. Make into a club sandwich and use as a filling between buttered toast slices.

Orange Cheese Sandwich

1 package cream cheese
2 tablespoons cream
Watkins Paprika
Grated rind of 1 orange
Salt
½ cup pecans or walnuts
Mayonnaise
Whole wheat or nut bread

Mash cheese to a soft paste, adding cream, salt, Watkins Paprika and orange rind. Spread bread with creamed butter, a little mayonnaise, then with cheese mixture. Cover with nuts and top with buttered bread.

Orange Toast

Blend 2 tablespoons orange juice and grated rind of 1 orange with ½ cup sugar and ⅛ teaspoon Watkins Ground Cinnamon. Spread on slices of hot buttered toast and place in a hot oven about 2 minutes. Serve hot.

Pineapple Cheese Crackers

3 ounces cream cheese
3 tablespoons mayonnaise
½ cup chopped pecans
½ cup drained crushed pineapple

Blend cheese and mayonnaise, add nuts and pineapple. Spread on crisp crackers or on slices of buttered bread. Cut into fancy shapes.

Orange Graham Cracker Sandwich

Blend 1 cup powdered sugar with 3 to 4 tablespoons orange juice and 1 teaspoon grated orange rind. Spread between Graham crackers. A children's favorite with a glass of milk or Watkins Cocoa.

Toasted Orange Sandwich

Orange mar-   Hot buttered
  malade   toast slices
Grated cheese

Spread orange marmalade on buttered toast. Sprinkle with cheese and place under broiler for cheese to melt.

Hot Pineapple-Cheese Sandwich

6 large slices   1 small package
  canned drained   Old English
  pineapple   cheese
Mayonnaise   6 slices cooked
Watkins Paprika   bacon

Cut crust from 6 slices of white bread and toast one side. Heat pineapple in oven. Spread untoasted side of bread with creamed butter, then with a little mayonnaise. Add a slice of pineapple, a slice of cheese, and top with a slice of crisp bacon. Place under broiler to melt cheese. Serve hot.

Ribbon Sandwiches

Cut crusts from both a white and a dark loaf of bread, then cut each loaf in lengthwise slices one-half to three-fourths inch thick. Fit slices together, alternating a dark and a white slice, and trim edges evenly.

Spread the first layer with creamed butter, then with cream cheese and crushed pineapple mixture. Spread second slice with creamed butter, adding a little minced parsley. Spread third slice of bread with creamed butter and use cream cheese and pineapple filling.

Or try a combination of orange marmalade for the first layer, blended cream cheese and chopped candied ginger for the second layer, and avocado paste for third layer.

Add top slice of bread, press together firmly, wrap in a dampened cloth, and chill. Slice just before serving.

Rolled Sandwiches

Cut crust from white bread, slice spread with creamed butter, cream cheese and nut filling. Roll and fasten with toothpick. Place under broiler and toast lightly on all sides. Remove toothpick and serve hot.

Toasted Rolled Sandwich

Cut bread in thin slices, remove crust, place slices together, wrap in a damp cloth and chill in the refrigerator several hours. Before serving, spread slice of bread with thin layer of soft creamed butter. Cover stalk of drained canned or freshly cooked asparagus with mayonnaise dressing; roll asparagus stalk in each slice of bread, fasten with toothpick and toast to a light brown. Turn to brown on all sides.

Russian Club Sandwich

Cut six thin round slices of sandwich bread, the smallest an inch and a half in diameter and the largest 4 inches. Place the largest slice on a salad plate and spread with plum jam or other fruit. Place the next largest slice on top and spread with cream cheese. On the next size slice, place crisp bacon or sliced chicken, with crisp lettuce. On the fourth piece lay a slice of ripe tomato and on the fifth, a slice or two of cucumber, made crisp in ice water and marinated in French dressing.

Each slice of bread should be spread with creamed butter, and each vegetable with a bit of mayonnaise.

Top with a ripe strawberry, or orange or grapefruit sections. Make sandwich secure by fastening with toothpicks.

Salmon Sandwich

1 small can
  salmon
2 tablespoons
  mayonnaise

2 teaspoons
  bottled
  horse-radish
Salt

Blend salmon, horse-radish and mayonnaise with salt and Watkins Paprika. Spread between slices of buttered bread or toast.

Toasted Sardine Sandwich

Place sardines between two slices of buttered bread, and toast. Remove top slice of toast, add a leaf of crisp lettuce, spread with cooked dressing, then add thin slice of tomato, a little Russian dressing, and the top slice of buttered toast.

Savory Sandwiches

6 sardines
3 sour pickles,
  minced
1 teaspoon Wat-
  kins Prepared
  Mustard
Salt

1 tablespoon
  olive oil
2 tablespoons
  vinegar
Yolks 2 hard
  cooked eggs
Watkins Paprika

Carefully remove bones, skin and tail from sardines and mash fish to a paste. Blend all ingredients and spread on buttered rye or white bread.

Spanish Sandwich Filling
(With a Salad)

2 tablespoons
  green pepper,
  chopped
2 tablespoons
  onion, chopped
1 tablespoon
  butter
½ teaspoon salt

¾ cup tomato
  pulp
1 cup soft,
  grated cheese
⅛ teaspoon Wat-
  kins Paprika
1 egg, beaten

Cook pepper and onion in butter to a light brown, add tomato pulp and simmer about 5 minutes. Over low heat, stir in grated cheese, salt, Watkins Paprika and beaten egg, and cook about 2 minutes. Spread thickly between slices of hot buttered toast.

Tongue Sandwiches

1½ cups chopped
  cooked tongue
½ cup minced
  sweet pickles

⅓ cup
  mayonnaise
Crisp water cress

Blend tongue, pickles and mayonnaise and use as a filling between slices of buttered white bread. Add sprigs of water cress.

Tuna Fish Sandwich

1 cup flaked
  tuna fish
1 tablespoon
  mayonnaise

Watkins Onion
  Seasoning
½ teaspoon
  minced chives

Cut bread ¼ inch thick, toast lightly on both sides. Spread toast with creamed butter, trim neatly, and spread with filling.

Tuna Fish Walnut Sandwiches

1 7-oz. can tuna
  fish
¾ cup walnuts,
  chopped
2 cups chopped
  sweet pickle

⅛ teaspoon salt
1 tablespoon
  minced green
  pepper
6 tablespoons
  mayonnaise

Slice white bread, spread with creamed butter. Flake tuna fish and add a little French dressing or lemon juice. Blend filling mixture and spread on buttered bread. Top with slice of buttered bread. Garnish with crisp water cress and pimientos.

Hot Tuna Fish Sandwich

1 small can tuna
  fish, flaked
¼ cup
  mayonnaise
½ cup stuffed
  olives, chopped

½ teaspoon
  Worcestershire
  sauce
Toasted bread
Grated cheese
Watkins Paprika

Blend fish, olives, mayonnaise, and add salt to taste. Spread untoasted side of bread with creamed butter, add sandwich mixture, sprinkle top with grated cheese and place under broiler to melt cheese. Serve hot.

Tuna Fish and Bacon Sandwiches

Flake fish, chill and moisten with French or a little Russian dressing. Blend with chopped crisp bacon and use as a filling between buttered slices of rye bread, toasted.

Vegetable Sandwich

Mix chopped cabbage or carrots with mayonnaise. Use as filling with buttered bread.

Vegetable Sandwich

1 cup carrots
⅓ cup parsley
1 cup diced celery
1 cup shredded crisp cabbage
2 medium-sized onions
1 package sharp cheese
Lemon juice
Worcestershire sauce
Salt

Put vegetables through food chopper using the finest blade; blend with a French mustard dressing and chill 1 hour. Slice whole wheat bread thinly, spread with creamed butter, then with cheese. Drain vegetables, add Worcestershire sauce, lemon juice and salt, if needed. Use as a filling and garnish plate with crisp water cress.

Walnut, Cheese and Olive Sandwich

1 3-oz. package cream cheese
2 small sweet pickles, minced
½ cup chopped walnuts
¼ cup chopped stuffed olives
½ cup mayonnaise
Watkins Paprika

Blend all ingredients and use as a filling for buttered bread. Add a crisp leaf of lettuce over filling.

Walnut and Date Sandwich

½ cup pitted dates
¾ cup walnuts
¼ teaspoon salt
2 tablespoons cream

Put dates and nuts through food chopper. Add salt, cream and blend well. Spread on buttered slices of white, whole wheat or cracked wheat bread.

Walnut and Ripe Olive Sandwich

1 cup chopped ripe olives
4 tablespoons mayonnaise
¾ cup walnuts
2 tablespoons minced canned pimiento

Chop nuts and blend with other ingredients.

Canapes - Appetizers - Hors d'Oeuvres

Canapes differ from hors d'oeuvres in that they are usually served on plain bread, on toast, or unsweetened crackers, a mere tid-bit that can be eaten in one or two bites. Canapes may be simple or elaborate and are attractively garnished for appetite appeal.

There are three kinds of canapes: first, the assortment served on trays and passed with cocktails preceding dinner; second, the spread-your-own, with assorted canape and cheese spreads, and a variety of assorted crackers; third, the single canape of a larger size, served on a small individual plate on the service-plate, as the first course for dinner, and eaten with a fork.

Prepare canapes just before serving. If served on toast, use day old bread, cut into ¼ inch slices in varied shapes, squares, rounds, crescents, triangles, or in long, narrow strips; and cut the bread in the desired shapes before toasting. Or the bread may be fried a golden brown and drained on a paper towel, or toasted under the broiler, or toasted on one side, then the untoasted side spread with creamed butter, and covered with the canape mixture. Or plain bread spread with creamed butter may be used, then the desired topping added.

Cracker-Base Canapes

Select fresh, crisp, unsweetened crackers packaged in tins or cartons and arrange on a tray, as a foundation for a canape spread. Ready-to-serve canape spreads may be purchased in tubes or jars. These include anchovy paste, caviar, pate de fois gras, minced chicken, tuna, crab meat, lobster, and shrimp, any of which can be quickly made into an appetizing paste-mixture.

Appetizers

Appetizers are savory relishes which precede the dinner and whet the appetite. Such appetizers include canapes, small open sandwiches with a well-seasoned paste of anchovies, caviar, lobster, cheese-spread, stuffed eggs, or a small salad, with assorted relishes. In California, the informal dinner begins with a salad, as an appetizer.

Hors d'Oeuvres

An old French cook book says: "Hors d'oeuvres are little light dishes which have the double advantage of decorating the table and keeping the guests patient until other courses are ready to be served." Hors d'oeuvres, called "Smorgasbord" by the Scandinavians, consists in an assortment of chilled vegetables, a variety of julienne strips of cooked chicken, ham, tongue, smoked salmon, herring, fish and stuffed eggs, with relishes to stimulate the appetite.

A complete list of hors d'oeuvres would fill a small book; but the most popular are fish, tiny sausages, smoked salmon, pate de foie gras, caviar, pink shrimp with a delectable sauce, strips of assorted cold meat, intriguing salads, raw and cooked well-seasoned vegetables, such as artichoke hearts, cucumber slices marinated in French dressing and garnished with gherkins, truffles, olives, and an unlimited variety of similar tid-bits.

If hors d'oeuvres are served as a first course at dinner, omit the salad. Canapes may be passed with the hors d'oeuvres, or crisp crackers or pastry sticks may be substituted.

The French Serve Fruit As An Hors d'Oeuvre

The French serve chilled fresh fruit juice as a refreshing aperitif before a meal. The favorite juices include orange, grape, grapefruit, pineapple, strawberries, raspberries and black currants. Pass assorted canapes.

Watkins Seasonings

Seasonings play an important part in the preparation of both canapes and hors d'oeuvres. To serve the perfect canape or hors d'oeuvres, keep a supply of Watkins choice seasonings on hand, as these appetizers require high seasoning. Use Watkins Pepper, Paprika, Red Pepper, Onion Seasoning, Celery Salt, and Spice Blend, as these richly flavored condiments give zest to any canape mixture.

Also for a quick snack, keep an assortment of relishes on hand, with green, ripe, and stuffed olives, sweet and dill pickles, capers, pickled onions, gherkins, and salted nuts, to serve with canapes. Parsley, water cress, minced chives, a dash of caviar, truffles, pimientos cut into fancy shapes, will add attractiveness as a garnish.

Hot Miniature Biscuit Canapes

2 cups sifted flour   ½ teaspoon salt
4 teaspoons   ¼ cup lard
   Watkins Baking   ⅔ cup milk
   Powder

Sift flour, salt and Watkins Baking Powder together. Add lard and blend as for pie crust. Add milk, a little at a time, to make a soft dough. Chill. Pat on a lightly floured pastry cloth to ½ inch thickness. Use a tiny cutter, about 1 inch in diameter. Bake 10 minutes in a hot oven, 425 degrees F. Keep biscuit dough chilled and bake as needed. Serve piping hot with your favorite assorted spreads Each guest breaks and spreads his own biscuit.

Cheese Beef Rolls

1 cup cottage   Dash Worcester-
   cheese   shire sauce
2 tablespoons   Watkins Paprika
   chili sauce   12 small slices
Salt   dried beef

Blend cottage cheese, chili sauce, and Worcestershire, add seasoning. Spread on dried beef, roll and fasten with toothpick. Chill. Will make 1 dozen.

Cheese Canape

½ cup grated   Watkins Paprika
   American   ¼ teaspoon
   cheese   Worcestershire
6 rounds bread   sauce
Creamed butter

Blend grated cheese, Worcestershire sauce and Watkins Paprika to a smooth paste. Spread bread with creamed butter and add cheese mixture. Garnish with a small piece of pimiento, or a slice of pimiento olive.

Puffed Cheese Tid-Bits

1½ inch cubes of   Melted butter
   white bread   Salt
Mixture of: Watkins Red
Melted cheese   Pepper
Lightly beaten   Dash Worcester-
   egg   shire sauce

Hollow out center of bread cubes; butter cubes inside and out. Fill cavity with blended cheese mixture and bake in a medium oven until bread is browned and cheese puffed Serve hot.

Cheese Sticks

1 cup chilled   4 tablespoons
   pie crust   grated cheese
Watkins Paprika

Roll pie crust thin, sprinkle one-half of dough with grated cheese, fold over the other half and roll again. Repeat three times. Cut into narrow strips. Place on a baking sheet and bake in a very hot oven, 500 degrees F., about 10 minutes. Will make 12 sticks.

Hot Cheese Nut Balls
(Will Make 15)

2 teaspoons flour
⅛ teaspoon
  Watkins Red
  Pepper
1 egg white
  stiffly beaten

½ teaspoon salt
1 cup grated
  American
  cheese
¼ cup finely
  chopped nuts

Blend flour, Watkins Red Pepper, salt and grated cheese. Fold in beaten egg white. Form mixture into small balls, roll in chopped nuts, chill. Just before serving, fry in hot deep fat, 375 degrees F., to a golden brown and drain on a paper towel. Serve hot on cocktail picks, as an appetizer, or with salad.

Deviled Cheese Crackers

1 cup grated
  American
  cheese
¼ teaspoon
  Watkins Dry
  Mustard
Salt

1 teaspoon
  Worcestershire
  sauce
½ teaspoon Watkins Paprika
Cream to moisten

Blend entire mixture and spread on crisp crackers or toast squares. Place under broiler just before serving, to melt cheese.

Chicken Liver Appetizers

6 chicken livers
2 tablespoons
  Watkins Prepared Mustard
6 slices bacon,
  cut in halves

2 tablespoons
  finely chopped
  olives
¼ cup fine bread
  crumbs

Cook chicken livers in boiling water 20 minutes, cut into half, spread with blended Watkins Mustard and olives. Wrap bacon around each piece, fasten with a toothpick, roll in bread crumbs and bake in a hot oven, 425 degrees F., 10 to 15 minutes, or until liver and bacon are done.

Dried Beef Appetizers

1 3-oz. package
  cream cheese
1 teaspoon bottled
  horse-radish
Salt

Watkins Onion
  Seasoning
Watkins Paprika
12 slices dried
  beef, chill

Blend cream cheese, horse-radish and seasoning. Spread each slice of dried beef with the cheese mixture, roll tightly and fasten with a toothpick. Chill.
Or chill chipped beef and roll minced cooked chicken with a little mayonnaise in the slice of chipped beef; chill and serve.

Dried Beef Rolls

Large even slices
  of dried beef,
  cut wafer thin
Mayonnaise
Chopped nuts

Soft cheese-
  spread, cream
  or American
  cheese
Minced ripe olives

Blend filling, spread on beef; roll dried beef tightly and chill. Cut in ½ inch lengths, place with cut-end-up on tiny squares (1½ inch) of buttered toast.

Eggs As Hors d'Oeuvres
(Hard-Cooked Eggs)

Anchovies	Olives, minced
Chopped cooked mushrooms	Mayonnaise
	Watkins Paprika

Blend egg yolks with anchovy fillets, trimmed and washed. Add soft butter and blend until smooth. Refill egg whites and garnish with parsley, olives and boiled mushrooms.

Variation:

Minced tuna fish marinated in French dressing and seasoned with mayonnaise may be blended with egg yolks.

French Onion Hors d'Oeuvre

24 small white onions	1 teaspoon tomato paste
2 tablespoons seedless raisins (plump raisins in hot water then drain)	1 tablespoon olive oil
	Dash Watkins Red Pepper
1½ tablespoons sugar	Bay leaf
	6 pepper corns
Few grains salt	Watkins Paprika
	White wine

Place ingredients in a saucepan, cover with a mixture of ⅔ white wine to ⅓ vinegar. Cook slowly until the liquid is reduced one-half. If onions are not tender, add a little boiling water and cook until done.

Pate De Foie Gras Canapes

3 tablespoons pate de fois gras	¼ cup cream
Watkins Red Pepper	Salt
	Parsley

Add cream and seasoning to the pate paste, put through a sieve and use as a canape spread, on small rounds of buttered toast. Garnish with parsley.

Variation:

Mix chopped cooked goose-liver with minced cooked crisp bacon and minced pickle. Use as a spread on plain or toasted bread.

Imitation Foie Gras

½ cup cooked chicken livers	1 tablespoon chopped chives
2 tablespoons butter	Watkins Celery Salt
Salt	Watkins Paprika

Blend liver, soft butter, seasoning and chill. Use as a spread for canapes.

Anchovy Canapes

Cut sandwich bread in oblongs and circles. Toast and spread with anchovy butter. Place narrow strips on anchovy fillets and a strip of pimiento on top of toast, alternating one with the other, either in lines or circles, depending on shape of toast.

Or spread toast strip with anchovy paste and place a curled anchovy in the center, with a tiny pearl onion as a garnish.

Or serve an anchovy on a slice of chilled ripe tomato or cucumber.

Anchovy-Cheese Balls

Mash three anchovy fillets with 2 tablespoons mayonnaise. Blend in 2 to 3 tablespoons cream cheese. Form into small balls and roll in minced parsley. Chill and serve.

Anchovy and Broiled Mushroom

Roll an anchovy in a broiled mushroom and serve with a cocktail toothpick.

Apple or Pineapple Appetizers

Chill, then cut an apple or canned pineapple in cubes, spread top with a mixture of cream cheese and minced chives, then skewer with a toothpick. Serve by placing toothpicks into an appetizer-holder or a large red apple.

Artichoke Hors d'Oeuvres

Cook small artichokes. Chill and marinate artichoke bottom in French dressing 1 hour. Garnish with egg stuffed with minced tuna fish, marinated in French dressing. Add a little mayonnaise to mashed egg yolk and add Watkins Paprika.

Bacon Appetizers

Wrap a thin piece of bacon around a pimiento olive, or a chunk of dill pickle, with a piece of American cheese in center, like a sandwich; fasten with a toothpick. Broil until bacon is crisp, turning to cook all sides, it will take about 10 minutes. Insert a fresh toothpick and serve canape piping hot.

Variations:

Remove black vein from shrimp and place pineapple wedges and shrimp together and roll with a piece of bacon. Broil until bacon is crisp. Serve on a toothpick.

Bacon and Camembert Spread

Cook 5 slices of bacon crisp, drain on a paper towel and chop fine. Blend bacon with 5 tablespoons Camembert cheese and add Watkins Paprika. Blend mixture and use as a spread on crisp crackers or toasted bread.

Beet Hors d'Oeuvres

Hollow out tiny pickled beets and fill with caviar. Sprinkle lightly with lemon juice; chill and serve.

Biscuit Canapes

Chill biscuit dough made a little thinner than usual; use a small cutter. Spread half the cut dough with melted butter, other half with grated cheese, or sardine-paste, minced cooked chicken, or ham. Fold dough over or cover with biscuit-round, and bake in a hot oven, 450 degrees F. just before serving.

Bottled Hors d'Oeuvres

Chill and serve tiny gherkins, sweet pickles, ripe, green and stuffed olives with canapes.

Caviar Canapes

Cut bread into quarter-inch slices then into oblongs 2 inches wide and 4 inches long; toast one side only. Spread one-half of each oblong on untoasted side with creamed butter and minced onion, and the other half with caviar. Garnish with a small piece of pimiento.

Caviar Canape

Blend soft butter and grated Holland cheese to a smooth paste; add a little Madeira wine and a slight flavor of Curacao. Use as a spread and top with caviar on toasted squares or rounds.

Canape Ball

Wash a large grapefruit, dry, then chill. Just before serving, place a row of stuffed olives (stuck on toothpicks) across the top and down the sides of the grapefruit. On each side of the olives place anchovies stuck on toothpicks. Continue the rows, parallel to the olives and anchovies, with cubes of American and Swiss cheese, the size of the anchovies. Add a row of pickled onions, if desired, or large ripe olives.

Stuffed Celery

Select crisp celery stalks about 2½ inches long and spread with any of the following mixtures:

Blend cream cheese with a little cream, add Watkins Paprika and chopped nuts.

Or blend a 3-oz. package of cream cheese with ¼ cup canned crushed pineapple, 1 tablespoon minced pimiento, and Watkins Paprika.

Or mix cream cheese with a little bottled horse-radish, minced chives, and lemon juice.

Or mix cream cheese with a little mayonnaise, chopped stuffed olives and chopped nuts.

Or put one green pepper, a medium-sized Bermuda onion, and a tender-carrot through a food chopper; blend with 1 tablespoon mayonnaise, 1 tablespoon catsup and ¼ teaspoon salt. Add Watkins Paprika.

Or spread celery with Roquefort cheese, olive, pimiento or cream cheese spread and add Watkins Paprika.

Cheese and Anchovy Squares

Toast one side of a thin slice of bread, cut into three strips, cover untoasted side with a thin slice of cheese (Old English), cut to fit bread, and add a curled anchovy in center. Toast under a low broiler flame until cheese is melted. Serve hot.

Cheese and Caviar Canapes

Use cream cheese as a spread on toast strips, and cover with caviar.

Cheese-Chutney Canape

Spread Melba toast or crisp crackers with cream cheese, and Watkins Paprika; top with East Indian chutney.

Cheese and Dill Pickle

Spread small finger-shaped slices of white bread with creamed butter, add grated cheese and a slice of dill pickle. Sprinkle grated cheese over pickle and place under broiler to melt cheese. Add a dash of Watkins Paprika. Serve hot.

Cheese Pecans

Roll any variety of spreading or cream cheese into balls, 1 inch in diameter. Press two large pecan or walnut halves, one on either side, of each ball. Chill and serve.

Toasted Cheese Rolls

Cut fresh bread in thin crosswise slices, trim off crusts. Spread each slice with any cheese mixture then roll like a jelly roll and fasten with a toothpick. Brush with melted butter and broil until a golden brown. Serve hot.

Cheese Roll

Slice white bread very thin, spread with cream cheese mixed with horseradish and pimiento. Roll and cut in small slices. Fry in butter or olive oil. Serve hot.

Cream Cheese Balls

Make cheese balls in advance, chill thoroughly, fry in deep hot fat and drain on a paper towel. Serve hot.

Or blend tiny croquettes of minced cooked chicken, salmon, ham, or crab meat mixture; shape into balls and fry in deep hot fat, just before serving.

Hot Cheese Balls

Thoroughly cream ½ cup butter and ½ pound grated American cheese. Mix with ¾ cup sifted flour, adding flour a little at a time, then add Watkins Onion Seasoning, Watkins Celery Salt, and a little tabasco sauce. Form into balls and chill. Bake at 375 degrees F. until puffed and lightly browned. Serve hot.

Cheese Toast Strips

On strips of buttered toast place small pieces of American, Parmesan, Sierra, or Camembert cheese. Place in oven to melt cheese. Add a dash of Watkins Paprika and serve hot.

Stuffed Cheese Olives

Cut large stuffed olives in half lengthwise. Cut American cheese into ½ inch squares, about ¼ inch thick. Place one square of cheese between olive halves and press firmly together. Chill and serve.

Toasted Cheese

Melt one cup American cheese, add white of one egg and Watkins Red Pepper. Spread on toast cut in fancy shapes. Glaze under broiler.

Chicken Liver and Bacon Appetizers

Cook chicken livers in boiling, salted water about 20 minutes, or until tender; drain. Wrap each cooked liver in ½ slice of thin bacon, cut crosswise. Fasten bacon with a toothpick. Broil until bacon is crisp or brown in a hot oven, 425 degrees F., turn once. Insert a fresh toothpick and serve hot.

Chicken Liver Canape Spread

Mix minced cooked chicken livers with heavy cream and season to suit taste. Add Watkins Paprika.

Corned Beef Canapes

Chop canned corned beef into small pieces, blend with enough chili sauce to moisten. Place filling in center of fried toast strips or squares. Serve cold or place under broiler a few minutes.

Cocktail Sausage

Buy cocktail sausages in 5-oz. cans, already cooked, and fry just before serving. Use a colored toothpick to serve sausage.

Use an electric chafing dish and keep little fried sausages or bacon curls crisp and hot. Have colored toothpicks handy so guests can spear their favorite.

Crab Meat Canape

Cook and stir 2 sliced fresh mushrooms and 1 diced green pepper in 2 tablespoons butter. Remove from fire, add 2 cups canned crab meat and enough mayonnaise to moisten. A little diced celery may be added. Spread on buttered toast rounds, add a small piece of American cheese to top canape and heat under broiler to melt cheese. Serve hot with a wedge of lemon and crisp parsley.

Crab Meat, Lobster and Shrimp Canapes

Remove black vein from shrimp. Blend into a paste equal parts of crab meat, lobster, and shrimp, add salad dressing to moisten. Spread mixture on small rounds of bread, cut thin and buttered.

Cracker Canape Spreads

Arrange assorted crisp crackers, toast triangles, and crisp potato chips, on a platter with cheese spreads, for guests to serve themselves. Serve caviar placed on ice with wedge pieces of lemon; anchovy paste, crab meat, shrimp, or lobster, moistened with a seasoned salad dressing, also pate de foie gras, or goose-liver paste.

Puffed Crackers for Canapes

Soak flaky square soda crackers in cold water 8 minutes, drain, place on paper towel then in a greased baking pan. Brush with melted butter, salt and Watkins Paprika. (Any canape butter spread as minced chives, may be used). Bake in a hot oven 450 degrees F., 10 minutes, then reduce heat to 350 degrees and bake another 20 minutes, or until lightly browned.

Cucumbers Served as Hors d'Oeuvre

Chill cucumbers, peel, slice, marinate in French dressing and chill. Remove from dressing, place a curled anchovy in the center, topped with a little anchovy paste or tuna.

Dill Pickle Slices with Cheese

Cut a slice from one end of each pickle, carefully remove center of pickle with an apple corer. Fill space with Old English cheese spread and pack firmly. Chill one hour, then cut into half-inch slices, crosswise, and serve as a border on a plate with pretzel sticks, or crisp cheese crackers.

Frankfurter Logs

Wrap cocktail frankfurters in very thin slices of bread and fasten with a toothpick. Spread outside of the bread with mustard butter (2 parts Watkins Mustard to 2 parts butter, creamed together). Place under broiler and brown. Serve piping hot.

Ham As Hors d'Oeuvres

Roll cooked ham cone-shape and chill. Fill with pate de foie gras and garnish with parsley.

Ham and Pickle Spread

Blend minced baked ham, chopped pickle relish and use as a canape spread.

Hot Ham Canapes

Blend ½ cup minced cooked ham and 1 tablespoon chopped pickle relish. Spread mixture on small squares or rounds of bread spread with creamed butter. Place a cube of cheese on top and place under broiler to melt cheese. Serve hot. Add a dash of Watkins Paprika.

South American Appetizer Boiled Ham

Spread soft cream cheese on a slice of Virginia boiled ham (remove all fat), add a little minced green pepper or chives, and wrap the ham around a small dill pickle. Fasten with a toothpick, cover with waxed paper and chill.

Herring Hors d'Oeuvres

Remove skin, tail and fins from smoked herring, soak herring in milk 1 hour then drain and dry with a clean cloth. Place herring in a deep dish in alternate layers with diced celery, slices of onion, gherkins, bay leaves, sprig of thyme. Add white wine or olive oil and a little vinegar. Cover dish and place in the refrigerator 3 or 4 days.

When ready to serve, remove herring and garnish with sliced onions and some of the dressing from the marinade. Garnish with hard-cooked quartered eggs, adding a little caviar and Watkins Paprika.

Herring Appetizers

Cut pickled herring in small pieces and skewer with a toothpick.

Liver Sausage Canapes

Mix liver sausage with one-third butter. Add Worcestershire sauce to taste, and a dash of Watkins Paprika. Spread on toast squares.

Lobster Canape

Chop cooked lobster meat very fine. Add lemon juice, salt, Watkins Paprika, and a few drops of Worcestershire sauce. Chill. Spread prepared bread or toast with the paste and garnish with a slice of pimiento olive or a strip of pimiento.

Mushroom Appetizers

Marinate canned or freshly cooked mushrooms (cooked in a little butter and drained), in French dressing several hours. Drain. Dip in fritter batter (see Watkins Cook Book, Page 72) and fry to a golden brown. Drain on a paper towel and serve hot with a colored toothpick.

Stuffed Olives In Anchovy Fillets

Chill large stuffed olives. Roll each olive in an anchovy fillet and fasten with a cocktail toothpick.

Stuffed Cheese Olives

Cut pimiento olives in half lengthwise, cut American cheese into ½ inch squares. Place one cheese-square between two halves of olive and press firmly together. Chill and serve.

Pinwheel Appetizers

Roll thin slices canned veal loaf around whole stuffed olive or whole sweet pickle, like a jelly roll. Fasten with a toothpick at ½ inch intervals. Cut in slices between the toothpicks. Serve appetizers stuck into an appetizer-holder or a large red apple.

Potato Chips and Cheese

Blend 1 4-oz. package spreading-Roquefort-cheese with 1 teaspoon minced chives. Spread thinly on crisp potato chips and add a dash of Watkins Paprika.

Potato Chip Appetizers

Spread crisp potato chips with anchovy paste.

Prima Donna Canapes

Make a rich pie crust, cut into small fancy shapes and bake until crisp and light brown in color. Spread with minced ham or anchovy paste and sprinkle with Watkins Paprika.

Or roll frankfurters in thin pastry and bake. Add a little Watkins Dry Mustard and Red Pepper to the unbaked pastry, to give a different flavor. Serve hot.

Prune Appetizers

Steam large prunes until pits can be easily removed. Fill with chopped pimientos, nuts, stuffed olives, and a few capers made into a paste. Put thin slices of bacon around each prune, fasten with a toothpick and bake in a hot oven. Or fill prunes with cheese and nuts. Chill and serve.

Stuffed Radishes

Carefully hollow out large radishes with a sharp pointed knife, then crisp in ice water. Drain and stuff with a blended mixture of caviar, lemon juice, onion juice, and a little mayonnaise. Chill and serve.

Salami Appetizers

Place small cubes of salami on colored toothpicks with a tiny pickled onion.

Roquefort and Cream Cheese Spread

Blend 1 4-oz. package Roquefort cheese and 1 3-oz. package cream cheese with 1 tablespoon minced chives and ¼ cup cream. Add Watkins Paprika. Chill. Use as a spread on toasted or buttered bread, or crisp crackers.

Salmon Canape Surprise

Roll square pieces of smoked salmon with a filling made of a little whipped cream, horse-radish and Watkins Paprika. Roll, fasten with a toothpick, cover with waxed paper and chill.

Salmon and Anchovy Canape

Cut toasted white bread in 2½-inch squares, spread top with creamed butter. Cover one-half with smoked salmon, the other half with anchovy filets. Serve with a wedge of lemon and crisp parsley.

Salmon Cornucopia

Make a cornucopia of smoked salmon. Stuff with sardine paste, caviar, or anchovy.

Salmon Canape

Butter thin slices of toasted white bread, cut into strips 1½ inch wide, cover with thin slices of smoked salmon. Add a sprig of parsley and arrange on a platter with wedges of lemon. A slight garnish of caviar may be added to the salmon.

Salmon, Shrimp, Crab Meat, Smoked Canned Fish for Canapes

Shrimp, crab meat, any smoked or canned fish, may be made into a paste; highly season, and use as a canape spread. Chill mixture before using.

Smoked Salmon Canapes

Drain, chill small sweet pickles, roll in cream cheese, then in a slice of smoked salmon, fasten with a toothpick and chill.

Sardine Paste Canape

Spread finger-length strips of bread with creamed butter, then with sardine-paste, moistened with lemon juice.

Sardines As Hors d'Oeuvres

Brittany sardines are favored by epicures. Remove skin and bones, make a paste of sardines and a little soft butter.

Use as a spread on canapes and add a few drops of olive oil and a dash of Watkins Paprika.

Shrimp Hors d'Oeuvres

Remove black vein from canned shrimp and chill shrimp. Just before serving insert a colored toothpick in each shrimp and arrange in a bowl on ice. On the tray have cracked ice and a glass container with a well-seasoned cocktail sauce, for guests to dip shrimp. Drained chilled artichoke hearts may be served as above.

Shrimp Curls

Add 1 teaspoon grated lemon rind to a little thin waffle batter. Split fresh cooked or canned shrimp lengthwise (remove black vein), dip in batter and bake on a hot waffle iron. Serve hot.

Smoked Sturgeon Canapes

Cover slice of toast with smoked sturgeon. Cut in four diamonds.

Swiss Canape

Spread triangular pieces of Pumpernickel bread with creamed butter, add Swiss cheese cut to fit bread, and fill open spaces with caviar.

Pumpernickel bread may be purchased in tins, and is delicious for a canape.

Tongue and Cheese Appetizers

Spread thin slices of cold cooked tongue, cut into squares, with cheese, adding a little mayonnaise or heavy cream. Bleu cheese is recommended. Add Watkins Paprika.

Tuna Fish Canape

Make a paste of flaked tuna fish, adding minced sweet pickle, a little mayonnaise and Watkins Paprika.

Tuna Fish and Cheese Canapes

Spread toasted rounds of bread with creamed butter, blended with a little grated horse-radish. Add flaked tuna fish blended with mayonnaise. Add grated cheese, place under broiler just before serving.

Hot Tuna Fish Canape

Cut squares from fresh puff paste, roll thin. Chill. Pound tuna fish to a fine paste, add 1 tablespoon cream a beaten egg white, lemon juice, salt and Watkins Paprika to suit taste. Spread on puff-paste squares, roll and bake just before serving, 400 degree F. oven.

Vienna Sausage Tid-Bits

Cut Vienna sausage into ¾ inch length. Place two pieces of sausage with a slice of stuffed olive or sweet pickle on the end of a toothpick.

A Raw Vegetable Hors d'Oeuvres Platter

A combination of chilled raw vegetables as relishes may be attractively arranged on a chop plate, and garnished with water cress or parsley. Include carrot sticks, carrot fans and curls, cauliflower flowerets, cucumber-fingers or slices, celery curls and sticks, green-pepper straws, radish roses and fans, chives, and gherkins. Garnishes should be thoroughly chilled.

Carrot Sticks

Wash and scrape young tender carrots, preferably deep orange well-flavored ones. Cut into quarters lengthwise, then into narrow strips. Wrap in a damp cloth and chill.

Variation:

Rub sliced carrot with a cut clove of garlic, cut into narrow strips 3 inches long. Wrap in a damp cloth and chill before serving.

Carrot Fans

Wash and scrape tender young carrots. Cut into quarters lengthwise. Use a sharp knife, cut each quarter into thin lengthwise slices, almost to the end. Spread in a pan of ice and chill.

Celery Club Style

Remove tough outer stalks from celery, wash thoroughly under cold running water. Trim root-end to an oval; if "club" is small, leave it whole, if large, cut into halves or quarters. Wrap in a damp cloth and chill.

Celery Curls

Select tender stalk of celery, cut into 3-inch lengths then cut each length into narrow, parallel strips, nearly to the end. Place in a pan with chopped ice and a teaspoon salt. As celery chills, the ends will curl.

Carrot Curls

Cut thin, lengthwise pieces from peeled long carrots. Curl around finger then place in ice water and chill. Dry and serve on cracked ice.

Cucumber-Fingers

Peel a narrow cucumber, cut into half lengthwise, remove seeds and cut solid portion into narrow strips, about 3 inches long. Place on a chilled plate, cover cucumbers with a damp cloth and chill at least an hour before serving. Add a dash of Watkins Paprika.

Green Pepper Sticks

Wash green pepper, cut out stem, remove center and seeds. Cut pepper in half, lengthwise, then in quarters, then into long narrow strips. Wrap pepper sticks in a clean damp cloth and chill at least an hour.

Radish Fan

Wash long radishes, cut thin crosswise slices nearly through radish. Chill in ice water and the slices will spread fan-shape.

Onion Rings For Sea-Food Cocktail

Cut large, mild onions into thin slices crosswise, drop into ice water and chill. Use a fork, loosen rings, drain, chill and serve.

Beverages

Learn the art of making a palatable beverage and the most simple meal will win high praise. A cup of well made, appetizing, hot coffee is an important part of any meal. It is urged that homemakers give thought and careful attention to preparing and serving hot drinks hot and cold drinks cold.

For real hospitality and good cheer serve a cup of hot steaming coffee, or a sparkling, refreshing iced drink. A chocolate, cocoa, or egg drink made with milk, is nourishing and will be a splendid "pick up" when you are tired in the mid-afternoon.

Hints In Making Coffee

There are four different types of coffee-making containers: percolator, drip, vacuum-type, and the coffee pot. Regardless of method used in making coffee, always use a standard measuring spoon and cup, and adhere to the proportion of 2 level tablespoons of coffee to 1 measuring cup of water. The measurements must be accurate.

Use soft, freshly drawn cold water in making coffee. If it is necessary to use hard or chlorinated water, boil it 3 minutes before making coffee. Make coffee in a spotlessly clean, fresh and sweet-smelling utensil. It is **important** that all coffee-making equipment be scrupulously clean.

After each brewing, wash the coffee-maker in hot soapy water, using a brush to clean the spout and crevices, and a powdered cleanser to remove stains. Rinse thoroughly in scalding water, wipe container dry, and air well. When using an electric coffee-maker, do not place the heating unit, if a part of the coffee pot, into a pan of hot suds, and do not wet the base, the plug connection, or the cord.

The coffee must be fresh. Buy coffee in small quantities in vacuum-packed containers, freshly roasted and freshly ground, because coffee deteriorates quickly. A fifteen-day-old coffee in the bean, is about equal in strength to ground coffee that has stood three days after roasting. To preserve aroma and flavor, keep coffee tightly covered in a tin container in the refrigerator; do not keep coffee at room temperature. Do not mix old coffee with the fresh supply; and do not let the coffee canister stand open, because the oxygen in the air destroys the flavor of roasted coffee. It is the caffee-oil which coffee contains, that gives the characteristic flavor.

Use the Right Grind of Coffee

Use the right grind of coffee, the one suited to your coffee-maker. Use regular or medium-grind for steeped and percolator coffee, drip-grind for the drip method, and fine-grind for the vacuum type.

Remove grounds as soon as the coffee is ready to serve, as they tend to absorb flavor and aroma. Pour freshly made hot coffee into hot cups for coffee must be hot to be appetizing. For iced coffee make the beverage double strength and pour while hot over ice cubes.

Make coffee fresh for each meal; do not serve left-over coffee re-heated. After each use, **scour, scald, dry,** and **air** coffee-maker, and **scald** coffee pot before using.

Selecting a Coffee-Maker

FROM THE UNIVERSITY OF VIRGINIA EXPERIMENT STATION

The Dripolator

In this type of coffee-maker, ground coffee is held in a perforated basket, and boiling water from a container drips over the coffee into the pot. This type of coffee-maker scored highest on quality of coffee produced, required more dry coffee, took a longer time in preparation, and would not percolate the finest grind.

Percolator Type

In this type of coffee-maker the water is spurted to the top of the pot then drips back through the coffee. A medium-grind coffee was found most satisfactory in this type of maker, and a smaller amount of coffee was required.

Vacuum Type

This coffee-maker has two glass bowls, one above the other, with a filter between. Water in the lower bowl is heated until forced, by steam pressure, to the upper bowl containing the coffee; then, when the heat is turned off, is drawn back through the filter by vacuum.

The vacuum-type coffee-maker is fragile, but it is the only type in which the finest grind of coffee could be used without producing sediment in the cup; it scored high for the quality of beverage and gave the largest measure of coffee.

If the drip-grind does not give a full strength brew in your vacuum coffee-maker, keep the heat on a little longer so that the water stays in contact with the coffee, a few extra minutes.

Careful washing, both of the glass parts and the cloth filter, is necessary for good coffee. The rubber gasket which makes the seal tight, may have to be replaced frequently. Cloth filters proved best for high quality and a clear beverage, but improved paper filters may soon be available.

Boiled Coffee

Use 2 level tablespoons of coarse or medium-grind coffee for each cup of water. To bring out the flavor, pour ½ cup of cold water over the coffee, before adding freshly boiling water. Add the exact amount of water, cold, hot or boiling, place over heat, stir mixture to blend, and bring to boiling.

To Make Coffee With Egg:

Add 1 teaspoon slightly beaten egg for each cup, and 1 extra tablespoon of coffee for the pot. Mix coffee and egg with a little cold water; add remaining water (exact amount) and the washed, crushed egg shell. Cover pot, bring slowly to boiling; stir twice during cooking. Remove from heat, let stand in a warm place, over low heat with an asbestos mat, and pour 2 tablespoons of cold water down the spout to settle the grounds. Use a strainer and pour the hot coffee into hot cups.

Coffee too finely ground will make a cloudy beverage.

Drip-Grind Recommended

Drip-grind coffee is considered best for all coffee-makers. Fineness of grind is important in improving the flavor and quality of the beverage.

Drip Coffee

Use 2 level tablespoons drip-grind coffee to each cup of water. Place the coffee in the proper compartment of the coffee pot, and pour fresh, vigorously-boiling water in the water compartment. If filter paper is used, adjust before adding the water. Let water drip through the coffee, keeping the pot over low heat; coffee should not boil. Remove coffee and water section, stir coffee to blend mixture, and serve hot in hot cups. If coffee must stand, place pot over low heat and use an asbestos mat.

Percolated Coffee

Use 2 level tablespoons regular-grind coffee for each cup of water. Use freshly drawn cold water and have coffee-maker at least half-full. Turn down the flame when water begins to percolate so that it functions slowly. Allow coffee to percolate from 10 to 12 minutes from the time the water begins to bubble. Remove container with grounds, as soon as the coffee is made.

Vacuum Type Coffee-Maker

Follow directions given by the manufacturer for the vacuum type coffee-maker. Use 2 level tablespoons drip-grind coffee to each measuring cup of water. The vacuum coffee-maker has a thermostatically controlled electric heater which keeps the coffee at the right temperature.

For Valve Type Vacuum-Maker:

Place coffee in the proper compartment with **cold** water for a better flavored coffee.

For Valveless-Type Vacuum-Maker:

Pour cold or hot water in the bottom of the percolator. To make 6 cups, percolate the coffee 10 minutes from the time when the liquid, coming through the tube, begins to show discoloration. If less than 6 cups are made, reduce the time of percolation to 7 minutes; a longer time will make the coffee bitter. Remove the coffee compartment as soon as the percolation stops, since coffee grounds absorb flavor and aroma, unless removed.

After-Dinner Coffee
Demi Tasse

Prepare strong coffee, using from 3 to 4 tablespoons of ground coffee for 1 cup freshly boiling water; the drip-method is preferred. Serve hot in small after-dinner cups.

Cafe Au Lait French Coffee

Make coffee double strength by any method, and prepare an equal amount of freshly scalded milk. Pour hot coffee and hot milk in equal amounts into heated cups and add a dash of whipped cream.

Iced Cafe Au Lait

Pour 1 cup strong, hot coffee over cracked ice in a tall glass. Add a scoop of vanilla ice cream and serve immediately.

Steeped Coffee

Measure water accurately, bring to full rolling boil, remove from heat, and add 1 level tablespoon of ground coffee to each cup of boiling water. Cover, and steep in a warm place 5 minutes. To settle grounds, pour 1/4 cup cold water down the spout and let stand 1 minute.

Steeped Coffee for Forty

Place 1 pound medium-grind coffee in a white cheesecloth or muslin bag, allowing space for coffee to double in bulk. Drop bag into a large kettle containing 2 gallons of freshly boiling water. Cover kettle tightly and let stand over a low flame about 10 minutes. When ready to serve, pour coffee into a coffee pot, rinsed thoroughly with boiling water. Serve in hot cups.

Iced Coffee

Make coffee twice the usual strength. Pour hot coffee over cracked ice in tall glasses, or over a block of ice in a large pitcher. Add ice cubes; top with whipped cream.

Or make coffee regular strength (2 tablespoons coffee to each measuring cup of water) and pour over coffee ice cubes; coffee ice cubes will not dilute the coffee.

To Make Coffee Ice Cubes:

Make coffee regular strength, cool, and pour into freezing tray of your automatic refrigerator and freeze. Iced coffee has a better flavor when the beverage is freshly made and poured hot over cracked ice.

To Top Iced Coffee
(When Cream Is Scarce)

Beat 1 egg white until stiff, fold in 2 tablespoons sugar and add a few drops of Watkins Vanilla. Add a little cream to the iced coffee and top with chilled egg fluff.

Coffee Briquettes

Postwar coffee in form of briquettes, will occupy 42% less shelf space than coffee in bulk. The coffee bean is prepared by roasting and grinding, then compressed at a temperature of 45 degrees below zero, in an atmosphere of carbon dioxide, to prevent oxidation.

The new coffee briquettes are about the size of a yeast cake, and each cake will make three cups of strong coffee. Crumble the coffee briquette into the heated coffee pot and prepare the usual way. This new improved "compressed coffee", is heat-sealed into a cellophane wrapped, air proof, and moisture proof container.

Instant Coffee

Soluble coffee was used successfully by our Armed Forces during World War II, and is recommended when coffee must be served quickly, or for only one person. Place a teaspoon of coffee powder (more for a stronger beverage) in a hot cup, stir and add vigorously boiling water and the coffee is ready to serve.

Iced coffee can be just as quickly made by adding boiling water, then ice cubes.

The new scientific process used in the manufacture of Instant Coffee pulverizes the coffee and the infusion is made. Carbohydrates in form of dextrose, maltose, and dextrines are added, to seal in the coffee flavor. The coffee is then filtered to insure a sparkling brew, after which it is spray-dried and milled, to reduce the coffee in bulk.

A four ounce jar will yield approximately the same number of cups as a pound of regular coffee, and at about the same cost, with the advantage that, when using Instant Coffee, there is no waste.

Two Types of Instant Coffee

There are two types of Instant Coffee, the filled and the unfilled. The unfilled types are pure coffee, brewed, filtered, dried and packaged. The filled types are pure coffee, with carbotose and dextrines added by an improved process, which retains the original flavor of the coffee bean.

Hints In Making Tea

Tea is graded according to the size of the leaf and packaged as Flowering Orange Pekoe, Orange Pekoe, Pekoe, Pekoe Souchong, and Souchong. Black, also called fully fermented tea, is most popular in the United States; Darjeeling tea from the Himalaya Mountains in India, is credited by experts as having the richest flavor.

Tea leaves may be purchased in tea bags; or if purchased in bulk, may be tied in a cheesecloth bag, with space allowed for the leaves to swell. Connoisseurs of tea do not use tea bags.

Use a china, earthenware or crockery teapot, not a metal container. Allow from 1 to 2 teaspoons of tea leaves to 1 cup of briskly boiling water. Place the tea in a scalded teapot, add freshly boiling water, cover the pot and steep in a warm place from 3 to 5 minutes. Strain the tea into a pre-heated serving pot and serve in hot cups.

Iced Tea

Prepare tea double strength, then pour hot tea over cracked ice, in tall glasses. To serve a large number, pour hot tea over a block of ice, using a large bowl or pitcher. Cool the tea quickly for a clear beverage, then pour into tall glasses over ice cubes.

Fruit Juices for Health

Next to milk, fruit juices are most important in the daily diet as a beverage because they contain essential health vitamins and minerals; natural fruit sugar is high in fuel value. Orange, grapefruit, grape juice, pineapple and lemon juice may be extracted from the fresh fruit, or may be purchased in tin containers.

Fruit juices are best served in combination (except orange juice) for a richer flavor, and are improved by standing in the refrigerator one hour before serving, to mellow.

To keep fresh fruit juice drinks clear, strain out all pulp and sediment. If fruit is added as a garnish, cut or slice the fruit in large enough pieces, to prevent the pulp from breaking or dissolving in the punch bowl or pitcher.

The difference between a thin fruit sugar water drink and a rich well flavored one, lies in the strength and quality of the ingredients, the proper blending, the thorough mixing, which gives the beverage palatability. Use a cocktail shaker to mix blended fruit and milk drinks. An improvised shaker may be made with a quart fruit jar, a tightly fitting lid, and a towel placed over the cover while shaking the mixture. Or pour the beverage quickly from one fruit jar to another until the beverage is well blended.

To whip milk and egg drinks, use a deep bowl and a rotary beater. Carbonated water added to a lemonade or a fruit drink, will give a froth and sparkle to a beverage.

Suggested Fruit Juice Combinations For a Beverage

Equal parts of pineapple and orange juice and ¼ as much lemon juice.

Equal parts of dry ginger ale and grape juice.

Grapefruit and grape juice.

Canned apricot nectar and canned grapefruit juice.

Cherry and pineapple juice.

Cherry and lemon juice.

Raspberry and grapefruit juice.

Apricot and peach juice.

Pineapple and apricot juice.

Orange and grapefruit.

Frosted Glasses for Fruit Juice

Just before filling glasses, chill them. Dip glass in lemon juice to a depth of half an inch, then dip glass immediately into granulated sugar, rotating glass until frosted.

Fruit and Milk Drinks

Blend any kind of fruit juice (except fresh pineapple juice) with whole milk, but canned pineapple juice may be used. Both the fruit juice and milk should be thoroughly chilled before blending. The exact proportion of fruit juice and milk varies with the acidity of the fruit, the usual proportion is one-third fruit juice to two-thirds milk. Serve in a tall glass iced cold, with straws.

Fruit Juice Ice Cubes

Freeze unsweetened pineapple juice, orange juice, or any canned fruit syrup diluted with water, and fill sections of the refrigerator tray, first adding a drop of Watkins Yellow, Green, or Red Color Mixture. Chill until firm.

Sugar Syrup for Sweetening Fruit Drinks

Make a syrup of equal parts of sugar and water, or use white corn syrup and water, stir the mixture until the sugar is dissolved, and boil 10 minutes. Cool and keep syrup in a covered jar in the refrigerator. Use the syrup to sweeten any beverage. To substitute sugar syrup for sugar, use 1¼ tablespoons of syrup for each tablespoon of sugar called for in a recipe. Sugar intensifies fresh fruit flavor, but the less the amount of sugar in a beverage, the less the drink can be diluted.

Mint Ice Cubes For Iced Tea:

Boil together 2 cups of water and ½ cup of sugar 5 minutes, then pour over ½ cup finely minced washed mint leaves and let stand until cool. Add the juice of 3 lemons, strain, and add a drop of Watkins Green Color Mixture. Pour into the freezing tray of the automatic refrigerator and chill until firm. Mixtures which contain sugar take longer to freeze.

Frozen Fruit for Instant Use

Fresh frozen fruit juice may be purchased in quart jars. A quart of quick frozen lime juice is equivalent to the juice of 20 medium-sized limes. Allow three hours to defrost a quart size block of fruit juice at room temperature. Frozen fruit juice placed in a punch bowl instead of ice, will keep the punch from being diluted. Frozen orange, grapefruit, or lemon juice, is a boon when serving a refreshing beverage to a large group.

Decorative Ice Cubes

To give a note of color to a lemonade or a fruit drink, freeze decorative ice cubes in the mechanical refrigerator. Fill the tray with cold water and freeze only until the bottom and sides of the ice cube is solid. With an ice pick break a hole in the top of the cube, empty the water, add a sprig of fresh mint, or a cherry, a strawberry, or a piece of orange or lemon, then refill the cube with ice water, and freeze until firm.

Banana-Pineapple Ade

1 ripe banana
1 cup pineapple juice
½ cup cream
1 cup shaved ice
Few drops Watkins Vanilla

Mash banana, stir in cream and ice. Shake briskly to blend, then add pineapple juice. Serve cold.

Cherry Juice

4 cups cherry juice
Juice 1 lemon
2 cups sugar syrup
4 cups water (Part pineapple juice may be used)

Make a sugar syrup of 1 part water and 2 parts sugar or white corn syrup; boil 5 minutes, cool. Blend cherry and lemon juice with chilled syrup, strain and chill.

Cherry and Grape Juice

1 cup grape juice, chilled
2 cups chilled cherry juice
Sweeten to taste
Chill and serve.

Cherry-Almond Cocktail

2 cups pitted
   sour cherries
½ cup blanched
   almonds
1 tablespoon
   lemon juice

⅓ cup cherry
   juice
½ cup con-
   fectioner's
   sugar

Blend and chill mixture. Serve in cocktail glasses.

Cherry Drink

2 cups cherry juice, chilled
Sugar to suit taste
4 cups ginger ale, chilled
Or 2 cups orange juice
Chill and serve.

Cherry Frappe

3 cups canned
   red cherry juice
⅓ cup sugar
3 cups hot tea
   slightly cooled

1 quart chilled
   ginger ale
2 quarts cracked
   ice

Stir sugar into chilled cherry juice. Pour tea over ice, stir in cherry juice. Chill. Just before serving, stir in ginger ale.

Cherry Freeze

4 cups cherry juice blended
   with pineapple and a little
   lemon juice
2 cups sugar syrup
4 cups water
Blend ingredients and pour over cracked ice.

Cider Mint Cocktail

2 cups sweet cider
¾ cup orange
   juice

½ cup canned
   pineapple juice
Juice of ½ lemon

Have all ingredients cold and serve in cocktail glasses. Garnish with a sprig of mint.

Chocolate Coffee Cream

1 cup sugar
¾ cup honey
1 cup corn syrup
¾ cup warm
   water
½ cup Watkins
   Cocoa

¼ cup strong
   coffee
1 teaspoon Wat-
   kins Vanilla
   Cream
Ginger ale, chilled

Blend sugar, honey, corn syrup and water, stir constantly and cook over low heat 5 minutes. Blend coffee and Watkins Cocoa, add to syrup and boil 3 minutes. Strain and use as sugar syrup; keep in the refrigerator. Place 2 tablespoons of cocoa syrup in a tall glass, add 1 tablespoon cracked ice and 1 tablespoon cream. Fill glass with ginger ale. Serve.

Chocolate Syrup

½ cup Watkins Cocoa or 2 squares (2 oz.) unsweetened chocolate, melted

1 cup sugar syrup
⅛ teaspoon salt
1 teaspoon Watkins Vanilla

To Make Sugar Syrup:
Boil 2 cups water and 1½ cups granulated sugar 5 minutes; cool, keep in a covered jar in the refrigerator ready for instant use. Place 1 cup of syrup, with salt, Watkins Cocoa, stir constantly, bring to a boil and boil 3 minutes. Cool, add Watkins Vanilla and use for chocolate drinks.

Chocolate Milk Drink

Use the proportion of 3 tablespoons chocolate syrup to a glass of cold milk and whip with a rotary beater.

Cocoa

(To Serve Six)

6 tablespoons Watkins Cocoa

¼ cup sugar
Few grains salt
1 cup water
5 cups top milk

Blend sugar, salt and Watkins Cocoa in a saucepan, add water, and boil 2 minutes. Add milk and heat slowly until scalded, just below boiling. Cover container and keep hot over hot water. Just before serving, beat Watkins Cocoa with a rotary whip, keeping the container over hot water. Serve in hot cups with a dash of whipped cream or a marshmallow.

Iced Cocoa or Chocolate

2 tablespoons Cocoa Syrup
1 cup milk

Drop Watkins Peppermint Extract

Whip cocoa syrup and milk with a rotary beater until frothy, add peppermint and pour over cracked ice in tall glasses. Add a dash of whipped cream.

Iced Mocha Cocoa

1 cup hot strong coffee
3 cups top milk, chilled

½ cup Cocoa Syrup
¼ cup whipped cream
Shaved ice

Blend hot coffee, milk and cocoa syrup. Use a rotary beater and whip briskly. Pour over ice and top with whipped cream.

Evaporated Milk in Cocoa Drinks

In making cocoa, chocolate and coffee drinks, use undiluted evaporated milk for a richer beverage.

Frosted Chocolate

2 tablespoons
cocoa syrup
1 cup milk,
chilled

1 scoop chocolate
ice cream

Whip syrup and milk with a rotary beater, pour into tall glasses and add ice cream. Shake briskly and serve.

Coffee With Whipped Cream

¼ cup evaporated
milk, chilled
1 quart hot coffee

1½ tablespoons
sugar
½ cup top milk

Whip chilled evaporated milk until stiff, beat in sugar. Add top milk to coffee, and sweeten to suit taste. Serve in hot cups and add a table-spoon whipped evaporated milk.

Frosted Coffee

Fill four iced glasses with chipped ice. Pour warm coffee over ice until glasses are three-quarters full. Add a heaping tablespoon vanilla ice cream and serve immediately.

Iced Coffee Shake

3 cups strong
coffee
3 drops Watkins
Almond Extract
2 cups top milk,
chilled

2 cups carbonated
water, chilled
Powdered sugar
to taste
Whipped cream,
or ice cream
to top

Blend all ingredients, shake well, and serve with cracked ice.

Mocha Iced Coffee

1 quart strong
coffee, cool
1 quart Watkins
Cocoa made
with rich milk,
cool

½ cup powdered
sugar
1 teaspoon Wat-
kins Vanilla
2 quarts crushed
ice

Blend coffee and cocoa, stir in sugar until dissolved. Pour over cracked ice.

Cranberry and Grapefruit Cocktail

2 cups bottled
cranberry juice
⅔ cup canned
grapefruit juice

Dash angostura
bitters or
lemon juice

Dip rims of cocktail glasses in lemon juice, then in powdered sugar to a depth of ¼ inch. Add chilled fruit juice.

Cranberry Juice Cocktail

2 cups cranberries
3 cups water
2 tablespoons lemon juice
½ cup sugar or white corn syrup

Wash, drain, cook cranberries with water until skins pop. Strain and return to saucepan. Add sugar, and simmer 5 minutes. Add lemon juice and chill.

For a variation in flavor, add ½ inch stick of cinnamon to juice and simmer 5 minutes. Remove spice, add lemon juice and chill.

Currant Fizz For Fifty

3 cups currant jelly
4 cups boiling water
5 cups orange juice
1⅓ cups lemon juice
3 quarts chilled ginger ale

Blend boiling water and jelly and whip with a rotary beater. Add fruit juices and chill. Just before serving, add chilled ginger ale. Add a large piece of ice to punch bowl.

Egg Nog

For 1 serving:
1 egg, beaten
Few grains salt
2 teaspoons granulated sugar
½ cup milk
½ cup cream
⅓ teaspoon Watkin Vanilla
Dash Watkins Nutmeg

Use a rotary beater and whip egg. Add salt, sugar, milk and Watkins Vanilla. Whip entire mixture, pour into a tall glass and add a dash of Watkins Nutmeg.

Chocolate Egg Nog

4 tablespoons cocoa syrup
1 cup rich milk
1 egg

Blend cocoa syrup with milk and add beaten egg yolk. Whip with a rotary beater. Fold in stiffly beaten egg white and pour over cracked ice. Will make 1 glass.

Honey Egg Nog

To Serve 6:
6 eggs
¾ cup honey
6 cups ice cold milk
½ teaspoon salt

Use a rotary beater and whip eggs until lemon colored. Stir in cold milk, honey and salt. Stir well and serve.

Frosted Cocktail

Add a teaspoon of any fruit ice, to each cocktail glass of chilled fruit juice.

Chilled Orange Egg Nog

Two Glasses:
1 egg, beaten
Few grains salt
1 cup milk

1 cup strained
  orange juice
Sugar syrup

Use a rotary beater and whip mixture, add enough sugar syrup to sweeten. Pour into freezing tray of an automatic refrigerator, with temperature control set at lowest point. Stir occasionally and serve when mixture is full of tiny crystals.

Fruit Drink

2 eggs, beaten
½ cup light
  corn syrup
½ cup chilled
  evaporated
  milk

Juice 2 oranges
Juice 1 lemon
Carbonated
  water, chilled
Ice cubes

Beat eggs, beat in syrup, juices and milk. Pour over cracked ice and add carbonated water.

Fruit Juice Cocktail

1 cup canned pineapple juice
1 cup canned grapefruit juice
1 cup bottled cranberry juice
1 cup canned apricot nectar
1½ teaspoons fresh or bottled
  lime juice
Chill and serve in cocktail glasses.

Fruit Punch

3 lemons, juice
½ cup sugar
  syrup
2 cups chilled
  ginger ale

2 oranges, juice
1 pint chilled
  charged water
1 cup grapefruit
  juice

Blend fruit juice, sugar syrup and chill. Just before serving, add ginger ale, carbonated water and serve with ice cubes.

Fruit Punch Bowl

2 cups sugar
1 cup water
2 cups canned
  pineapple juice
2 cups orange
  juice

⅓ cup lemon
  juice
4 quarts chilled
  ginger ale or
  carbonated
  water

Boil sugar and 1 cup water 5 minutes, add fruit juices and chill. Just before serving, add chilled ginger ale and ice cubes.

Fruit Punch For Fifty

1 cup chopped
  pineapple (pulp
  and juice)
2 cups sugar
1 cup boiling
  water
1 cup lemon juice

1 cup hot tea,
  strain
2 cups grape juice
1 quart chilled
  Apollinaris
3½ quarts ice
  water

Add pineapple pulp to boiling water and cook gently 5 minutes, add sugar and boil another 5 minutes. Add freshly made tea, and fruit juices; chill 30 minutes then strain. Add ice water and Apollinaris just before serving and pour over a block of ice.

Fruit Punch For Fifty
(7 Quarts)

2 quarts strong
  tea, chilled
1½ quarts pine-
  apple juice,
  chilled
Juice 10 lemons
Juice 10 oranges,
  chilled
1 quart ice water

Large piece of ice
1 cup sugar
6 bottles (9 oz.)
  pale dry ginger
  ale, chilled
1 cup raspberries
Slices of orange,
  quartered

Blend all ingredients except ginger ale and chill several hours. Add ice and ginger ale just before serving. For ½ cup serving in sherbet glasses.

Fruit Punch With Tea Base
(To Serve Fifty)

2 cups lemon
  juice
1 quart sugar
  syrup
1 quart orange
  juice
2 quarts water

2 quarts strong
  tea
2 quarts shaved
  ice
Fresh pineapple
  strips

Blend lemon juice, sugar syrup, and orange juice, chill 1 hour. Just before serving blend all ingredients and pour over ice. Add a thin strip of pineapple and a maraschino cherry to each glass.

Ginger Ale Flip

2 cups grape juice
½ cup lemon
  juice
Cracked ice

3 tablespoons
  powdered sugar
3½ cups chilled
  dry ginger ale

Blend fruit juices, stir in sugar then chill. Just before serving add ginger ale and ice.

Ginger Ale Punch

Juice of 4 lemons
1 quart chilled
  ginger ale

1 pint grape juice
Sugar-syrup to
  suit taste

Blend fruit juice and syrup. Chill. Just before serving, add chilled ginger ale.

Ginger Ale With Cream

1 cup light cream　1 tablespoon
1 teaspoon Wat-　　powdered sugar
　kins Vanilla　　Pale dry ginger
Cracked ice　　　ale, chilled

Blend cream, Watkins Vanilla and sugar. Pour mixture into 3 glasses, add ice and fill glass with ginger ale. Stir mixture and serve.

Ginger Ale With Ice Cream

Add a scoop of vanilla ice cream to a tall glass then slowly fill glass with chilled ginger ale.

Grapefruit Ale

2 cups canned grapefruit juice
3½ cups dry ginger ale, chilled
Cracked ice
Blend mixture and serve cold.

Grapefruit and Orange Cocktail

1 cup grapefruit juice
1 cup orange juice
⅓ cup lemon juice
Sugar to taste
Chill and serve.

Grapefruit Flip

2 cups canned grapefruit juice
3½ cups pale dry ginger ale
2¼ cups pineapple juice
Cracked ice
Have ingredients cold and serve with cracked ice.

Grapefruit-Loganberry Flip

2 cups canned loganberry juice
2 cups canned grapefruit or
　pineapple juice
1½ cups chilled dry ginger ale
Cracked ice
Blend thoroughly and serve cold.

Grapefruit-Mint Julep

¾ cup granulated　1 pint carbonated
　sugar　　　　　　water, chilled
Fresh mint leaves　Shaved ice
Juice 6 grapefruit

Crush mint leaves with sugar and add fruit juice. Add carbonated water, ice, a sprig of mint and a green minted cherry.

Grape Juice Cocktail

Wash purple grapes and boil until skin, pulp and seeds separate. Press through clean cheesecloth. To 1 pint juice add ½ cup sugar or sugar syrup and boil 20 minutes. Chill and serve with ice cubes.

Grape Juice Cup

Serve chilled grape juice in tall glasses filled with shaved ice and add ½ the quantity of chilled carbonated water. A little lemon juice may be added.

Grape Juice Punch

2 cups grape juice Juice 4 lemons
2 cups water   Juice 2 oranges
1 cup sugar syrup

Chill all ingredients, blend, and serve in cocktail glasses.

Grape Juice Punch
(For Fifty)

2 cups strong,   2 quarts chilled
  hot tea   grape juice
1 cup lemon juice   1 quart car-
4 cups water   bonated water,
½ cup sugar   chilled
4 oranges, wash,   1 quart orange ice
  slice, remove   Fresh mint
  seeds

Prepare just before serving. Blend all ingredients and pour over ice cubes. Garnish with fresh mint.

Grape Juice Rickey

½ glass chilled   2 tablespoons
  grape juice   sugar
Juice of ½ lime

Use a shaker, add crushed ice and chilled carbonated water to fill glass.

Fruited Lemonade

Keep left over syrup from canned fruit in a covered fruit jar in the refrigerator. Add lemon juice to flavor and pour into a glass with ice cubes. Add a sprig of mint and a slice of orange.

Lemonade

6 lemons   1 to 1½ cups
3 cups ice water   sugar syrup

Wash, roll lemons, squeeze juice. Add sugar syrup, ice cubes and stir in ice water. Serve cold. The amount of sugar used depends on the acidity of the lemons.

Berry Lemonade

To each glass of lemonade add 2 tablespoons crushed fresh or canned berries—loganberries, blackberries, raspberries or strawberries. Strain fruits with seeds. Add ice cubes and top with a whole berry.

Limeade

Juice ½ to 1 lime per glass (depending on size of glass)
1 to 2 tablespoons sugar or
    sugar syrup
¼ glass crushed ice
Ice water
Shake or stir, and serve cold. (Keep limes in refrigerator.)

Lime Juice Punch

2 cups cold tea infusion
2 quarts sweet cider, chilled
Juice 2 lemons
2 oranges, sliced
1 cup granulated sugar
Fresh mint
1 quart sparking lime juice,
    chilled
Cracked ice
Have all ingredients cold. Add lime juice and cracked ice just before serving.

Lime and Orange Juice Cocktail

1 12-oz. bottle carbonated
    lime beverage, chilled
1 cup canned or fresh
    orange juice

Loganberry Cocktail

2 cups loganberry juice, chilled
1 cup orange juice
Juice 1 lemon
1 cup ice water
¼ cup sugar syrup
Blend all ingredients and serve cold.

Serve Watkins Sweetened Malted Milk

Chocolate Flavored   With Sunshine Vitamin D

For a Nourishing Drink

Hot Malted Milk Drink

For each cup, blend 3 rounded teaspoonfuls of Malted Milk with 1 tablespoon boiling water and stir to a smooth paste. Add ¾ cup hot milk heated in top of a double boiler. Whip mixture with a rotary beater and add a few drops of Watkins Vanilla.

Cold Malted Milk

For One Glass:

Blend 3 rounded teaspoonfuls of Malted Milk with 1 tablespoonful of boiling water and stir to a smooth paste. Add one glass of cold milk and whip mixture with a rotary beater. Add a drop or two of Watkins Vanilla.

Malted Egg Nog

For each cup, blend 3 rounded teaspoonfuls Malted Milk with 1 tablespoonful boiling water and stir to a paste. Add well beaten egg yolk and a few drops of Watkins Vanilla. Add ¾ cup hot or cold milk, whip with a rotary beater, and add stiffly beaten egg white. Shake briskly and serve.

Malted Milk Ice Cream Drink

Place 1 to 2 tablespoonfuls vanilla ice cream in a shaker, add 1 cup blended cold malted milk drink—following recipe for Cold Malted Milk. Shake until ice cream is dissolved.

Malted Ice Cream Soda

Blend 3 to 4 tablespoonfuls Malted Milk with 2½ tablespoons boiling water, to make a smooth paste. Add a few drops Watkins Vanilla, 1 tablespoon heavy cream, and 2 to 3 tablespoons vanilla ice cream. Put mixture in a large glass, fill remainder of glass with chilled carbonated water. Stir mixture and serve.

Milk Punch

1 cup top milk, chilled
2 tablespoons sugar or sugar syrup

¼ cup carbonated water, chilled
½ teaspoon Watkins Vanilla

Whip milk, Watkins Vanilla and sugar with a rotary beater. Just before serving add carbonated water and pour mixture from one glass to another. Serve cold.

Milk Shake

¼ teaspoon Watkins Vanilla or 2 tablespoons fruit juice or chocolate syrup

⅔ glass cold milk
Sugar to taste
Finely chopped ice

Fill glass two-thirds full of rich cold milk, stir in sugar and flavoring. Fill glass with chopped ice, shake vigorously and serve.

Banana Milk Shake

1 ripe banana
½ cup orange juice
1 tablespoon lemon juice

Sugar syrup or 2 tablespoons honey
Dash of salt
2 cups rich milk

Mash banana, add ingredients in order given (except milk) and chill. When ready to serve add milk and whip mixture with a rotary beater.

Chocolate Banana Milk Shake

4 sieved ripe bananas
4 cups milk

½ cup Watkins Malted Milk
Ice

Put bananas through sieve, add milk, sugar to suit taste, and cracked ice. Shake well and serve.

Coffee Egg Milk Shake

3 cups cold strong coffee
3 eggs, beaten
6 cups rich chilled milk
½ cup cream

Sugar to taste
½ teaspoon Watkins Vanilla
Iced carbonated water

Combine all ingredients in a shaker; blend thoroughly and add enough iced carbonated water to each glass to foam on top.

Fruit Milk Shake

1 large banana
½ cup orange juice
¼ cup lemon juice

1 cup canned pineapple juice
1 cup evaporated milk, chilled

Mash banana, add fruit juices and chill. Pour into chilled evaporated milk and whip with a rotary beater. Serve cold.

Mint Julep

1 cup lemon juice
1 bunch fresh mint
1½ cups sugar

½ cup water
3 pints ginger ale, chilled
Ice

Add mint leaves, sugar and water to lemon juice and let stand 30 minutes. Pour over a large piece of ice and add ginger ale. Serve in small glasses.

Mocha Float

6 tablespoons chocolate syrup
3 cups coffee brewed double strength

4½ cups milk
⅛ teaspoon salt
1 pint vanilla ice cream

Blend chocolate syrup with coffee and chill. Add cold milk and mix well. Pour into tall chilled glasses and top each glass with a table-spoon of ice cream.

Watkins Nectar Drinks

A sparkling, richly flavored fruit drink can be quickly made with Watkins Nectar Bases. There are several different flavors—Watkins Lemon, Cherry, Grape, Orange, Strawberry and Pineapple. All are delicious and wholesome to serve any day in the year.

As a summer beverage, serve a refreshing, tasty, colorful cold drink that will quench your thirst. Watkins Nectar Base drinks give heat resistance in the hot weather—they are satisfying, have a rich fruit flavor and are more economical than imitation drink flavors.

Keep a Supply of Watkins Nectar Base

Keep a supply of the different flavored Nectar Bases on hand to serve to your family or when unexpected guests arrive. Let the children make and enjoy a fruit drink because there is nothing synthetic or imitation in the nectar base. Watkins Nectar Bases contain a concentrated mixture and that is why they are economical. Two teaspoons of your favorite Nectar Base with sugar or sugar syrup, a glass of cold water and ice will make a delicious drink. Cool drinks lower the temperature of the body and give new energy.

Uses for Watkins Nectar Base

A special recipe folder is around every bottle of Watkins Nectar Base with recipes for Sherbet, Fruit Punch, Salad, Pudding Sauce, Cake Icing, a Dessert Gelatin or an Ice to serve with the meat course or as a dessert.

Watkins Fruit Punch

Blend Watkins Cherry, Lemon and Orange Nectar Bases in equal proportions. Add sugar syrup to suit taste and ice cold water. Serve with ice cubes.

Sweeten Watkins Nectar Drinks With Sugar Syrup

Use sugar syrup to sweeten Nectar Base Drinks instead of plain sugar. The base may be made in any quantity, stored in a covered fruit jar ready for instant use. Sugar syrup will completely dissolve while plain sugar will remain in the bottom of the glass.

Make Watkins Nectar Base Ice Cubes for Your Summer Drinks

Will Not Dilute Beverage.

Follow recipe for making Nectar Base drinks, with or without sugar. Add Watkins Color Mixture to suit taste. Blend thoroughly and pour into refrigerator trays and freeze. Use Watkins Yellow Color Mixture for the Lemon and the Red Color Mixture for the Cherry Nectar Base.

Or use colorful ice cubes in Watkins Lemon drinks. A little of the Watkins Red or Green Color Mixture added to the water in the freezing tray, will give an attractive color effect for Lemon Nectar Base drinks. Pieces of fruit as a few strawberries, cherries or raspberries may be frozen in the ice cubes.

Nectar Punch

½ cup Watkins
  Lemon Nectar
  Base
Sugar syrup to
  suit taste

3 cups iced water
  or iced tea or
  carbonated
  water

Blend Nectar Base and sugar
syrup. Stir in chilled liquid, mix
well and serve with ice cubes.

Lemon, Orange, Cherry or Grape

2 tablespoons
  Watkins Nectar
  Base (any
  flavor)

⅔ glass iced
  water
Sugar syrup to
  suit taste

Blend above mixture, shake vigorously and pour over cracked ice.

Orangeade

6 oranges
2 lemons
5 cups ice water

1½ cups sugar
  syrup
Shaved ice

Blend fruit juice with syrup and
stir in ice water. Pour over ice.

Orange Cream Drink

2 cups milk
2 cups light cream
1 cup orange juice
1 teaspoon lemon
  juice

Scant ½ cup
  sugar
4 egg whites,
  beaten stiff

Blend milk, cream, orange and
lemon juice, add sugar to suit taste
and chill. Fold in stiffly beaten
egg whites and serve.

Orange Flip

½ cup white
  grape juice
1 teaspoon sugar

2 tablespoons
  orange juice
Cracked ice

Fill glass half full with shaved ice.
Add grape juice, orange juice, sugar
and ice water. Add sprig of mint.

Orange-Lime Fizz

2 cups strained
  orange juice
½ cup granulated
  sugar
⅓ cup lime juice

1½ cups chilled
  carbonated
  water
Cracked ice

Heat 1 cup orange juice to boiling,
stir into sugar and add sprigs of
mint cut fine. Cool, strain, add
orange and lime juice. Chill. Just
before serving, add carbonated
water and shaved ice.

Orange Mint Cocktail

Juice of 6 oranges
Fresh mint
Powdered sugar
3 tablespoons lemon juice
2 tablespoons granulated sugar
Chill thoroughly and serve

Iced Peach Nectar

2 cups canned peach juice
2 cups strong tea
1 cup orange juice
⅓ cup currant jelly

Pour hot tea over jelly and stir until dissolved. Chill. Add juices and pour over cracked ice.

Pineapple Frappe

½ cup sugar
2 cups water
½ cup grape juice
Juice 1 orange
2 cups pineapple juice
Juice 2 lemons

Boil sugar with 1 cup water 5 minutes then cool. Add fruit juices and pour over cracked ice. Add second cup of water. Garnish with a thin wedge of pineapple and maraschino cherry.

Pineapple and Grapefruit Cocktail

½ cup water
2 cups pineapple juice
½ cup sugar
1 cup grapefruit juice

Boil sugar and water 5 minutes, stir to dissolve sugar. Cool, add fruit juice and chill.

Pineapple and Grape Juice Cocktail

2¼ cups canned pineapple juice, chilled
1 cup grape juice, chilled
1 cup chilled carbonated water

Blend fruit juices and chill. Just before serving add chilled carbonated water. Serve in cocktail glasses.

Pineapple Mint Julep

4 tablespoons mint jelly
4 tablespoons sugar
Juice 4 lemons
4 cups tea infusion
2 cups canned pineapple juice, chilled
1 pint ginger ale, chilled
Fresh mint

Make tea strong, allowing 1 teaspoon of orange pekoe for each cup boiling water; let stand 5 minutes and strain. Pour hot tea over mint jelly, stir in sugar. Cool. Add pineapple, lemon juice, and ginger ale.

Pineapple Cream Frappe

Break an egg into a mixing glass, add 4 tablespoons pineapple syrup and a scoop of vanilla ice cream. Shake briskly and fill glass with chilled carbonated water. Add extra ice cream just before serving.

Pineapple Fruit Punch

1 quart pineapple juice	Juice 1 lemon
Juice 3 oranges	Juice 1 grapefruit
½ cup sugar syrup	½ cup crushed pineapple

Blend all ingredients, add ice cubes and serve cold.

Pineapple-Tea Drink

2 cups pineapple juice	Sugar syrup
Juice 3 lemons	1 to 2 cups strong tea
1 quart ice water	Ice cubes

Blend all ingredients; sweeten to suit taste.

Raspberry Cocktail

1 cup raspberries	1 cup tea
1 cup currants	2 cups boiling water
1 lemon	
1 cup sugar syrup	

Crush raspberries and currants and strain through clean cheesecloth. Pour boiling water through the pulp in the cloth but do not squeeze, as the juice will be cloudy. Add sugar syrup, blend all ingredients and chill.

Raspberry-ade

4 quarts raspberries	1 quart cider vinegar

Pick over berries, wash in a wire basket under running cold water, cover with vinegar, cover container and let stand 4 days. Strain. To each cup of juice add 1 cup sugar. Boil 15 minutes and bottle.

To serve, blend one part raspberry juice syrup with three parts ice cold water. Fill tall glass with crushed ice, then add raspberry-ade.

Rhine Wine Punch

(To Serve 20)
3 tablespoons
 sugar
½ cup cold water
6 tablespoons
 maraschino
4 bottles Rhine
 wine
2 oranges, quar-
 tered and sliced

2 lemons, quar-
 tered and sliced
1 small pineapple,
 peeled, sliced
 and diced
1 quart car-
 bonated water,
 chilled
1 large piece of
 ice for punch
 bowl

Blend sugar, water and maraschino. Add wine, fruit, carbonated
water and blend all ingredients.

Spiced Fruit Juice Cocktail

1 cup orange juice
½ cup pineapple
 juice
⅓ cup sugar
 syrup
⅔ cup ice water

½ teaspoon Wat-
 kins Nutmeg
¼ teaspoon Wat-
 kins Cinnamon
1½ pints sweet
 cider

Add spices to fruit juice and sugar
syrup, chill 2 to 3 hours. Strain,
then just before serving add ice
water and sweet cider, stir briskly
and serve with cracked ice.

Iced Lemon Tea

1 cup lemon juice
½ cup sugar
2 quarts strong
 tea, strain and
 cool

2 quarts crushed
 ice
Slices of orange
Bunch crisp mint

Blend lemon juice and sugar, stir
in tea and pour over the cracked
ice. Garnish with slice of orange
and a sprig of mint.

Tomato Juice Cocktail

3 cups chilled
 tomato juice
½ teaspoon salt
¼ teaspoon sugar

5 teaspoons lemon
 juice
5 drops tabasco
 sauce

Blend all ingredients and chill.
Add a wedge of lemon to each glass.

Tomato-Lime Cocktail

½ cucumber
1 can (14 oz.)
 tomato juice
⅓ teaspoon salt

1 tablespoon fresh
 lime juice
Dash Watkins
 Celery Salt

Peel, chop cucumber fine and add
to chilled tomato juice. Chill 1
hour. Strain and force cucumber
through sieve. Just before serving,
add salt and fresh lime juice.

Vegetable Juice Cocktail

Serve chilled canned vegetable cocktail, a blend of several vegetable juices, and add a dash of Watkins Celery Salt and Watkins Onion Seasoning.

Vegetable Juice Cocktail

1 No. 3 can tomatoes	1 sliced minced onion
Sprig bay leaf	1 chopped carrot
1 cup minced celery leaves	2 cups water
3 celery stalks	1 teaspoon salt

Simmer mixture a half hour, strain, rub pulp through sieve. Add a dash of Worcestershire sauce and chill. Add a little lemon juice before serving. Watkins Seasonings will add a rich flavor to vegetable juice.

Venice Flip

1 cup boiling water	¼ canned pineapple juice
16 marshmallows	¾ cup lemon juice
¾ cup orange juice	1 cup ice water

Add marshmallows to boiling water and let them melt. Cool, add fruit juices and water. Add crushed ice and chill.

Vienna Grape Drink

Pour chilled grape juice into a tall glass, add a scoop of vanilla ice cream or one of lime, lemon or orange ice. Stir until dissolved. Serve at once.

Popular
American and French Desserts

The desserts listed on a French menu are not numerous because the popular demand is for fruit, cooked in a sugar syrup, with wine as the flavoring. This is called Compote of Fruit and includes peaches, pears, cherries, apricots, strawberries and fresh pineapple; the fruits are cooked separately and chilled.

In Paris, the term French Ice Cream is applied to ice cream containing a high percentage of egg or egg yolk, a rich custard with heavy cream. In the United States, the term "French" is applied to an ice cream of higher butterfat content than standard ice cream contains.

Frozen desserts made in the home are divided into two main groups: those frozen with stirring, and those frozen without stirring.

French Desserts Frozen Without Stirring

Biscuit

A parfait mixture with stiffly beaten egg whites added. The mixture is stirred until partly frozen, then packed in individual paper cases. The molds are then placed in trays in the mechanical refrigerator, or the molds are packed in a freezer, with layers of waxed paper, and chilled until firm.

Bombe

A combination of two or more frozen mixtures, packed in layers in a covered mold and chilled in a freezer, packed with salt and ice, and chilled from 3 to 5 hours. The chilled mold is lined with a frozen ice or ice cream, then filled with a rich custard and whipped cream, and chilled until firm.

Mousse

A sweetened flavored whipped cream, packed in a chilled mold and frozen without stirring. Softened, dissolved gelatin may be added, to make a stiffer dessert. Pack mold in a freezer, with 4 parts ice and 1 part salt; chill several hours.

Parfait

A hot thick syrup is poured over well beaten egg yolks or stiffly beaten egg whites, with sugar and Watkins flavoring. Whipped cream is folded into the mixture, then packed and frozen without stirring, until firm.

Neapolitan

Two or more kinds of ice cream and ices (previously frozen by stirring), are arranged in lengthwise layers and chilled in a mold by packing in a freezer, with a mixture of 3 parts ice and 1 of salt.

Desserts Frozen With Stirring

American Ice Cream

Generally, American ice cream is a mixture of custard, sugar and cream, with flavoring; a less rich dessert than French ice cream.

Philadelphia Ice Cream

A frozen rich dessert made with coffee cream (no eggs), sugar and flavoring.

Junket Ice Cream

Milk is first blended with a dissolved rennet tablet, then cream, sugar and flavoring are added; a smooth ice cream with less butter-fat than American or French ice cream.

Frappe

A water-ice frozen to a mush, by using a high proportion of salt in the freezing, to give a coarse granular texture.

Frozen Pudding

American type ice cream made with the addition of fruits and nuts, in which either American or Philadelphia ice cream may be used as the base.

Ice as a Dessert

A frozen mixture of water and sugar, with fruit juices added.

Sherbets and Sorbets

A dessert made with several kinds of blended fruit; such as an ice made with fruit juice, sugar and water, or fruit juice, sugar and milk. An ice is a sweetened fruit juice frozen; a sherbet is a plain ice with stiffly beaten egg whites added. Milk sherbet, blended with a little lemon juice and fresh fruit juice, is called a Velvet Sherbet, a dessert of smooth velvety texture.

Almond Ice-Box Cake

¾ cup butter
1¼ cups sifted powdered sugar
3 eggs
½ teaspoon Watkins Almond Extract
12 macaroons
1 cup chopped toasted almonds
1 cup heavy cream
1½ dozen lady fingers or sponge cake

Cream butter thoroughly, gradually add sugar and mix well. Add Watkins Almond Extract and beaten egg yolks. Add stiffly beaten egg whites, chopped nuts and fold in whipped cream.

Line a three pint mold with waxed paper; place a layer of macaroons on the bottom with whole toasted almonds. Line sides of mold with lady fingers arranging them vertically. Place half the cream mixture in mold, cover with macaroons; cover with remaining cream custard, and chill 24 hours. Unmold on a chilled platter and garnish with sweetened whipped cream put through a pastry tube.

Chocolate Ice-Box Cake

Follow recipe given above and add ½ pound grated sweet chocolate, melted, to the creamed butter and sugar. Substitute Watkins Vanilla for Almond Flavoring.

Almond Custard

1 teaspoon Wat-
kins Almond
Extract
Shredded
almonds or
macaroon
crumbs

2 eggs, beaten
1¼ cups
powdered sugar
2 cups milk
⅛ teaspoon salt
1½ cups cream

Make a custard in top of double boiler with beaten eggs, sugar, milk and salt. Stir and cook over boiling water until mixture begins to thicken. Cool. Add cream, Watkins Almond Extract, and almonds. Freeze. Will make 1 quart.

Apricot Ice-Box Cake

1 sponge cake
3 cups cooked,
sweetened
apricots
1 teaspoon gelatin
softened in
2 tablespoons
cold water

1 egg, beaten
2 tablespoons
sugar
½ teaspoon Wat-
kins Vanilla
1 cup whipping
cream

Line bottom of refrigerator tray with sponge cake. Heat apricots and add softened gelatin, stir only to dissolve gelatin. Cool, then spread over cake. Beat egg, beat in sugar and Watkins Vanilla, fold in whipped cream and spread mixture over apricots. Chill 2 hours. Serve with Apricot Puree Sauce.

Apricot Puree Sauce

Cook fully ripe apricots in sugar syrup (the proportion ½ cup sugar to 1 cup hot water), and cook fruit gently until tender. Remove apricots and put through a sieve. Add fruit pulp to syrup and continue cooking until mixture thickens. Cool, then chill and serve over a Rice Conde or vanilla ice cream. If canned apricots are used, cook until soft, in the drained canned syrup; remove fruit, put through a sieve, add fruit pulp to syrup and continue cooking until mixture thickens.

Apricot or Peach Dessert

2 tablespoons
lemon juice
1 cup sweetened
fresh or dried
fruit (cooked—
drained) pulp,
chilled

1 cup irradiated
evaporated
milk
½ teaspoon Wat-
kins Lemon
Extract

Chill milk thoroughly and whip. Add lemon juice and whip very stiff. Fold in chilled fruit pulp and Watkins Lemon Extract. Pour into freezing tray, set control to coldest point, and chill mixture until firm.

Apricot Sherbet

¾ cup canned
   apricot juice
1 tablespoon
   honey

16 marshmallows
4 egg whites,
   beaten stiff

Place cut marshmallows and apricot juice in top of a double boiler and heat over boiling water until melted. Remove from the fire. Add lemon juice, fruit pulp and honey. When cold pour into freezing tray. Chill. When mixture begins to freeze stir in the stiffly beaten egg whites. Freeze until firm.

Banana Date Roll

1 cup whipping
   cream
½ lb. marsh-
   mallows—
   cut fine
½ lb. finely
   chopped dates
3 ripe bananas,
   sliced

½ cup nuts, cut
8 Graham
   crackers,
   crushed
1 teaspoon grated
   lemon rind
1 teaspoon Wat-
   kins Vanilla

Whip cream until stiff. Fold in cut marshmallows, Watkins Vanilla, dates, nuts and bananas. Form into a roll, 3 inches in diameter. Roll in Graham cracker crumbs mixed with lemon rind. Chill about 4 hours. Cut into 1 inch slices and serve with whipped cream.

Baked Alaska

Place an 8x6 inch sponge cake on several thicknesses of heavy paper on a baking sheet. Cover cake with one quart vanilla ice cream firmly frozen. Let cake extend ½ inch beyond edge of ice cream.

Beat 5 egg whites until stiff, then gradually beat in ½ cup sugar until well blended. Spread meringue over entire cake and ice cream and sprinkle ¼ cup powdered sugar completely over meringue. Bake in a hot oven 400 degrees F., about 5 minutes, or until lightly browned.

Individual Baked Alaska

Scoop out center from thick rounds of sponge cake and fill center with vanilla ice cream. Heap meringue on sides and top and place on several thicknesses of heavy paper on a baking sheet. Bake in a hot oven 400 degrees F., about 2 to 3 minutes, just to a light brown.

Place sifted flour in a mixing bowl, make a hollow in the center. Soften compressed yeast in warm (not hot), milk and pour into hollow. Cover and let stand 5 minutes. Add beaten eggs, mix with dough and knead 5 minutes. Cover bowl with a clean towel and let stand in a warm place 30 minutes.

Melt butter over hot water and cool, then add to dough with sugar and salt. Beat dough and turn on a lightly floured board. Toss and knead five minutes. At first the dough will be stringy but continue the kneading and it will become smooth. Do not add more flour. Pat evenly into a greased tube pan, cover pan and let rise in a warm place to double in bulk. Bake in a moderate, 375 degree F. oven 40 minutes, or until done. Loosen from side of pan while warm and invert on a cake rack. Serve with rum sauce. If desired, bake in muffin tins; grease tin, fill half full with dough. Let rise to double in bulk, then bake in a hot oven, 400 degrees F., 25 minutes or until done.

Baba Au Rhum Dessert

2 cups sifted all-purpose flour
1 cake compressed yeast
¼ cup warm milk
⅓ cup melted butter
3 eggs, beaten
1½ tablespoons sugar
Few grains salt
1 teaspoon Watkins Vanilla

Blend sugar and water, cook over low heat to dissolve sugar, then boil 2 minutes and cool. Add rum and stir to blend. Place cake on serving platter, bottom-side up, and carefully spoon the sauce evenly over surface. Let cake stand 1 hour, then turn right side up. Cut into slices about 1 inch thick and serve.

Rum Sauce

1 cup granulated sugar
½ cup water
½ cup rum

Variation:

Top with vanilla ice cream or sweetened whipped cream. A combination of rum and any fruit sauce may be used over cake, or peach pulp, strawberries or any wine instead of rum sauce.

Biscuit Tortoni

8 egg yolks	1 cup sugar
1 quart whipped cream	2 teaspoons Watkins Vanilla

Beat egg yolks with a rotary whip adding a few grains salt. Gradually beat in sugar. Stir constantly and cook mixture in top of a double boiler until mixture thickens. Remove from fire, set in a pan of cold water until cold. Add Watkins Vanilla, fold in whipped cream. Turn into individual molds, sprinkle top with crumbled macaroons and chill in automatic refrigerator tray until firm. Allow several hours to chill.

Charlotte Russe

2 cups heavy cream	½ cup sherry
½ cup sugar	2 tablespoons cold water
2 tablespoons gelatin	Lady fingers

Whip cream, gradually beat in sugar, then stir in wine. Soften gelatin in cold water 5 minutes then stir over hot water to dissolve. Cool. Stir into whipped cream, beat well and chill. Line a chilled pudding mold with single lady fingers, then fill center of mold with cream mixture. Chill until firm. Unmold and decorate with sweetened whipped cream, maraschino cherries, or ripe strawberries.

French Cherry Cake

4 eggs	½ cup sugar
2 egg yolks	2 cups sweet cherries, pitted
1 cup sifted cake flour	1 teaspoon Watkins Lemon Extract
¼ cup butter, melted	

Beat eggs and egg yolks lightly. Add sugar and heat over very low fire until just lukewarm, stirring constantly. Remove from heat and whip with a rotary beater until mixture doubles in volume. Sift flour, a little at a time, over egg mixture and fold in alternately with melted butter. Turn into a buttered and lightly floured baking pan (9x12). Drop cherries over entire top and bake in a moderate, 350 degree F. oven, about 50 minutes or until cake shrinks slightly from edge of pan. Serve with a cherry sauce.

French Cherry Sauce

⅓ cup port wine
⅓ cup sherry wine
1 4-oz. glass currant jelly
Juice 2 oranges

Juice 1 lemon
2 tablespoons butter
2 cups sweet cherries

Blend wine, jelly, fruit juices, and butter and place over low heat, stir to dissolve jelly. Add cherries, heat and serve.

Delicious Cheese Cake

6 egg yolks
¾ cup granulated sugar
Juice 1 lemon
Grated rind of 1 lemon
3 tablespoons sifted flour
2 lbs. cottage cheese, put through ricer
1 cup heavy cream

Few grains salt
¼ lb. butter blended with an extra ⅓ cup sugar
6 egg whites, beaten stiff
1 teaspoon Watkins Vanilla
24 zwieback (1 package) rolled

Beat egg yolks in a large bowl until creamy, gradually beat in the ¾ cup sugar and blend thoroughly. Add lemon juice and rind. Add flour and mix well. Use a wooden spoon and add cottage cheese. Add salt, then fold in cream. Fold in stiffly beaten egg whites.

To Prepare Spring-Form Cake Pan: Use a pan 2½ inches deep by 10 inches.

Melt butter over hot water, cool slightly then stir in sugar and zwieback crumbs with 1 tablespoon Watkins Cinnamon. Blend mixture throughly and spread over bottom, sides, and around center of cake-tube, reserving ¾ cup of the zwieback-butter-sugar-mixture to sprinkle over top of cake before baking. Fold cheese mixture into spring-form mold and sprinkle top of cake with crumb mixture.

Light oven (do not pre-heat) and set control at 375 degrees F. Bake cake 1 hour then test with a straw, if done, turn off heat. **Important:** Open oven door slightly and support door with handle of a broom. Let cake remain in oven, until cold. When almost cold, run a knife around the edge of the pan. When cold, lift cake on to a serving plate by unfastening spring at side of pan. Splintered toasted almonds may be placed over top of cake. Cover cake loosely with waxed paper and keep in tin box first day, then keep in refrigerator.

French Chocolate Mousse

6 oz. dark sweet chocolate
½ oz. bitter chocolate
4 tablespoons cold water
1 teaspoon Watkins Vanilla
3 egg yolks
3 egg whites, stiffly beaten

Break chocolate, place in pan with water, and stir over low heat until dissolved. Remove from fire, stir in Watkins Vanilla. Add unbeaten egg yolks one at a time and beat well. Add stiffly beaten egg whites and blend thoroughly. Pour into sherbet glasses and chill 3 hours.

Coconut Glace Dessert

Grate meat of 2 coconuts, add 1 quart whipping cream blended with 2 cups powdered sugar. Add 2 teaspoons Watkins Vanilla and fold in stiffly beaten whites of 4 eggs. Whip mixture and freeze.

Coffee Bavarian

1½ tablespoons gelatin
3 tablespoons cold water
1 cup sugar
⅓ cup water
3 egg yolks
Dash salt
½ cup strong coffee
2 teaspoons Watkins Vanilla
2 cups evaporated milk, chilled and whipped

Soften gelatin in 3 tablespoons cold water. Boil sugar with ⅓ cup water to thread stage and beat hot syrup into beaten egg yolks. Add salt. Dissolve softened gelatin in hot coffee and stir into egg mixture. Cool and add Watkins Vanilla. When mixture begins to set, add milk beaten stiff. Turn into a mold and chill.

French Compote of Fruit

To poach fruit—apricots, peaches, cherries, strawberries, pears—make a sugar syrup in the proportion of ½ cup sugar to 1 cup hot water, and cook 10 minutes. Add ripe fruit and cook slowly, covered, without stirring, until fruit is tender. Peaches, pears or apricots may be halved, or cooked whole, if desired. Carefully remove fruit so as not to disturb its shape, and chill. Continue cooking syrup until thick, remove from fire, add a little Kirsch and pour over fruit. A little lemon juice added to the syrup in cooking pears will keep the fruit white.

Coupe Jacques

Pack chilled ice cream mold with a lining of ice cream or a hard-frozen ice, add a filling of fruit puree (see apricot or peach puree sauce), or add strawberries, marrons or macedoine of fruit. Add several thicknesses of waxed paper over mold then add the cover. Pack in a freezer with 4 parts ice and one of salt and chill several hours. Garnish with whipped cream and fresh whole berries.

Cranberry Ice

4 cups cranberries Few grains salt
3 cups water ½ cup orange
2 cups sugar juice

Wash, drain, then cook berries and water 10 minutes. Add sugar, salt, orange juice and stir until sugar is dissolved. Put mixture through sieve and force as much pulp as possible. Cool. Turn into refrigerator tray and freeze. When slightly frozen, remove to a chilled bowl and whip with a rotary beater. Return mixture to tray and freeze until firm.

Creme de Menthe Ice

1⅔ cups sugar 3 cups water
½ cup lemon ¼ cup creme de
juice menthe syrup

Cook sugar and water together 5 minutes and cool. Add lemon juice and creme de menthe and freeze in refrigerator tray until firm. Stir mixture several times during freezing.

Crepe Dessert

1 egg, beaten 2 tablespoons
3 tablespoons brandy
flour Enough milk for
Dash salt a very thin
Little grated batter (pour
lemon peel like milk)

Place a little olive oil in a small frying pan, heat and keep shaking pan to avoid burning. Pour in a little batter to make a thin coating, and brown. Sprinkle with powdered sugar, or spread with currant jelly; roll and serve hot. The thinner the crepes, the better.

Crepe Suzettes (French Pancake)

1 cup sifted flour 2 tablespoons
½ teaspoon salt melted butter
3 eggs, beaten 1 teaspoon grated
1 cup milk lemon rind

Mix and sift together flour and salt. Blend beaten eggs and milk, stir in butter and lemon rind, and stir into flour mixture. Fry on a hot greased griddle, making cakes 3 inches in diameter. Re-heat in Suzette sauce and serve hot on a hot plate.

Suzette Sauce

6 lumps sugar	¼ teaspoon
1 lemon	Watkins Vanilla
1 orange	1 pony of brandy
¼ cup sweet	and 1 pony of
butter	cointreau, if
¼ cup powdered	desired
sugar	

Rub lumps of sugar over orange and lemon, then add juice from orange. Place butter in a hot chafing dish, add sugar, orange juice, Watkins Vanilla. Reduce heat. Add baked crepe Suzettes and cook until sauce is reduced to a heavy syrup. Fold crepes in quarters, sprinkle with powdered sugar. **Use care in removing top of chafing dish from fire.** Pour brandy and cointreau on cakes and serve 3 to a person, as you light the brandy.

Custard Cheese Cake

1½ cups sifted	1 teaspoon salt
cake flour	1 egg, slightly
½ cup butter or	beaten
margarine	¼ cup milk

Filling:

½ lb. cottage	4 eggs
cheese	3 tablespoons
⅓ cup melted	raisins
butter	½ cup sugar
1 cup sour cream	1 teaspoon
	Watkins Vanilla

Mix and sift flour and salt. Cut in shortening with a pastry blender. Beat eggs, stir in milk, and add in small amounts to flour. Use a fork and stir lightly to blend. Shape into a ball and roll about ⅛ inch thickness on a lightly floured board. Line a 7-inch spring mold with the pastry.
Blend cheese, shortening, cream, beaten egg yolks, raisins, sugar and Watkins Vanilla; fold in stiffly beaten egg whites. Turn into pastry lined pan and bake in a moderate, 350 degree F. oven about 45 minutes or until custard is set.

Ginger Caramel Cakes

1 can sweetened	24 ginger snaps
condensed milk	1 teaspoon
1 cup chopped	Watkins Vanilla
walnuts	Whipping cream

Place unopened can of condensed milk in boiling water, have cover tight and boil 3 hours, cover pan. Cool. Open can and whip milk until creamy, then beat in nuts. Use 4 ginger snaps for each cake. Spread the caramel, Watkins Vanilla, nut mixture between ginger snaps and press together. Spread top and sides with whipped cream and chill in the refrigerator.

Banana Ice Cream
(Hand Freezer)

2 egg yolks, beaten	1 cup milk
⅓ cup sugar	1 cup banana pulp
1 teaspoon gelatin	1 tablespoon lemon juice
2 tablespoons cold water	3 cups light cream

Beat egg yolks, gradually beat in sugar and milk. Heat in double boiler. Soften gelatin 3 minutes in cold water and stir into hot milk. Cool. Mash ripe bananas and add lemon juice. Add to milk mixture, then add cream. Freeze in hand-freezer, using 8 parts ice to one of salt. Let stand 1 hour to flavor.

Bisque Ice Cream

Add 1 cup toasted macaroon crumbs to your favorite ice cream mixture before freezing.

Chocolate Ice Cream
(Hand Freezer)

2 squares unsweetened chocolate	½ cup sugar
	1 egg yolk
	1 quart cream
2 tablespoons honey	2 teaspoons Watkins Vanilla

Melt chocolate over hot water, add sugar and honey and mix well. Blend beaten egg yolk with ¼ cup cream and add to warm chocolate mixture. Stir and cook mixture over hot water until smooth and slightly thickened. Cool. Add Watkins Vanilla. Stir in remaining cream. Whip with rotary beater. Pour into freezer using 4 parts ice to 1 of salt. When firm, remove dasher and pack, using 3 parts ice to 1 part salt. Let stand 1 hour to flavor.

French Ice Cream

1 pint cream	1 cup sugar
1 quart milk	2 teaspoons Watkins Vanilla
8 egg yolks	

Heat milk and half the sugar in top of a double boiler. Beat egg yolks with a rotary whip until lemon colored, gradually beat in remaining sugar. Stir in 1 cup hot milk and blend with beaten egg yolks, then stir egg mixture into hot milk. Stir and heat over low heat until creamy, do not boil. Cool and chill. Add cream, Watkins Vanilla and freeze.

Havana Ice Cream

To any rich ice cream mixture, add ½ cup chopped black walnuts and 1 cup chopped raisins soaked in a little brandy.

Neapolitan Ice Cream

Pack ice cream tinted in three colors and differently flavored, in layers in a pudding mold with tight cover. Pack mold in a freezer with 4 parts ice to 1 of salt and chill several hours or until firm. May be made of two layers ice cream and one layer of sherbet.

Peach Ice Cream
(Hand Freezer)

1 pint cream
1 quart milk
8 egg yolks
1 cup sugar

1 pint peach pulp
1 teaspoon Watkins Almond Extract

Put milk and one-half of sugar (stir mixture) in top of a double boiler, heat. Beat egg yolks with a rotary whip, beat in remaining sugar, a little at a time. Add a little of the hot milk to beaten egg yolks, then stir egg mixture into hot milk. Stir and heat over low heat until creamy **but do not boil.** Remove from fire and chill. Add peach pulp, almond extract, and freeze. Use 8 parts ice to 1 part salt. Let stand one hour to flavor.

Peppermint Ice Cream
(No Sugar Required)

½ lb. peppermint stick candy
1 cup milk

2 cups cream
1 teaspoon Watkins Vanilla

Grind candy, soak overnight in milk, in refrigerator. Stir in whipped cream or whipped chilled evaporated milk. Add Watkins Vanilla. Pour in refrigerator tray and freeze several hours until firm.

Quick Peppermint Ice Cream
(No Sugar)

20 marshmallows
1 cup hot milk
1 cup crushed peppermint candy

1 cup heavy cream, whipped
1 teaspoon Watkins Vanilla

Cut marshmallows and stir into hot milk, when dissolved remove from fire, cool then chill. Fold marshmallow mixture into whipped cream and beat until smooth. Fold in crushed candy and Watkins Vanilla. Turn into freezing tray of an automatic refrigerator and freeze 3 to 4 hours or until firm. Stir twice during freezing. For Sunday dinner, make and chill overnight.

Pineapple Ice Cream

Follow recipe for Peach Ice Cream and substitute 1 part canned, crushed pineapple for the peach pulp, and Watkins Vanilla or Lemon Extract or Almond Flavoring.

Pineapple Sherry Ice Cream Refrigerator

20 marshmallows
⅔ cup milk
½ cup drained canned crushed pineapple
⅛ teaspoon salt
4 tablespoons sherry
1 cup heavy cream

Add cut marshmallows to milk, stir and melt over hot water. Chill until mixture is slightly thickened. Stir in pineapple, salt and sherry. Fold in whipped cream. Pour into automatic freezing tray and freeze until firm.

Italian Dessert

8 fresh ripe peaches
1 cup almonds, blanched
1 tablespoon finely cut candied orange peel
3 bitter almonds
¾ cup sugar
½ cup water
2 teaspoons rose water
4 tablespoons sherry

Peel, halve, remove stone from peaches, crush 4 peach halves to a pulp. Pound almonds to a paste. Add rose water, ¼ cup of sugar, orange peel and peach pulp. Fill remaining peach halves with this mixture. Place in a buttered baking dish and bake in a moderate, 350 degree F. oven, 30 minutes or until tender. Baste frequently with a syrup made of the remaining ½ cup sugar, ½ cup water and sherry. Chill.

Lemon Chiffon Pie

1 cup water
⅞ cup sugar
1½ teaspoons grated lemon rind
Watkins Yellow Color Mixture
½ teaspoon salt
¼ cup cornstarch
3 tablespoons lemon juice
4 egg whites
1 baked (9 inch) pastry shell

To make yellow coloring, add 1 drop Watkins Yellow Color Mixture to 1 teaspoon water, and use ½ teaspoon of this mixture.
Dissolve cornstarch in lemon juice. Blend water, 6 tablespoons sugar, salt, lemon rind and the yellow color. Bring to a boil. Add dissolved cornstarch and cook until mixture boils and thickens, stirring constantly. Remove from heat. Beat egg whites until stiff, gradually beat in remaining ½ cup sugar and beat until sugar is dissolved. Fold cornstarch mixture into egg whites. Pour filling into baked chilled pie crust. Chill and serve.

Sherry Lemon Pie

½ cup butter	Juice 2 lemons
1 cup sugar	⅛ teaspoon Wat-
½ tablespoon	kins Nutmeg
flour	3 eggs, separated
½ wine glass	1 standard recipe
sherry	plain pastry

Cream butter, beat in sugar and flour and mix well. Add lemon juice, sherry and Watkins Nutmeg. Add well beaten egg yolks and whip until light. Fold in stiffly beaten egg whites. Turn into a pastry-lined pie pan and bake in a hot oven, 450 degrees F., 10 minutes, reduce heat to 325 degrees F., and bake to a nice brown and center is firm when tested with a knife.

Macaroon Bavarian Cream

¾ cup sugar	1 teaspoon
2 egg whites	Watkins Vanilla
½ cup boiling	1 cup heavy cream
water	½ cup
Few grains salt	maraschino
1 tablespoon	cherries cut
gelatin softened	into eighths
in 2 tablespoons	½ cup
cold water	macaroons,
5 minutes	crumbled

Boil sugar and water 5 minutes, add softened gelatin. Remove from fire. Slowly add to stiffly beaten egg whites and whip constantly until cold. Fold in Watkins Vanilla and whipped cream. Add macaroons and cherries. Chill several hours. Unmold and serve with whipped cream and whole cherries.

Macedoine of Fresh Fruits

Wash, drain, and cut fresh pears, apricots, plums, cherries and small berries such as strawberries and raspberries. Add sugar syrup to sweeten, flavored with a little Kirsch, Orange Curacao or Maraschino. Place in the refrigerator, cover dish with waxed paper, and chill at least one hour.
VARIATION:
COUPE JACQUES:
Arrange strawberry or lemon ice as a lining in a dessert bowl and fill center with macedoine of fresh fruit.

Mint Ice

2 cups sugar	Watkins Pepper-
4 cups water	mint Flavoring
Juice 2 lemons	¼ teaspoon salt
Dash Watkins	2 egg whites,
Green Color	beaten stiff
Mixture	

Boil sugar and water together 5 minutes. Cool. Add lemon juice, mint flavoring and Watkins Green Color Mixture. Freeze in refrigerator tray until firm. Remove to chilled bowl and whip briskly. Fold in stiffly beaten egg whites adding salt. Freeze mixture until firm.

Maple Almond Mousse

1 cup maple syrup
1 cup salted almonds, chopped
4 eggs
2 cups whipping cream
1 teaspoon Watkins Vanilla

Rub salt from almonds. Heat maple syrup to boiling, reduce heat and simmer. Add chopped almonds and stir to prevent burning. When syrup begins to thicken, beat mixture and slowly add syrup to the well beaten eggs. Place in top of double boiler, stir and cook 3 minutes. Cool. Fold in whipped cream and add Watkins Vanilla. Pour into freezing tray and freeze until firm.

Marron Glace

1 pint whipping cream
½ cup marron glaces
¼ cup syrup from marrons
½ cup sherry

Whip cream until it thickens. Stir in marrons cut into pieces. Add syrup and sherry. Pour into an automatic refrigerator and freeze. Stir once or twice during freezing. Serve in chilled glasses; top with cut marrons.

Orange Bavarian Cream

1 tablespoon plain gelatin
¼ cup cold water
¾ cup boiling water
⅛ cup sugar
½ cup orange juice
2 teaspoons lemon juice
½ cup light cream
Macaroon crumbs

Soften gelatin in cold water 5 minutes then stir and dissolve over boiling water. Dissolve sugar in fruit juice and stir into gelatin. Chill until mixture thickens but is syrupy. Whip with a rotary beater until fluffy and fold in cream. Brush a dessert mold with salad oil and dust with macaroon crumbs. Pour in dessert and chill until firm. Unmold on a chilled platter and garnish with orange sections.

Orange Bisque

1 pint heavy cream
4 egg yolks
½ cup sugar
4 egg whites, beaten stiff
1 teaspoon Watkins Vanilla

Use a rotary beater and whip yolks until creamy. Beat in sugar a little at a time. Add whipped cream and Watkins Vanilla. Fold in stiffly beaten egg whites. Pour into a chilled mold, cover top with waxed paper, add tightly fitting cover and rub seal with margarine. Pack in a freezer with cracked ice and salt and chill several hours or until firm. Just before serving, sprinkle top with pistachio nuts.

Orange Sherbet

2 egg whites,
  beaten stiff
¾ cup light
  corn syrup
Juice of 1 lemon

½ cup orange
  juice
2 cups evaporated
  milk—chill
  and whip

Beat egg whites until stiff, then slowly beat in the corn syrup and fruit juices. Beat in milk. Blend well and pour mixture into refrigerator tray. When half frozen, beat until smooth, using a chilled bowl. Return to refrigerator tray and freeze until firm.

Peach-Almond Ice Box Cake

½ cup butter
1¼ cups
  confectioner's
  sugar
3 eggs
1 cup mashed
  fresh peaches
1 cup whipping
  cream

¾ cup chopped
  toasted
  almonds
½ teaspoon Watkins Almond
  Extract
12 lady fingers
12 macaroons,
  crushed

Cream butter thoroughly, gradually beat in sugar. Add beaten egg yolks, peaches and almonds. Fold in stiffly beaten egg whites; add whipped cream and flavoring. Line a mold with lady fingers and crushed macaroons. Pour in filling and chill several hours or overnight. Unmold and serve with whipped cream. Sprinkle top with toasted chopped almonds.

Peach Melba

Make a syrup with ½ cup sugar to 1 cup water, and boil 10 minutes. Add carefully peeled peaches cut into halves, cover pan and cook until fruit is tender; remove fruit and chill. Serve a peach half, filled with vanilla ice cream, pour raspberry sauce over the peach and ice cream, and sprinkle with sliced blanched almonds.

Peach Melba Raspberry Sauce No. 1

Put washed ripe raspberries into a saucepan with a little butter, add sugar to taste, and a very little water. Cook over a slow fire, stirring to prevent burning. Mash through a sieve as for a puree. Remove from fire, and add a little Kirsch.

Peach Melba Raspberry Sauce No. 2

1 cup strained
  raspberry pulp
Juice 1 lemon

½ cup powdered
  sugar

Blend, let stand overnight. Chill. Beat occasionally until smooth. Add more sugar if needed. Keep covered in the refrigerator.

Peach Bombe

Carefully line a chilled melon mold with well frozen peach ice cream. Pack all curves and corners with a thick layer of the ice cream. Fill center with a peach mousse mixture. Add waxed paper, then tight fitting cover. Rub margarine around seal to prevent salt entering. Pack in a freezer with 4 parts ice to 1 part salt, and chill 4 to 5 hours. Or pack in trays of the automatic refrigerator and allow 4 to 5 hours to freeze.

Peach Mousse

1 envelope
   unflavored
   gelatin
¼ cup cold water
1½ cups peach
   pulp
2 cups cream or
   chilled
   evaporated
   milk, whipped

½ cup
   confectioner's
   sugar
1 tablespoon
   lemon juice
¼ teaspoon salt
½ teaspoon Watkins Almond
   Extract

Soften gelatin in cold water 5 minutes, then stir over boiling water until dissolved. Peel and mash ripe peaches, put through strainer, stir in sugar, gelatin, and fold in whipped cream. Add lemon juice, salt and Watkins Almond Extract. Turn .into refrigerator tray and freeze several hours, or overnight for a luncheon. Or place in a chilled mold, cover with waxed paper, add cover, rub seal with margarine and pack in ice and salt for 4 hours.

Peach Sherbet

3 cups canned
   peaches
1 tablespoon
   peach syrup
1 tablespoon
   lemon juice

12 marshmallows
2 egg whites
⅛ teaspoon salt
2 tablespoons
   granulated
   sugar

Drain peaches, mash pulp and reserve juice. Blend syrup with juice, add cut marshmallows and heat over hot water until marshmallows are melted. Cool. Add lemon juice and mashed peaches. Pour mixture into freezing tray and freeze until firm around edge. Fold in stiffly beaten egg whites whipped with the salt and sugar. Continue freezing and stir briskly two or three times during freezing.

French Pear Conde

Form a ring of well cooked rice cooked in milk (see Rice Conde), then place poached pears or peaches in center of mold. Pour quite thick apricot sauce over pears and add a dash of whipped cream when serving.

Pineapple Conde

Place half slices of fresh ripe pineapple in sugar and Kirsch and cook until tender. Cool, then chill and serve.

Rice A La Conde

French Rice Dessert with Fruit Compote

1 cup first quality rice	Dash salt
2 cups milk	4 egg yolks, beaten
½ cup sugar	1½ tablespoons butter
1 teaspoon Watkins Vanilla	

Wash rice thoroughly in cold water, then blanch the rice by putting the washed drained rice in cold water and bringing to a boil. Drain immediately by placing the rice in a colander, and let lukewarm water run through it.

Then add milk, sugar and salt, and Watkins Vanilla to rice. When mixture begins to boil, cover pan immediately, place in oven and cook gently 25 minutes. Do not touch rice to stir. Gradually add rice to well beaten egg yolks, using care not to break grains. Add butter.

Form a ring of the cooked rice, place poached pears or peaches over mold and cover with apricot sauce.

Frozen Rice Pudding

½ cup raw rice	3 eggs, beaten
¾ cup sugar	1 teaspoon Watkins Vanilla
½ teaspoon salt	
¼ teaspoon Watkins Nutmeg	1 cup whipping cream
4 cups milk	

Wash rice thoroughly and cook in boiling water 5 minutes, then drain. Stir in sugar, salt and Watkins Nutmeg; add milk. Cook about 40 minutes, or until tender, in top of double boiler. Add beaten eggs and cook 5 minutes longer. Cool. Add Watkins Vanilla and fold in whipped cream. Turn into refrigerator tray and freeze with temperature control set at lowest point.

Rum Pudding

1 tablespoon gelatin	4 egg yolks, beaten
2 tablespoons milk	3 tablespoons rum
2 cups light cream, scalded	1 cup sweetened peach pulp or fresh strawberries
½ cup sugar	

Soften gelatin in cold milk 5 minutes. Add scalded cream, and stir to dissolve gelatin. Beat egg yolks and sugar, and add to gelatin cream mixture. Cool. Add rum and pour into one large or individual molds. Chill. Unmold and serve with sweetened strawberries or sliced ripe sweetened peaches.

Rum Pie

½ cup cream,
   heated in
   double boiler
3 egg yolks
3 tablespoons
   sugar
1 tablespoon
   gelatin

3 tablespoons
   milk
⅓ cup rum
½ cup sugar
1 cup cream,
   beaten
3 egg whites

Put ½ cup cream into top of a double boiler and heat. Beat 3 egg yolks and add 3 tablespoons sugar. Stir into cream and cook until mixture coats a spoon.

Soften gelatin in cold milk 5 minutes, then stir into hot custard. Add rum; when mixture is lukewarm, add stiffly beaten egg whites blended with ½ cup sugar. Chill. Fold in 1 cup whipped cream, pour into baked pie shell and chill in refrigerator for one hour.

Top with ¾ cup cream whipped stiff, adding 1 tablespoon sugar and 1 to 2 tablespoons rum. Sprinkle with 2 rolled Graham crackers. Chill and serve.

Sambaglione, or Creme Italienne

1 after dinner
   coffee cup of
   rum or Madeira

6 egg yolks
½ cup sugar

Beat egg yolks with rotary beater until thick, gradually beat in sugar, then add rum, beating constantly. Stir over hot water until mixture is frothy. Serve immediately while warm in sherbet or frappe glasses.

Schaum Torte

6 egg whites
2 cups sugar
1 teaspoon
   vinegar
Ice cream

1 teaspoon
   Watkins Vanilla
Fresh or canned
   drained peaches
Whipped cream

Beat egg whites stiff, fold in sugar, vinegar and Watkins Vanilla and blend well. Turn into a lightly greased spring-form pan. Bake 1 hour in a slow oven, 300 degrees F. Cool in pan. When cold and ready to serve, fill torte with ice cream, cover with fresh peaches and garnish with whipped cream.

Fresh Strawberry Coupe

Choice ripe
   berries
Powdered sugar

Maraschino
   liqueur
Vanilla ice cream

Add powdered sugar and maraschino to washed, drained and chilled berries. Just before serving, fill sherbet glasses half full of chilled berries, pour little juice over fruit, then fill glass with vanilla ice cream. Top with a ripe strawberry.

Souffle Pudding Desserts

Dessert souffles are usually made from a foundation of thick white sauce to which is added flavoring, sugar, beaten egg yolks, then stiffly beaten egg whites are folded into the mixture, poured into a buttered baking dish and baked at moderate temperature until firm. All souffles are baked with the casserole in a pan of hot water. Souffles should be served immediately when done; serve hot. Souffles when served as a dessert are generally unaccompanied, but ripe strawberries, peaches or berries may be added with the dessert if desired.

Souffles made from fresh or canned fruit should be flavored with Kirsch or Kummel. Souffles made from cream are flavored with liqueurs such as rum, curacao, Watkins Vanilla, or anisette.

Just before removing a souffle from the oven, sprinkle it with powdered sugar and leave a moment or two in oven to glaze.

Hints in Making a Souffle

1. Make a smooth paste of flour, butter and milk, or cornstarch, milk and sugar. Stir well and quickly during cooking.

2. Cool sauce and add flavoring. Beat in the egg yolks, one at a time, and beat until smooth. Beat egg whites until stiff, then turn egg yolk mixture into the bowl of stiffly beaten egg whites—near the edge—so as not to crush the puff of egg whites. Use a metal mixing spoon and fold the yolks and whites of eggs; blend lightly and quickly—the secret of making a souffle.

3. Use a heavy baking dish so that the souffle will bake slowly and evenly. If glassware is used, or some other light material which heats quickly, place the container in another pan of hot water.

4. Have a moderate, 350 degree F. oven. For the average size souffle, bake 35 to 40 minutes; if firm to the touch, serve immediately. Cut the souffle quickly and gently with a fork and lift each portion with a spoon.

5. A souffle contracts when cold air is let into the mixture and it is important to serve "from the oven to the table".

Cherry Souffle

1½ cups cherries, pitted
4 eggs, separated
½ cup sugar
4½ teaspoons cornstarch
Grated rind of ½ lemon
1½ teaspoons Watkins Vanilla or Lemon Extract

Arrange cherries in bottom of a buttered quart casserole. Beat egg yolks until thick. Mix sugar and cornstarch together, and add gradually to well beaten egg yolks, beating well. Add flavoring and lemon rind, then fold in stiffly beaten egg whites. Pour mixture over fruit and bake in a moderate, 350 degree F., oven from 30 to 45 minutes, or until firm. Serve immediately.

Chocolate Souffle

2 tablespoons butter
2 tablespoons flour
1½ squares chocolate, melted

1 cup milk
½ cup granulated sugar
¼ teaspoon salt
4 eggs, separated
½ teaspoon Watkins Vanilla

Melt butter over hot water, stir in flour, gradually stir in milk and stir and cook until thickened. Remove from heat, stir in melted chocolate, sugar and salt; mix well and cool. Beat egg yolks until thick and add to milk mixture. Beat egg whites until stiff but not dry and carefully fold into egg yolks. Add Watkins Vanilla. Pour into a buttered 2 quart casserols, place in a pan of hot water and bake in a fairly slow oven, 325 degrees F., about 50 minutes or until firm to touch. Serve immediately.

VARIATION:

For Pineapple Souffle, omit chocolate and add 1 cup well drained crushed pineapple and 1 tablespoon lemon juice to the cooled mixture. Follow Chocolate Souffle recipe.

Fruit Souffle

1 cup fruit pulp
Sugar to suit taste

3 egg whites
Few grains salt

Any fresh fruit, peaches, pineapple, strawberries or other berries may be used. (Drain canned fruit from syrup before using in a souffle).

Press fruit pulp through a sieve, add a few grains of salt, sugar to taste, and heat mixture. Remove from stove and while hot, fold in stiffly beaten egg whites. Pour into a buttered casserole and set dish in a pan of hot water. Bake at 375 degrees F., about 25 to 30 minutes or until firm in center. Serve at once with whipped cream.

Lemon Souffle

4 eggs, separated
¼ cup hot water
2 teaspoons grated lemon rind

1 cup sugar
½ teaspoon salt
¼ cup lemon juice

Beat egg yolks with a rotary beater until thick. Gradually add water, sugar, salt, lemon rind and lemon juice, beating constantly. Fold in stiffly beaten egg whites. Pour into a buttered baking dish and set dish in a pan of hot water. Bake in a moderate, 350 degree F., oven about 30 to 45 minutes, or until firm. Serve immediately with lemon or eggnog sauce.

Lemon Souffle
(Variation)

3 tablespoons
butter
3 tablespoons
flour
¾ cup scalded
milk
3 eggs, separated
⅓ cup sugar

Few grains salt
1 teaspoon Wat-
kins Lemon
Extract
Powdered sugar
Lemon sauce
Grated rind
½ lemon

Melt butter and stir in flour. Stir constantly and gradually add milk; blend until smooth. Beat egg yolks with a rotary whisk, beat in sugar and salt. Stir hot milk slowly into beaten egg yolks (first adding 3 tablespoons of the milk to the beaten egg yolks). Cool. Fold in stiffly beaten egg whites (do not beat until dry). Sprinkle inside of the buttered baking dish with powdered sugar. Turn in mixture and bake about 35 minutes in a hot oven, 400 degrees F., until nicely browned. Serve with a hot lemon sauce.

Lemon Sauce

½ cup sugar
1 tablespoon
cornstarch
1 cup boiling
water
1 teaspoon grated
lemon peel

¼ teaspoon salt
3 tablespoons
strained lemon
juice
2 tablespoons
butter

Blend together sugar, cornstarch and salt, then gradually stir in hot water and cook until mixture is smooth and thick, about 15 minutes, stirring constantly. Add lemon rind, juice and butter.

Eggnog Sauce for Souffle

2 egg yolks,
beaten
1 cup sifted
confectioner's
sugar

½ cup heavy
cream, whipped
3 tablespoons
brandy

Beat egg yolks with a rotary whisk, gradually add sugar and beat until smooth. Stir in brandy with a spoon, and fold in whipped cream. Chill. Serve over Orange or Lemon Souffle.

Pineapple Souffle

⅓ cup butter
½ cup sugar
1 cup bread
crumbs

2 eggs, separated
1 cup grated
pineapple
(drained)

Cream butter, gradually beat in sugar and mix thoroughly. Add beaten egg yolks, then bread crumbs and pineapple. Fold in stiffly beaten egg whites and turn into a buttered baking dish. Place in a pan of hot water and bake in a moderate oven, 350 degrees F., about 35 minutes or until firm. Serve immediately.

Peach Souffle

8 macaroons,
crumbled
1 cup peach pulp
2 cups milk
4 eggs, separated

6 tablespoons
sugar
½ teaspoon Watkins Almond
Extract

Combine macaroons and peach pulp. Cook milk, beaten egg yolks and sugar in top of a double boiler, stir mixture and cook to the consistency of a thick custard. Beat egg whites stiff, fold in the custard, then add peach and macaroon mixture. Turn into buttered custard cups and set cups in a pan of hot water. Bake in a moderate, 350 degree F., oven about 45 minutes. Serve immediately.

VARIATION:
1 cup apple sauce may be substituted for the peach pulp.

Strawberry Souffle

1½ cups crushed
ripe strawberries
¾ cup sugar
1 tablespoon
powdered sugar

4 egg whites
Few grains salt
½ teaspoon Watkins Lemon
Extract

Pick over, wash berries, drain and crush; add sugar and salt and let stand 5 minutes. Beat egg whites stiff then fold in the strawberry mixture. Fill a buttered baking dish ¾ full of the mixture, sprinkle lightly with powdered sugar and bake in a slow oven, 325 degrees F. until firm in center, about 30 minutes. Serve immediately.

Vanilla Souffle Pudding

¾ cup thick
white sauce
(see below)
3 eggs, separated
⅔ cup granulated
sugar
¼ teaspoon Watkins Lemon
Extract

1 teaspoon
Watkins Vanilla
½ cup heavy
cream, whipped
⅓ cup toasted
almonds
Little powdered
sugar

WHITE SAUCE:

4 tablespoons
butter
4 tablespoons
flour

1 cup rich milk
or light cream
½ teaspoon salt

Melt butter, stir in flour until smooth; gradually stir in milk. Cook until mixture thickens, then cook 3 minutes longer, stirring constantly. Add salt. Place over hot water to keep hot and cover tightly to prevent a crust from forming on top.

For vanilla souffle, use ¾ cup white sauce. Stir in well beaten egg yolks, granulated sugar and flavoring. Fold in stiffly beaten egg whites. Pour into a buttered baking dish sprinkled with a little powdered sugar. Place in a pan of hot water and bake about 50 to 60 minutes, or until firm. Serve immediately from baking dish or serve in sherbet glasses. Add sweetened whipped cream and sprinkle top with toasted almonds.

Strawberry Cream Puff

Split a cream puff (see Watkins Cook Book, page 206) into halves and fill with vanilla ice cream. Add a few macaroon crumbs and a tablespoon brandy; add fresh strawberries blended with powdered sugar, or sliced ripe peaches. Serve one-half to each person.

Strawberry Bavarian Cream

1 tablespoon gelatin	¾ cup powdered sugar
2 tablespoons cold water	1 teaspoon Watkins Vanilla
1 cup crushed strawberries	Lady fingers
1 cup heavy cream, whipped	Ripe berries to garnish

Soften gelatin in cold water 5 minutes, then stir over hot water until dissolved. Stir into sieved strawberries and chill until mixture slightly thickens. Whip cream until stiff, fold in sugar and blend. Chill thoroughly. Line chilled parfait glasses with lady fingers, add chilled dessert and top with whipped cream and a strawberry.

VARIATIONS:

Substitute 1 cup fresh apricot or peach puree for strawberries or 1 cup crushed ripe sieved raspberries.

Strawberry Shortcake

4 cups sifted all-purpose flour	2 tablespoons sugar
8 teaspoons Watkins Baking Powder	1 cup shortening
½ teaspoon salt	1¼ cups rich milk
	2 eggs, beaten

Sift dry ingredients, cut in shortening and blend. Mix lightly, add milk, a little at a time, then beaten eggs. Divide mixture into half. Place dough on lightly floured board and pat into a cake pan. Place first layer in pan, brush top with melted butter, covering entire surface, add second layer of dough and bake in a hot oven, 400 degrees F., about 20 minutes.

STRAWBERRY FILLING:

1 cup whipped cream	1 teaspoon Watkins Vanilla
2 teaspoons confectioner's sugar	1 quart ripe strawberries
	½ cup granulated sugar

Whip cream, fold in confectioner's sugar, add Watkins Vanilla. Pick over, wash and hull berries, reserving large ones to garnish top. Crush remaining berries and blend with sugar, let stand 30 minutes to flavor and to dissolve sugar. Separate shortcake layers. Spread bottom layer with sweetened whipped cream, top with crushed berries. Add second layer, spread with whipped cream and garnish with whole berries.

French Tea Cakes

1¾ cups sifted
   flour
½ cup butter
1 cup powdered
   sugar
¼ cup almond
   paste (from
   bakery)

2 teaspoons
   Watkins Vanilla
2 tablespoons
   milk
4 eggs
2 additional egg
   yolks

Sift flour on waxed paper six times to incorporate air. Cream butter thoroughly, gradually beat in sugar, mix well, then add Watkins Vanilla. Blend almond paste with milk and stir into butter mixture. Gradually add beaten egg yolks, then beaten egg whites. Fold in flour, a little at a time. Turn batter into a greased 6½x10 inch pan lined with heavy paper and again greased. Push dough up along sides for a flat top cake. Bake in a 350 degree F. oven about 35 minutes. Remove from oven, cool on wire rack.

When cold, cut into small cakes or make Petits Fours, and cover with thin frosting. Decorate with chopped nuts, candied cherry, or small pieces of candied pineapple. Or cut into four squares and put together with your favorite frosting.

Velvet Fruit Sherbet

3 lemons, juice
3 oranges, juice
3 bananas, put
   through ricer

3 cups sugar
3 cups milk
3 cups cream

Blend entire mixture and use a hand freezer with 4 parts ice to 1 part salt. Let stand 1 hour to flavor.

Wine Jelly Dessert

1½ tablespoons
   gelatin
⅔ cup white wine
3 eggs, beaten

½ cup sugar
3 cups milk, scald
   in top double
   boiler

Soften gelatin in wine. Beat eggs and beat in sugar, a little at a time. Stir constantly and gradually add milk. Stir and cook over hot water until mixture coats a spoon. Remove from fire, stir in softened gelatin. Turn into a mold and chill until firm. Add a dash of whipped cream when serving wine jelly in sherbet glasses. Serve with lady fingers or macaroons.

INDEX

WATKINS PRODUCTS
Daily-Used Necessities for Home and Farm

FOOD PRODUCTS
Baking Powder
Chocolate Malted Milk
Cocoa
Cream of Tartar
Pectin Mix
Prepared Mustard
Root Beer Extract
Saccharin Tablets

Desserts
Butterscotch
Chocolate
Lemon   Tapioca
Vanilla
Color Mixture, Red

Dietary Food Supplements
Iron & Yeast Tablets
Multi-Vitamin Capsules
Multi-Vitamin Tablets
Vitamin A & D Tabs.
Vitamin B Complex
  Tablets

Beverage Bases
Grape   Lemon
Orange   Pineapple
Strawberry
Cherry

Spices
Allspice
Celery Salt
Chili Powder
Cloves
Imitation Pepper
Imitation Cinnamon
Garlic Seasoning
Ginger
Mixed Spices
Mustard   Nutmeg
Onion Seasoning
Paprika
Poultry Seasoning
Red Pepper
Sage   Spice Blend

Extracts and Flavors
Almond Extract
Banana Flavor
Black Walnut Flavor
Lemon Extract
Lemon Flavor
Maple Flavor

Mixed Fruit Flavor
Imit. Coconut Flavor
Orange Extract
Peppermint Extract
Pineapple Flavor
Vanilla Flavor, Imit.
Vanilla, Vanillin and
  Coumarin

HOUSEHOLD MEDICINES
Acotin Tablets
Adhesive Tape
Aspirin
Castoria
Corn Pads
Cough Balsam
Cough Syrup
Cr. of Cam. Liniment
Digestive Comp. Tabs.
Diuretic Stimulant for
  Kidneys (Tabs.)
Ephedrine Nasal Jelly
Herb Tablets
Inhalant
Laxative Cold Tablets
Laxative Wafers
LINIMENT
Menthol-Camphor
  Ointment
Milk of Magnesia
  Tablets
Nose & Throat Drops
Panol
Protective Skin Balm
Petro-Carbo Salve
Sarsaparilla
Sparkling Salts
Tonic   Unguent
Vapor Balm

TOILET ARTICLES
Mary King
Bath Salts
Creme Cologne
Deodorant Powder
Dusting Powder
Lavender
Lilac
Lipstick
Lotion for Hands and
  Skin
Make-Up
Perfume   Rouge
Skin Freshener

Shampoo
Sachet Powder
Superla Lotion
Talcum Powder

Creams
All Purpose
Cleansing
Foundation
Hand
Lemon
Peach Bloom
Vanishing

Face Powders
Natural   Peach
Rachel   Tru-Tan
Sun Brown

General Line
Aftershave Lotion
Antiseptic and Foot
  Powder
Baby Gift Box
Bath Salts
Brilliantine Hair Oil
Fragrant Pomade
Hair Beautifier
Lemon Lotion
Liquid Cleansing
  Lotion
Mouth Wash (Red)
Razor Blades
Sachet Powder
Scalp Zest
Service Kits
Shampoo, Coconut Oil
Shaving Cream
Shaving Cream,
  Brushless
Shave, Liquid
Shaving Soap
Talcum for Men
Tooth Brushes
Tooth Paste
Tooth Powder
Violet Talcum

TOILET SOAPS
Garda   Iodide
Green Palm
Lavender Complexion
  Mary King

Pine Tar   Pumisope
Sanisope

CLEANSERS
Cleanser
Granular Soap
Hand Cleanser
Washing Compound

HOUSEHOLD AIDS
All Duty Polish
Cleaner, Liquid
Disinfectant
House. Fly Sprayer
Liquid Wax
Machine Oil
Metal Polish
Moth Crystals
Pencils
Perfumed Starch
Polish
Spot Remover

INSECTICIDES
Bug Powder
Cryolite Insect Dust
Dry Insecticide
  (Dry Dip)
Fly and Moth Spray
Fly Spray
Fly Sprayer
Insect Dust
Insecticide, Dip & Disin-
  fectant (Stock Dip)
Louse Killer
Pheno. Emulsion
Pheno. Powder
Rat Killer
Roost Paint

MINERAL COMPOUNDS
Hog   Stock
Poultry

VETERINARY PREPS.
Calf Capsules
Cattle Grub Powder
Mange Oil
Niacin Yeast Mix
Nico Sulpho Tablets
Poultry Inhalant
Poultry Wormer
Tonaphysic
Veterinary Salve